Finding Your Ethical Research Self

Finding Your Ethical Research Self introduces novice researchers to the need for ethical reflection in practice and gives them the confidence to use their knowledge and skill when, later as researchers, they are confronted by big ethical moments in the field.

The 12 chapters build on each other, but not in a linear way. Core ethical concepts like consent and confidentiality once established in the early chapters are later challenged. The new focus becomes how to address qualitative research ethics when confidentiality and consent take on a limited form. This approach helps students understand that the application of concepts always requires thoughtful adaptation in different contexts and the book provides guidance on how to do this. Classroom/workbook exercises develop alternative solutions to create process consent, internal confidentiality, and engage reference groups, as examples. The first eight chapters allow students to develop their ethical research self before thinking through how they might address formal ethics review. Formal ethics review is deliberately not introduced until Chapter 9. Chapter 10 offers practical help to elements of review, before Chapter 11 emphasises the key message by providing examples of researchers' dilemmas in the field using vignettes and discussion. By providing these examples, students become aware that these can arise, explore how they might arise, and recognise how they might deal with them in the moment when they are unavoidable.

With numerous examples of ethical dilemmas and issues and questions and exercises to encourage self-reflection, this reflexive, learn-by-doing model of research ethics will be highly useful to the novice researcher, undergraduate, and postgraduate research student.

Martin Tolich is Associate Professor, Sociology, Gender and Social Work, Otago University, New Zealand. He is a specialist in qualitative research and research ethics, publishing books for Sage, Oxford University Press, Pearson, and Routledge, and in 2008 founded the independent New Zealand ethics committee.

Emma Tumilty is a bioethicist at Deakin University, Australia. Her work in research ethics is informed by time on ethics review committees, providing research ethics consultation services, and developing her own ethical practice. She is a member of AEREO (https://www.med.upenn.edu/aereo/) and a book review editor for the *International Journal of Feminist Approaches to Bioethics*.

"*Finding Your Ethical Research Self* is engaging and effective, avoiding a dry conceptual approach to key issues, instead, bringing the topic 'alive'. Student feedback was very positive, suggesting they found the book's workshops to be highly effective in addressing key tenets of qualitative research ethics facilitating their learning." – *Associate Professor Mark Falcous, School of Physical Education, Otago University, New Zealand*

"The workshop gave students a rich opportunity to discuss real-life dilemmas that qualitative researchers typically experience. It also turned out to be a valuable experience to engage with a set of essential principles for those who do qualitative research, such as belonging to a reference group, within which researchers can reflect on and discuss ethical issues inherent to research." – *Dr. António Pedro Costa, University of Aveiro, Portugal*

Finding Your Ethical Research Self

A Guidebook for Novice Qualitative Researchers

Martin Tolich and
Emma Tumilty

Routledge
Taylor & Francis Group

LONDON AND NEW YORK

First published 2021
by Routledge
2 Park Square, Milton Park, Abingdon, Oxon OX14 4RN

and by Routledge
52 Vanderbilt Avenue, New York, NY 10017

Routledge is an imprint of the Taylor & Francis Group, an informa business

British Library Cataloguing-in-Publication Data
A catalogue record for this book is available from the British Library

Library of Congress Cataloging-in-Publication Data
Names: Tolich, Martin, author.
Title: Finding your ethical research self : a guidebook for novice qualitative researchers / Martin Tolich and Emma Tumilty.
Description: Abingdon, Oxon ; New York, NY : Routledge, 2021. | Includes bibliographical references and index.
Identifiers: LCCN 2020043725 (print) | LCCN 2020043726 (ebook) | ISBN 9780367174774 (hbk) | ISBN 9780367174781 (pbk) | ISBN 9780429056994 (ebk)
Subjects: LCSH: Qualitative research–Moral and ethical aspects. | Social sciences–Research–Moral and ethical aspects.
Classification: LCC H62 .T56 2021 (print) | LCC H62 (ebook) | DDC 174/.900142–dc23
LC record available at https://lccn.loc.gov/2020043725
LC ebook record available at https://lccn.loc.gov/2020043726

ISBN: 978-0-367-17477-4 (hbk)
ISBN: 978-0-367-17478-1 (pbk)
ISBN: 978-0-429-05699-4 (ebk)

Typeset in Bembo
by SPi Global, India

Dedicated to our students who have taught us so much about research ethics while demonstrating a willingness to reveal and recalibrate their moral compass.

Contents

Acknowledgements

This book would not have been possible had not so many courageous people written reflections on their research practice in methodological statements (Alice Goffman, William Foote Whyte) or memoirs (Sudhir Venkatesh) or painful reflective notes (Carolyn Ellis, Scheper-Hughes) or paradigmatic reflective shifts (Guillimen and Gillam). Readers of this book must acknowledge that the way forward is on their shoulders. Many of the learning moments in this book have emerged from reflections on Tolich's ethical practice.

CHAPTER 1

The one-minute ethicist

Why write the text, the cartoons [Figures 1 and 2] say it all.

Professor Emeritus

Figure 1 documents the origin of this book. It illustrates a real event when one of the authors was teaching a postgraduate class in qualitative research ethics at the University of Otago in 2016. The class began on day one with a provocation to see if the five postgraduate students could identify ethical conundrums that may not sit well with them and to see if they could come up with some solutions to this conundrum. As the cartoon shows, they did. This book developed from that single moment. Tolich assigned no reading for the first class. His goal was to make the students central to their own learning (Harland & Wald, 2018; Kilburn et al., 2014; Lewthwaite & Nind, 2016). The five students were novices to research ethics (Tolich et al., 2017) and self-confessed no knowledge of qualitative research ethics. They said:

- I knew pretty much nothing. I knew a little about ethics committees, but nothing about the actual lived ethics experience.
- Prior to class, the only understanding of [research] ethics I had was a standard textbook definition: conducting research ethically means to do research in a safe and secure manner where participants' wellbeing and interests are safeguarded during the pursuit of knowledge.
- My prior knowledge of qualitative ethics was limited to writing a paragraph for "ethical consideration" for undergrad courses.
- I began this class with what I felt was a reasonably comprehensive knowledge of the basic ethical concepts that might be encountered within quantitative social science research. What I quickly learnt is just how different qualitative and quantitative research ethics are.
- As I did not understand the amount of theory that goes behind qualitative ethics, I found myself expecting this course to be more about applying for ethics approval.

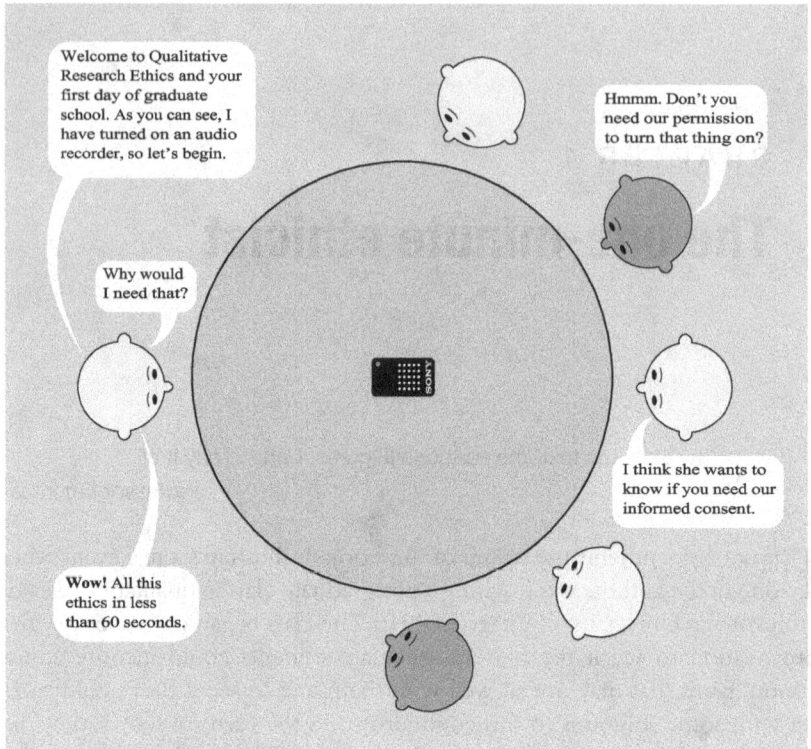

Figure 1 What are the two lessons learned from this situation? The first relates to an ethical concept. The second relates to a behaviour. Understanding these two lessons goes a long way to finding an ethical self.

The goal of this provocative and constructivist style of teaching was a *student as researcher* pedagogy, seeking to establish a culture of free expression within the class setting. Using this experiential learning technique (Lewis & Williams, 1994) students were challenged to perform as (ethical) agents in the moment rather than merely observe practices or receive knowledge, as is often the case in research ethics teaching. Tolich (Tolich et al., 2017) vividly recalls these events:

> After a little housekeeping, brief introductions and handing out course outlines, I took a digital recorder from my pocket and placed it on the tabletop. I then did something awkward; I switched on the recorder and a tiny red light blinked. With it, the room fell into an uneasy silence.

The reactions were instantaneous. Adam's[1] reflection (Tolich et al., 2017, p. 246) recalled the pushback capturing the tenseness of the situation the audio-recorder created in the first minute of the class. He said:

The walls seemed at once to close in, and disappear altogether. I felt watched, judged even, and painfully aware of the small device now listening to my every sound. With tightness rising in my throat, nerves and thoughts collided. My immediate reactions ranged from inquisitive to cautious, playful to suspicious, when out of all the consternation emerged a singularly clear voice. "Is this ethical?" asked one of my fellow students. "That's a great question" responded the lecturer. "What do you mean is that ethical?" Again silence reigned, the lecturer abdicated the floor. As if to help the lecturer out another student translated the question. "She means do you need our consent to have that tape recorder on?" "That is a good question", the lecturer said. "Do I?"

Are these students' reactions universal? Would all students have had a gut reaction to the presence of this audio recorder? Would the reader have identified the lecturer's placement of the audio recorder as a problem? That perception may be the easy bit. Would the reader have had the courage to challenge the lecturer by asking him "What are you doing?" The (Figure 1) cartoon reveals two of these students did have that courage. They both observed a problem and had the mettle to challenge the teacher. In a very short time, the culture of challenging the lecturer was established. This provocation was deliberate. With this action, Tolich sought to disrupt the students' normal *frame of reference* for learning, to have them question and critically assess what was going on; the first step in the pathway of transformative learning theory to becoming an autonomous thinker (Mezirow, 1994).

Our *frames of reference* develop over a lifetime of experience; from these experiences we have learned a set of assumptions about the world and how it functions, and our actions and understanding of experience are shaped by these assumptions (Mezirow, 2000). New experiences are measured against established assumptions, and resulting assumptions are rejected or assimilated accordingly, based on fit. Occasionally, a new experience challenges our assumptions and causes a revision or overhaul of our frame of reference. This table-top exercise was meant to be one such experience.

What is notable in this 60-second intervention is that the students in the class did not have to be prompted or taught about ethics, they naturally evoked their moral intuition, henceforth ethical intuition (defined in this chapter),[2] to say to the teacher, "That's not right". They assumed that it was a requirement that humans ask permission to take or record other people's ideas. Furthermore, one student translated their concern into an ethical concept called consent. "She means, do you need our informed consent to have that audio recorder on?" In this way, these students were active researchers in their own authentic learning (Rule, 2006). That is the philosophy of the course and this book; it is committed to the idea that to be ethical, one has to recognise ethically salient phenomena, develop one's assessment of its ethical rightness or wrongness, and lastly, but most importantly, take action.

This situation tested the students' ability to respond to the activation of the audio recorder. Replications of these tests occur in many of the scenarios in this book where the reader can analyse accounts of research in the same way the students did. In some of these examples of qualitative research presented to the class, the researcher in the case did not gain informed consent.

Turning on the audio recorder was a pivotal point in the students' learning about ethics. It is worth repeating that this moment had two parts. First, the students demonstrated they had an intuition of what is right and wrong, and second, they were willing to voice their beliefs on what they witnessed in the class. It would be pointless to learn ethics but never use them or feel obliged to act on them to protect others.

Tolich's (Tolich et al., 2017) response to the two student comments engaged the class further. Without offering a direct response to the query "Do you need our consent?" he eased tensions by affirming that he would need consent if he ever planned to listen to the audio recording, but he had no plans to do that. The audio recording was solely for their collective benefit. He then invited the five of them, all students on the first day of their postgraduate careers, to use these audio recordings to co-write a journal article based on their experience in this lesson and the rest of the course. The audio recordings would or could be their data. He labelled the five students as researchers; they were writing a journal article. They were researching their own education. The suggestion to them that they write a journal article came as much as a surprise as the positioning of the audio recorder in the first place.

To provide some space for their deliberation about what they wanted to do, the audio recorder was turned off and Tolich left the room for a few minutes while the five of them considered the proposal of their working as a group to use the audio recording to write a journal article about their learning of research ethics. When he returned to them, they collectively and enthusiastically agreed to his proposal. They saw benefit in the idea. Why wouldn't they, since they wanted to co-write a journal article? For all of them, this would be their first article. It was published as Tolich, M., Choe, L., Doesburg, A., Foster, A., Shaw, R., & Wither, D. (2017). Teaching research ethics as active learning: Reading Venkatesh and Goffman as curriculum resources. *International Journal of Social Research Methodology*, *20*(3), 243–253.

The classes that followed in the ensuing weeks were embryonic of how this book developed. All class discussions were audio recorded as the students reviewed a number of fictitious and published ethnographic accounts of research practice, always asked to take the perspective of participants in these studies. The students were responding to these texts individually as well as pooling their responses collectively on audiotape in the class. Now that they knew their brief, these *students as researchers* were equipped to examine how they would feel (and react) if they had been one of the participants, in the various studies, they read. By provoking their ethical intuitions and challenging their moral integrity, henceforth ethical integrity (to act), in the first session, Tolich had disrupted their *frame of reference* (Mezirow, 2000), therefore provoking a different engagement with each of the subsequent cases discussed in the class.

The students were tasked with identifying ethical conundrums in the various texts provided to them. They were supported to come up with solutions for how the research examples could be done without causing unease to them or the participants in the study. Over the next 13 weeks, the students repeatedly came into the class showing a grasp of what was right and wrong in research. Intuitively, they could identify and resolve complex ethical problems with some support. The teacher's task was to expand or reinforce their knowledge and encourage them to use it both in the classroom and later when they were in the field.

Writing now, two years later, the pathway the class followed seems obvious, but it was not so clear at the time. It took Tolich some months to grasp the innovative pedagogy of this type of learning in discussion with Tumilty. Postgraduate students are adult learners, often with some practical experience in the workforce or community. Ethical practice in research speaks to the way researchers are in the world and relate to others while conducting research. Ethics education has often either focused on abstract principles or theories sometimes applied to cases or on the rules and regulations relevant to a postgraduate student's (future) environment.

These kind of approaches arguably do not help students feel they are or can become ethical actors in the "real" research world. By using authentic learning techniques (Rule, 2006) within a transformative learning framework (Mezirow, 1994), this book's approach recognises the need to support novice researchers to become autonomous, ethical research practitioners. As said earlier, their first encounter in the class disrupted their *frame of reference* (Mezirow, 2000) and engaged their moral imagination (henceforth ethical imagination).

Ethical imagination is a mixture of empathy and creativity; the ability to consider the lives of various others affected by dilemma in all their complexity and think of, and through, the ethical solutions (Narvaez & Mrkva, 2014). By allowing and encouraging the challenging of the teacher in the first session, the student's power and voice is supported from the start. Practising the act of speaking up and out, based on one's ethical position within a low-stakes environment, helps one to develop the ability for future situations where the stakes may be much higher (Gillespie & Brown, 1997).

The pattern embodied within the one-minute ethicist is metaphorically that of an inoculation. In medicine, a small dose of bacteria (measles) builds antibodies sufficient to ward off a measles attack. After 60 seconds in this class, the students inoculated themselves against research conducted without informed consent. "Hmmm. Don't you need our permission to turn that thing on?" Tasks set for the students in the second class followed on from this, allowing the students to test these antibodies in hypothetical and real examples of research conducted without informed consent.

In their second class in 2016, after five minutes reading a hypothetical case study describing a researcher conducting research without informed consent, the five students had both the knowledge and the confidence to challenge the integrity of the case study. Over the semester, this learning was scaffolded (Hauhart & Grahe, 2015; van de Pol, Volman & Beishuizen, 2010); at the same time, they identified new ethical conundrums and sought to resolve potential harm. In so doing, the students self-inoculated against new ethical dilemmas.

While the inoculation was limited to specific situations, it served as starting point. The necessity of informed consent in research became second nature to these students, yet they found informed consent was not always possible. In Chapter 4, the virtual reality research examples presented not only failed to provide informed consent for participants, but such consent would have been inappropriate. These situations encouraged students to find alternative ways of protecting participants.

A notable development during the semester was how the students' learning was cumulative: each new ethics concept identified was used in the immediate task (evaluating a scenario or journal article), but then incorporated into the evaluation and treatment of subsequent exercises. It would take some time before this cumulative learning formally integrated itself as part of the class's learning objectives. Student-centred pedagogy proved a success. The students were learning, and Tolich, the teacher, was learning from them.

The outcome of the 13-week course was a collectively written first draft of the journal article based on the audiotaped classroom discussions. Some of these discussions are presented with students' permission, in subsequent chapters. The audiotapes allowed the students to recall both their unease with the scenarios or readings and how they found solutions to ethical conundrums.

Tolich's role in this initial drafting of the article was minimal. It was not until the revise and resubmit stage that he was required to assist the students, placing their ethnographic description of the class discussions into a wider pedagogical discussion that framed their learning. Up until the penultimate draft, his name did not appear as an author. The pushback from journal editors required his participation. Three of these students went on to use this high-impact journal publication (Tolich et al., 2017) as the basis of their successful PhD scholarship application.

An astute reader could question the ethics of surprising students with both the audio recorder and the offer to write a journal article, specifically in relation to their autonomy. Later cohorts reviewing Figure 1 would ask whether the offer of collectively writing a journal article diminished the students' autonomy. Was the request coercive, or an inducement? Did the request come from a person who was in a superior power position to the students? These questions are valid and are discussed later in this book.

THE FIVE-MINUTE ETHICIST

In 2018, a new cohort of postgraduate students took the same class, and Tolich was adamant that he did not want to write another journal article with this cohort. Tolich used the same ruse, initiating the audio recorder with these students in the qualitative research ethics graduate class as he had done in 2016. When he turned on the audio recorder to test the waters, the conditions that established the one-minute ethicist intervention were not evident. The intervention fell flat. None of these five students rose to the provocation. However, there seemed to be a technological reason for this change of behaviour.

Tolich was not fully cognisant of a major technological enhancement in undergraduate teaching at the University of Otago. In the previous two years, all undergraduate teaching lectures were audio recorded (Otago Capture) and posted online, accessible for any student enrolled in a class who could not attend the class in person. When he switched on the audio tape in 2018 and the red light illuminated, he had not made the connection to the ubiquity of audio recording. As it turned out, for the first few minutes of the class, the audio recorder did not register as a problem for the 2018 students.

Initially, he was somewhat disappointed, taken aback by this non-response. Unlike the 2016 class, none of the students said anything about the audio recorder. However, a few moments into the class as the students went around the room to introduce themselves, Rachel, one of the five students in the class, did raise a concern with the audio recorder (Figure 2). It was not so much the recording of the conversation that concerned the student, but the storage of the conversations and their eventual use. She wanted to know who would have access to the audio recording given that some of the classroom discussion she was likely to share would record private information.

In response to Rachel's concern, Tolich explained his motivation for the audiotaping. As the course was discussion, not lecture-focused, he wanted these students to have ready access to the recordings when writing their assignments. He also envisaged them giving their full attention to participation in the classroom discussion and not making copious notes. In effect, this was something akin to the "Otago Capture" recording process. Again, he had no plan to listen to the audio recordings. However, Rachel's concern

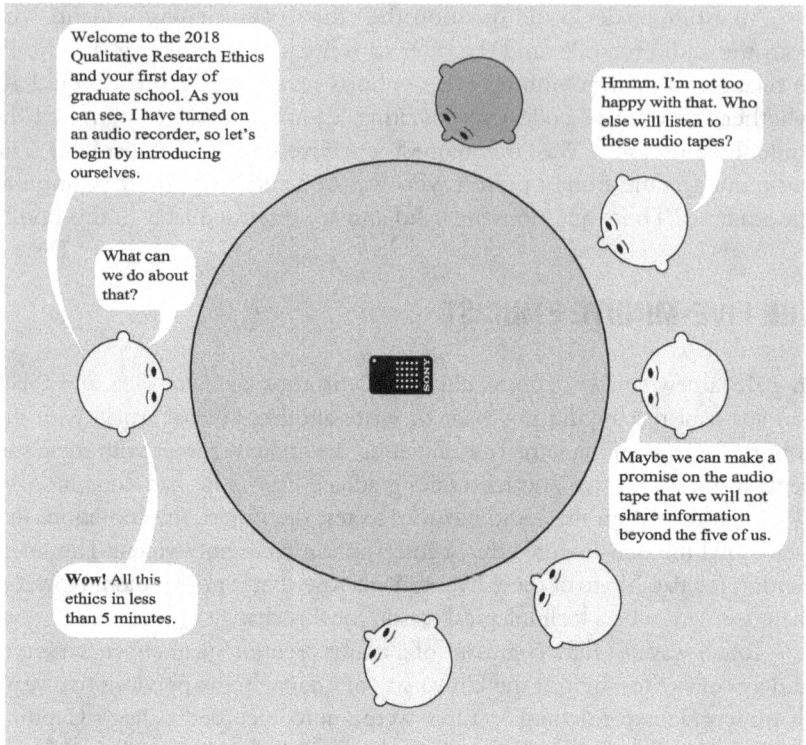

Figure 2 What are the two lessons learned from these students below? Much like in Figure 1, the first relates to an ethical concept. The second relates to a behaviour. Understanding these two lessons, helps students find an ethical self in research and is the purpose of this book.

was real, and Tolich recognised the opportunity. He asked the group, "Who could listen to the tapes?" This question raised an excellent issue that organically began a discussion about privacy, confidentiality, and the ethical considerations used in small group interviews. And so, while the disruptive experience stemmed from a different ethical concern, the same pedagogical experience had been replicated. The students had recognised an ethically salient phenomenon, considered what was at stake ethically, and acted on it – challenging a figure of authority.

Concerns with the confidentiality of the stored data were similar in form to the practicalities of consent issues raised in the 2016 class with the audio recorder turned on. The 2018 students saw the storage of the audio recording as a potential threat to their privacy. Keeping faith with the *student as researcher* pedagogy, Tolich asked them what the class should do about that. Rather than this being a hypothetical example, this was real, an authentic learning experience, pre-empting those they would need to consider as independent researchers. This was their problem; they now needed a solution.

The five members of the class immediately addressed this issue, deciding among themselves to give an oral consent to one another. They would share the audio recordings only with one another, spontaneously pledging on the audio recorder not to disclose anything discussed in class with other people. They would use the recordings only to assist writing assignments. To this discussion, Tolich promised not to reveal to others outside the group what individual students had said. Rachel's name is used here with her permission.

An astute reader will have once again noticed that this discussion within the 2018 class was something akin to discussing the ethics of running a focus group. Like so many moments in the class, some of the issues the students raised were tabled for later discussions. For example, see Chapter 6 for a discussion that asks how researchers should, or can, promote and protect confidentiality in focus groups.

In a real way, the students in 2016 and 2018 were establishing the learning objectives of their course and for this book on qualitative research ethics. It took Tolich, as the teacher, some time to comprehend fully the book's scope, found in Figures 1 and 2. Consent raised by the 2016 students asking, "Is that ethical? Do you need our consent?" is not only one of the book's dominant themes; it is a dominant theme in qualitative research ethics (Tolich, 2019). Sometimes the rich concept of consent is conflated with the administrative step required for regulatory purposes. As a dominant theme in this book, we are not interested in the process of gaining informed consent in the administrative sense, but in the idea of consent as a mediator of participant vulnerability and power within a qualitative research setting. Equally, "Who is going to listen to these tapes?" raises the central concern of confidentiality.

Tolich confesses it is humbling to realise that the students in a matter of minutes established this book's goals based solely on their ethical intuitions. However, it took them the rest of the two courses to grasp the nuance of these two concepts. In the first minutes of the 2016 and 2018 classes, the students demonstrated how they, unskilled in formal ethics training, could respond in an instinctual way identifying and labelling ethical concepts central to qualitative research. What follows in this book stems from their willingness to identify ethical concepts and to voice their concerns about them.

In the rest of this book, while outlining an approach to ethics education, we highlight the robust nature of the two concepts confidentiality and consent as well as their limits. For example, can confidentiality assurances be realised in small group research when people know who is being quoted in the research article and can guess through a process of elimination who said what? (Tolich, 2009). Informed consent is also malleable (Tolich, 2004). It is not always possible to give informed consent, and in some cases, it is difficult to keep it when new research topics emerge. In these circumstances, qualitative researchers must be sufficiently resilient to offer other ethical solutions.

A PEDAGOGICAL IDIOCULTURE

Finding Your Ethical Research Self focuses equally on what to learn and how to learn it. The pedagogy represented establishes a culture whereby students in 2016 and 2018 were expected to challenge practice. This was not just a classroom technique, but an expectation that to be a successful qualitative researcher, researchers must be capable of acting on their ethical beliefs in conducting their own or reviewing other's research practice.

This course and book take a refreshing pedagogical approach to research ethics. Assigning students five journal articles could have allowed the students to read and capture some notion of informed consent. But that was not the pedagogy adopted here. Before 2016, the following journal articles or book chapters were compulsory reading:

Brinkmann, S., & Kvale, S. (2008). Ethics in qualitative psychological research. *The Sage handbook of qualitative research in psychology*, *24*(2), 263–279.

Israel, M., & Hay, I. (2006). *Research ethics for social scientists*. London: Sage. (Particularly Chapter 5, Informed Consent.)

Miller, T., & Bell, L. (2002). Consenting to what? Issues of access, gate-keeping and "informed" consent. In M. Mauthner, M. Birch, J. Jessop, & T. Miller (Eds.), *Ethics in qualitative research* (pp. 53–69). London: Sage.

Sieber, J., & Tolich, M. (2013). Informed consent and process consent. Chapter 7 in *Planning ethically responsible research* (pp. 115–140). Thousand Oaks: Sage.

Stacey, J. (1991). Can there be a feminist ethnography? In S. B. Gluck & D. Patai (Eds.), *Women's words: the feminist practice of oral history* (pp. 111–119). New York and London: Routledge.

Wax, M. L. (1982). Research reciprocity rather than informed consent in fieldwork. In J. E. Sieber (Ed.), *The ethics of social research* (pp. 33–48). New York: Springer.

By 2016, Tolich sought to generate resources for the students to discuss by promoting student responses. He hoped the students would take the bait and respond to the audio recorder, and they did. What this demonstrated was that they were capable of using ethical intuitions of what was right and wrong to research their own world. They knew when something was wrong. Turning on the audio recorder without asking permission was wrong in their eyes. The first task in 2016 had been to establish precedent, and their response to the audio recorder created that precedent.

In 2018, the different cohort of students did not respond to the intrusiveness of the audio recording, but one student chose to respond idiosyncratically to the privacy implications in the storage of data. Who would get to listen to these private thoughts? Thus, collectively in 2016 and

2018, the students' response shaped a culture within the classroom similar to what Gary Alan Fine (1979) labels an idioculture. He discovered idiocultures in a study of a Little League baseball team. Fine found that although all Little League baseball teams were governed by rigid rules (for example, nine players and three strikes), each team's *idioculture* created its own rules. He said:

> Idioculture consists of a system of knowledge, beliefs, behavior, and customs *shared by members of an interacting group to which members can refer* and that serve as the basis of further interaction.
>
> (Fine, 1979, p. 734, our emphasis)

An *idiocultural item* illustrating Fine's concept of the power of the group to establish rigid, practically God-given rules at the outset of a group formation is drawn from the Little League team's first practice. A player missing from a team's inaugural practice would, at the second practice, be inducted into rules established in his absence (e.g., one's arrival at practice determined the batting practice order).

It was fortunate that on the first day of class in both 2016 and 2018, all five students attended and Tolich did not have to explain to any absent student what was achieved in the first class. Tolich wonders if it would have been difficult to explain the mechanics of this cultural development. Would the latecomer student experience the same shift in *frame of reference*? Later, in subsequent two- and five-hour workshops, the two cartoons (Figures 1 and 2) provided a good starting place for students to imagine themselves in the class creating their idioculture.

What Tolich was trying to do in 2016 and 2018, in the most basic sense, was to generate behaviour that would serve as *the basis of further interaction* or the new *frame of reference* for this group (Mezirow, 2000). His goal here was not short-term but long-term; establishing a culture for the entire course. Qualitative researchers were not only expected to identify ethical issues but also required to act on them, both in the classroom and later in the field.

TESTING INTEGRITY

By 2018, it was common for Tolich to ask students in the semester-long class or in the shorter two- to five-hour workshops if they knew about the two-line perception test, where one line was shorter than the other. Drawing two lines on a whiteboard invariably led to more than one student identifying the diagram as the Asch experiment, showing a willingness to explain the rudimentary research design to other students. This general query approach stayed true to the pedagogy of *student as researcher*.

Solomon Asch's experiment asked his research subjects to assess different lengths of lines.

> Asch (1956) studied conformity by telling participants that they were participating in a perception experiment in which each member of their group would select the line believed to be the same length as the standard line. Unknown to the person being studied, the other seven members of the group were confederates (i.e., part of the research team). On the first two trials, most of the seven confederates made the correct match. From the third trial on, the confederates all agreed on the wrong answer. Asch reported that the (real) subjects looked bewildered and anxious. Seventy-five percent of them gave the same wrong answer as the confederates in at least one trial, while the rest gave the correct answer despite obvious feelings of discomfort and confusion. The 75% error rate in the false majority condition was in sharp contrast to the 7% error rate in the condition without the confederates. Most subjects doubted their own judgment, and three-quarters of them caved in to the majority opinion. Following each subject's participation, a sensitive debriefing was conducted in which the procedure was fully explained and subjects were assured that their responses to conformity pressures are normal.
>
> (Sieber & Tolich, 2013, p. 49)

Applicability of the Asch conformity study is focused not on conformity, but on an emphasis on integrity. In other words, employing the Asch experiment gets to the heart of an ethical practice that relies on a person's integrity and courage. Knowing how the concept of informed consent operates does not mean the researcher is willing to use the concept. Without integrity, ethical issues dissolve; they become meaningless, if not implemented.

Unpacking the Asch experiment focuses attention on the 75% who knew the correct answer but chose to follow the crowd and give an incorrect answer. Asch would say the 75% basically conformed. But this example can be framed in a different way, for a different purpose, surrounding qualitative research ethics. Only 25% had the integrity to speak out. The number one lesson for qualitative researchers is the need to be reflexive, continually asking themselves when conducting research whether the research behaviour is ethical. If it is not ethical, it is incumbent upon the researcher to rectify that situation, often when they are on their own in the field. Thus, a prerequisite for qualitative research is that qualitative researchers are required to identify and respond to ethical issues on the fly. This is the norm, rather than the exception, and it is a task practised throughout the book, as it was in the first 60 seconds of the 2016 course. "Hmm. Don't you need our permission to turn that thing on?"While fieldwork and interviews are often done alone, many qualitative researchers work in teams, and many students will be junior members of teams at the beginning of their careers. Here as in their own practice, they need to respond to ethical issues and act on them, often in what will be very challenging situations. Having training that establishes a norm or idioculture, of questioning ethical decisions and practice, continually and somewhat naturally helps to strengthen their integrity "muscles", their confidence in speaking up and expressing their concerns.

Learning what is ethical is only one part of the equation. When a researcher identifies an ethical conundrum but chooses to ignore it, they are worse than being conformist – they lack integrity. Acting on the identification of the ethical conundrums is a matter of integrity. Doing something about it doesn't necessarily follow from identification as day follows night. Qualitative researchers need to commit to being in the 25% who acted on what they saw, not the 75% who identified the issue but failed to act. Trusting the visceral or gut feeling is an excellent starting point to identify ethical issues both in the scenarios in this book and later researching in the field.

Thomas Scheff (1988) reworked the Asch experiments, casting them as exemplars of human emotion, typically referred to as *peer pressure*, by describing situations in which people feel shamed by being seen in the minority. Scheff's dissection of the Asch experiment located subjects' motivation to lie as an avoidance of shame. Scheff (1988, p. 31) found:

> Asch reported that as the division between the majority and the individual continued, the individual became more tense, flustered, nervous, and anxious. A reaction that occurred both in independent and yielding subjects indicated the fear that they were suffering from a defect, and that the study would disclose this defect: "I felt like a silly fool. ... A question of being a misfit. ... they'd think I was queer. It made me seem weak-eyed or weak-headed, like a black sheep".
>
> Many of the comments show negative viewing of self from the point of view of the others: "You have the idea that the attention of the group is focused on you. I didn't want to seem different. I didn't want to seem an imbecile. They might feel I was just trying to be out of the ordinary. ... They probably think I'm crazy or something". These comments are all markers of overt shame.

Learning about ethical concepts and acting on that concern in isolation promotes integrity in research:

> Since much of what [researchers] do occurs without anyone else watching, there is ample scope to conduct ourselves in improper ways. For instance, researchers can fabricate quotations or data or getting information under false pretences. No one might ever know.
>
> (Israel, 2015, p. 3)

An assumption of this book is that the book is marketed to readers who want to be in the 25% group: those with the intuition to recognise ethical problems, the ethical imagination to consider responses and reason through them, and the integrity to address them.

THE FIVE-HOUR ETHICIST

Besides teaching semester-long versions of this course, in December 2018, Tolich experimented with the presentation, teaching the course as a day-long workshop in Christchurch. Subsequently, he has taught the course in shorter two-hour blocks as well as in other five-hour courses with students with whom he had no previous teaching history in New Zealand, Portugal, and Spain.

The Christchurch workshop students were all graduate students, and most had some research experience. In these workshops, Tolich did not have unlimited time, so he chose not to rely on provoking the students about informed consent or confidentiality by turning on the audio recorder. Instead, he used cartoon re-enactments (Figures 1 and 2) of the 2016 and 2018 classes as a starting point, asking the workshop students to analyse what had happened in these first classes. Did they grasp the learning about informed consent and confidentiality? Did they comprehend the establishment of an idioculture where students were expected and encouraged to challenge the teacher? In both cases, they could.

The workshop students immediately discussed the various nuances of the cartoon representations. They had the confidence to analyse the Figure 1 cartoon even though it involved a seemingly awkward moment, knowing the teacher depicted in the cartoon was their instructor. The students identified with the 2016 students, saying that the students were right to question the teacher's placement of the audio recorder. They were also not surprised that all of this interaction happened within 60 seconds of the class beginning. Informed consent was so obviously missing that this group went further than either the 2016 or 2018 classes.

The Christchurch workshop students went beyond the initial comments made by the 2016 students, characterising the term informed consent as a relationship between two strangers – the researcher and the researched, with a focus on the latter and their ability to be informed, as well as the relationship between being informed and consenting. They questioned what informed meant: i.e., was being informed a dichotomous concept (You are? You are not?) or something more akin to a range? And, depending on which, how does this affect our ability to recognise and obtain informed consent?

These comments further widened the gap between the words informed and consent. They believed researchers had a responsibility to check on the participant's ability to give that consent. The example they used was gaining consent from a child. Here the Christchurch workshop students were prying open the door to the concept of autonomy and diminished autonomy without labelling it as such or recognising that they were enunciating the Nuremberg code and the Belmont Report. Israel (2015, p. 36) summarises these codes, stating:

> Like the Nuremberg code and the declaration of Helsinki, the Belmont report gave emphasis to autonomy, incorporating convictions that, where possible, individuals should be treated as autonomous agents and those with diminished autonomy (for example, the mentally disabled) are entitled to protection.

The formal distinction between autonomy and diminished autonomy would come in later exercises when returning to questions asking if children, prisoners, or those with learning or neurological disabilities were capable of giving their consent. The words the workshop students used were not autonomy or diminished autonomy; their words aligned more to active and passive designations.

Was the person sufficiently confident to give active consent?

As the opening minutes of the Christchurch workshop proceeded, the discussions about the cartoons produced further insights. One student took the class back to Figure 1 asking if the placement of the audio recorder by the teacher was a provocation that would challenge any audience. He saw this provocation for what it was, a deliberate attempt by the teacher to create precedent within the class, making it both easy and acceptable for the students to criticise the teacher or the subject matter under review. These students were correct in this assessment. The provocative use of the audio recorder sought to establish a sustainable idioculture. The workshop students demonstrated they could learn from the 2016 students represented in the cartoon.

The dual learning objectives in the workshop were: (1) to teach research ethics, and (2) establish a behaviour in which students would feel comfortable critiquing research as if it was their own. The cartoon tropes validated these objectives, further provoking the students' ethical intuitions.

Ethical intuitions are important in that they are the recognition of some ethically salient experience occurring, and they serve as great starting points for ethical evaluation of a situation and what should be done. They are the flare to help researchers pay attention to something. Using their ethical imagination, researchers can then develop a deeper capacity to understand and explore possible decisions and actions and their justifications. By reasoning through these possibilities and their justifications, they can arrive at an acceptable course of action. Acting on a decision is the final step and requires integrity. This book begins with the premise that all students have these abilities, but much like muscles, they can be strengthened and developed by targeted exercise.

By teaching research ethics cumulatively, this book provides multilayered learning. On the one hand, it provides the opportunity to develop these ethical skills and behaviours (intuitions, imagination, reasoning, integrity) as one proceeds through the book; on the other, it teaches that research ethics learning is an ongoing process that can always be added to, improved, and adjusted.

In sum, the placement of the audio recorder in 2016 and the storage of data in 2018 were provocative for the students. Their representation in these cartoons were sufficiently clear for other students to grasp the significance. Each of these subsequent cohorts came to the same conclusion, seeing the audio recorder as an intrusion, in need of informed consent. From these introductions, the basic ethical concepts of consent and confidentiality were established. In the chapters that follow, these concepts are tested, finding them both robust and flimsy.

Identifying ethical concepts was an important task, but so too was having the courage to speak up. Speaking up was made more difficult because it required the students to question a person in authority. Yet the students demonstrated an ability to do that, revealing their moral courage. Moral courage was not taught in this class; it was just unleashed and then corralled.

The students learned the researcher's role in any qualitative research is that of learner, and the informant the expert (Lofland and Lofland, 1971). The same relationship occurred in these classrooms. Students were the teachers, and Tolich was the learner. Their responses and questions informed this book. However, the students had a lot to learn. Having grasped the concept of confidentiality and consent, the students' next tasks, in the lessons that follow, were to understand that there are limits to these concepts. For readers of this book, the same path lies ahead. Inside every concept, like informed consent, there is another concept that may contradict the understanding. What does a researcher do in Chapter 4, when a fully developed informed consent is not possible in virtual reality research?

NOTES

1   The name is real and used with permission of the student.
2   We introduce such terms as they are commonly known, "moral intuition", but then replace them with "ethical intuition" throughout. While disagreement about the distinctions between the two terms is ongoing, we consider them interchangeable.

CHAPTER 2

Organising the reader

Tolich and Tumilty have seen and been involved in teaching research ethics at various institutions, to various groups, to various fields for some time. Research ethics education, where it forms a minor part of another qualification, can be elective or mandatory, but in either scenario it is often afforded little time in the learning program and may only focus on the process of gaining ethical approval for research. Ethics teaching may also be isolated from other relevant learning such as research design and methodology. Where it attempts to do more than cover the regulatory process, it takes as its starting point the idea that students are naïve or unaware of ethics. Ethics teaching normally includes a mixture of three core things: (1) a rehearsal of some of the key cases of ethical misconduct through history; (2) at best a discussion, at worst a description of ethical theories, concepts, and principles; and (3) some reading of or discussion of cases to which to apply those concepts, principles, and theories. In some settings, students may be asked to complete mock information sheets or application forms, or they may undertake activities that mimic being an ethics committee member. This perspective assumes students know nothing about ethics in research, and the focus is on gross misconduct, ethical principles, regulation, and the process of ethical approval. We speak generally here – there are, of course, those who are innovative in this space and who are more careful about introducing nuance and discussions of power. Despite the degree of thoughtfulness or innovation in the teaching, in general, they all treat the students as "ethics-naïve" in relation to the research context.

What is put forward here, and introduced as a transformational learning pedagogy in Chapter 1, is the idea that we start by recognising students as moral actors with ethical intuitions. They may, depending on their background, be "research-naïve" and even "ethical theory/principle-naïve", but to conflate this with "ethics-naïve" is a misstep. That is, students are capable of recognising ethically salient situations, and when they do, they have a sense of what might be the right or wrong thing to do. These intuitions may not be perfect; that is, there may be recognition of something wrong but imperfect identification of what exactly it is, or there may be identification but no clear approach to developing an appropriate response. Importantly, however, there is ethical intuition. When we think about teaching from this starting point, when we recognise that our students have this ability, how should we then approach helping them develop these intuitions into ethically reasoned decisions that support action? And not only support action, but create an imperative to act? When we appreciate that students, novice researchers, and experienced researchers will encounter ethical situations in their research, whether in the field or their interactions with others, that require them to act dynamically and with integrity, how do we prepare them for this?

As the authors discussed Tolich's experience with his class and these broader issues of ethics education, it became clear that there was a new way to approach teaching research ethics. While some things could stay the same – the use of cases and discussion of big missteps – the roles and relationships between educator and learner had to change. The role of the educator in this setting is not the transference of ethical knowledge and regulatory requirements, but the facilitation of the key things needed to be an ethical research practitioner. We think these things are:

1. Recognising ethical intuitions and being able to identify their causes.
2. Recognising the limitations of intuitions (biased or incomplete) and developing relationships and skills to hone and expand them.
3. Using information gathering and ethical imagination to consider possibilities for action supported by reasoned ethical justifications.
4. Exercising moral courage to act on or speak up about one's ethically justified resolution or decision.

This book aims to set out ways in which educators can help students identify themselves as ethical actors and help them develop the skills to practice research ethically no matter how challenging the situation. We feel this is especially important for qualitative researchers who are by the nature of their work positioned more relationally with their participants and communities and so are much more likely to have to make immediate and responsive decisions to the situations that may arise.

This *student as researcher* pedagogy (Harland & Wald, 2018) fits with the unique epistemological positioning of qualitative research that is best characterised as emergent and iterative. Qualitative research is different from the linear, more predictable, quantitative research. In the absence of predictability, the qualitative researcher begins any course of research knowing at the outset that their research question is likely to evolve as the various iterations of data are collected and analysed. A core assumption of this book, and of this student as researcher pedagogy, is that as the research question in qualitative research develops, so do the project's research ethics. Students witness the course as "change is a constant". These changes invariably arise when the researcher is in the field, far from any ethics committee. Punch (1994) highlights this isolation of a qualitative researcher, saying:

> [Ethical issues] often have to be resolved situationally, and even spontaneously, without the luxury of being able to turn first to consult a more experienced colleague. [Moreover], the generality of codes does not help us to make fine distinctions that arise at the interactional level in participant observation studies, where the reality of their field setting may feel far removed from the refinements of scholarly debate and ethical niceties.
>
> (p. 89)

The responsibilities for qualitative researcher reflexivity are part of the primacy of the method. Normally this primacy refers to a qualitative researcher having to collect data and analyse data simultaneously – in quantitative research, the primacy is the research instrument, and in mixed methods, the primacy is the dictatorship of the research question (Tashakkori & Teddlie, 1998).

In qualitative research this primacy goes beyond data collection and analysis and extends to responsibilities for ethical consideration that arise in the research design, as well as when the researcher is in the field. On-the-spot ethical assessment and implementation is an essential responsibility for the qualitative researcher. Thus, learning about ethics in a way that helps empower students to recognise their own ethical agency within an interactive classroom setting, or as outlined in this book, promotes ethical responsibility for the Other. This responsibility is integral to the primacy of the research method for qualitative research. In what follows, readers are asked to analyse scenarios about research identifying issues that cause them unease, reflecting on rectifying the situation, and taking ultimate responsibility for the protection of those involved in research projects.

Using this "learning by doing approach" (Silverman & Marvasti, 2008) means students not only have to understand research ethics, they have to know that ethical considerations are changeable. Most importantly, it is they, as researchers, who are tasked with recognising an ethical consideration and having the courage to address it.

Figures 1 and 2 demonstrate researchers accepting the responsibility to identify ethical considerations and to act on them. In 2016 and 2018, the students accepted this task spontaneously. Subsequent cohorts have been able to review these cartoons and come to the same conclusion.

This mode of teaching developed intuitively over a decade, moving away from a traditional pedagogy with a prescribed reading list of books, chapters, or journal articles. It evolved. By 2015, the essay topics the students wrote about were less likely to be found in the course outline and more derived from classroom discussion and nuanced out of the student's own research interests. These students were active participants rather than detached critics. They were challenged to go beyond criticism focusing on the conditions under which the studies they read could have been conducted more ethically. In this learning by doing pedagogy, they were expected to treat the texts they read as research and solve these problems as if they were their own problems. This approach to teaching is one of co-creation. It recognises students as valuable contributors with unique perspectives and the role of educators as one of facilitating their development and growth.

This intuitive course development evolved to follow what educational philosophers call a student as researcher pedagogy:

> [S]tudents start research training from the first day they enter university, and this apprenticeship thread runs through the 3 years of study. Students learn to formulate original research questions, write grant applications, design experiments, carry out fieldwork, evaluate data, review the work of peers, give seminars, and write reports and articles. This curriculum is modelled on the way in which academics themselves learn, and in particular knowledge of the postgraduate student experience serves as a guide to curriculum decisions and teaching.
>
> (Harland & Wald, 2018, p. 616)

This philosophy places the student at the centre of their learning. The students have the responsibility for driving their research learning. Authentic learning activities promote the student's transition to professional. In Figure 1, provocatively turning on the audio recorder to see what would happen was a leap of faith. As discussed in Chapter 1, it has the potential to provoke a shift in a student's *frame of reference* (Mezirow, 1994), challenging them to consider the experience of participants by being positioned as participants. It can also shift the teacher's frame of reference, challenging them to recognize students as ethical agents rather than passive recipients of ethical knowledge and regulation. This book, in itself, is a leap of faith. The student's response "Hmm, do you need permission ..." confirmed that the lecturer's faith was not unfounded. They were up to the task.

The book's challenge employs this student as researcher pedagogy and transformational learning theory in a series of interactive exercises allowing any teacher to present the puzzles/conundrums/scenarios/lessons throughout their course, thrusting the students into the centre of their learning and removing the teacher from their position of total authority. The expectation is that any reader, either in a classroom setting or in independent learning, can readily take an active part in the exercises in each of the chapters, leading to a natural interactive learning extension.

Engaging your Ethical Research Self assumes senior undergraduates and postgraduate students taking a research methods course have the prerequisite skills allowing them to decipher a range of scenarios and to reach conclusions based on their sense of moral unease with what they have read. Recognising this unease is the precise learning objective of the book. Linking that unease with core ethical concepts within an incubator environment is a second key learning objective. A further learning objective stems from the realisation that the most important ethical issues qualitative researchers face happen when they are alone in the field. An ethics code of practice, such as the one developed incrementally in the review exercises at the end of each chapter, identifies the reader's ethical self and develops confidence in it. This is crucial in being able to act responsively when out in the field.

The book's most basic learning objective is distinguishing between recognising an ethical fault and having the pluck to act upon it. Having knowledge about ethics is one thing; having the integrity to act on it is a completely separate challenge. In *Finding Your Ethical Research Self* the Asch experiment (discussed in Chapter 1) provides a continuous backdrop, not in terms of conformity but in terms of integrity; being part of the 25% who can identify an ethical issue and act on it.

The emergent, iterative epistemology underpinning qualitative research requires researchers to self-police these ethical issues *in situ*. In some situations, as documented in Figure 1, it took less than a minute to establish both the pedagogy and the learning outcomes. The students had the ability to act on their unease – in fact, this was encouraged – and they had the tacit knowledge to identify key ethical issues and attempt to resolve them.

This student as researcher pedagogy both centres and challenges the reader. Most ethics textbooks assume the learner is an empty vessel needing to assimilate core ethical concepts; for example:

Iphofen, R. (2011). *Ethical decision making in social research: A practical guide.* London: Palgrave Macmillan.

Israel, M. (2015). *Research ethics and integrity for social scientists: Beyond regulatory compliance* (2nd ed.). London: Sage.

Macfarlane, B. (2010). *Researching with integrity: The ethics of academic enquiry.* London: Routledge.

van den Hoonaard, W. C. & Hamilton, A. (Eds.). (2016). *The ethics rupture: Exploring alternatives to formal research-ethics review.* Toronto: University of Toronto Press.

Wiles, R. (2012). *What are qualitative research ethics?* London: Bloomsbury Academic.

In the past when Tolich and Tumilty have taught courses, they have conformed to the assumption students were an empty vessel; in this book based
on Tolich's work, they turn that assumption on its head. The goal in this
book is to harness and develop the students' inbuilt ethical agency, encouraging them to use case studies in the classroom to accumulate confidence in
their agency and tools to use later in the field. The use of case study scenarios is not original, but it is effective.

Swazey and Bird (1997, pp. 7–8) claim

> case [study] teaching can be an extremely effective method to foster
> the students learning the analytical skills needed to address ethical
> issues in scientific research, as well as gaining knowledge about the
> context of those issues. ... Interactive group discussion of cases or
> scenarios ... transmit professional values and ethical standards of the
> discipline to students and in the process clarifying conventions.
> [These] scenarios that provide a true to life example of problematic
> situations are especially useful as a catalyst to group discussions.

The book is *not* a primer for ethical theorising, but the historical precedents
that produced the need for research ethics codes at Nuremberg and Tuskegee
(see the Belmont Report, National Commission for the Protection of
Human Subjects of Biomedical and Behavioral Research, 1979) are discussed, as are the research scandals conducted by Milgram and Zimbardo.
From past teaching experience, most graduate students have some familiar-
ity with these exemplars and can be drawn upon to begin a conversation
about each exemplar. This knowledge can be expanded upon without
usurping the *student as learner* pedagogy.

If there is a theoretical position taken on ethics in the book, it is more
sociological than philosophical. In 25 years serving as chair or committee
person on ethics committees, Tolich has yet to witness a debate or discussion
couched in philosophical terms by ethics review committee members (see
also Stark, 2012). Ethics are more the sociological negotiation of unequal
power among parties; between researchers and those that are researched,
between qualitative research and quantitative research, between social science
and the biomedical model, between ethics committees and researchers. These
are not philosophical conflicts, but stem from imbalances in power that are
essentially embroiled in relationships. Ethics committees operate as idiocultures (Stark, 2012), making decisions without accessing ethics codes. The
decision-making then becomes the precedent for future decision-making.

This book is *not* focused on research design or epistemology, yet it
reviews how epistemological demarcations between quantitative and qualitative research exhibit divergent ethical considerations. The deductive, linear
form of quantitative research produces predictability in ethical issues prior

to beginning the research. It is still important for researchers using quantitative measures to recognise themselves as ethical agents and act accordingly (discussed in Chapter 5), but this looks quite different when compared to qualitative research. The use of a standardised questionnaire makes formal ethics review anticipate subsequent ethical issues. Qualitative research epistemology, on the other hand, with its emergent research design and an iterative interview guide, means that formal ethics review is only ever partial. Ethical considerations invariably change, and the researcher needs to be trained to adapt to this flux in real time. In Chapter 11 we present a series of ethical conundrums that review how ethical considerations can change.

This book is *not* an introduction to qualitative research, but along the way, the book discusses various techniques used by qualitative researchers in great detail, as well as how these techniques manifest different forms of ethical considerations. Focus groups and autoethnography use completely different ethical considerations. For example, in Chapter 6, readers are asked to decide if focus groups actually have any ethical considerations in terms of informed consent or confidentiality. Is the researcher's promise to keep focus group participants' opinions in confidence binding? If it is, should focus group participants sign a confidentiality statement promising not to share private conversations with others outside the focus group? Equally, autoethnographic research offers an inherent puzzle when authors' stories involve other people without gaining their consent. Do authors own their own story about growing up because they tell it? Students found the answer was no and yes.

The focus of the book, especially the first eight chapters, is *not* on what Guillemin and Gillam (2004) label *procedural ethics* – formal ethics review. The focus is on post-procedural ethics, what Guillemin and Gillam designate as *ethics in practice*. Procedural ethics are important for a qualitative researcher, but qualitative researchers need to know that any research approved by an ethics committee is iterative, likely to change when research questions change in the field. Current research ethics education and the way that we talk about research ethics approval sets up researchers to believe that once they have approval, they have "done" ethics for their project. In reality, what were previously only ethical considerations in the design phase become real ethical situations once out in the field, when the researcher comes into contact with participants and communities. At that point there is no ethics committee to turn to. The qualitative researcher must find solutions within their ethical self. This book incubates this ethical self by recognising there is little that is predictable in qualitative research, except that once research has begun, not only will the research design change, so too will the research's ethical issues. For epistemological reasons, qualitative researchers must be trained to recognise how new ethical issues arise in the field and made familiar with how to address those issues.

The first eight chapters of the book *do not* discuss ethics committees or procedural ethics. The focus of these chapters is on the primacy of the method, how in qualitative research the researcher is responsible for pastoral care of those who volunteer to take part in their research. Although, the sensitivity for ethical issues in research over the years has led to the formation of large numbers of codes of ethics and the establishment of ethics committees in many areas (Flick, 2006, p. 45) mandatory ethics review is not universal. New Zealand, Canada, Australia, Brazil, and the United States all have mandatory ethics review; other countries do not. This book, at least Chapters 1 to 8, assume research can be conducted without formal ethics review if the researcher has developed an ethical self. There is also a pedagogical reason for this delay in introducing formal research ethics review.

Placing discussions of formal ethics review too early in a book designed for novice researchers is counterproductive, encouraging readers to abdicate responsibility to an ethics review board. Once ethics approval is gained, the researcher may assume their ethical responsibilities are over. However, this is not the case in qualitative research. Ethics review, introduced in Chapter 9, takes place only after the reader has established their own code of ethical practice and shown a willingness to use that knowledge. It's also not hard to imagine that by developing students as ethical agents prior to thinking of ethical approval, this might improve their experience of ethical approval. If through such work they are better able to conceptualise the needs of their participants and explain what considerations they owe those participants as a researcher, then this could be beneficial in their approach to research ethics review.

Engaging Your Ethical Research Self is organised around 12 chapters with a multitude of puzzles that work cumulatively. These puzzles allow the reader to immerse themselves in research situations, learn by doing, and then accumulate that learning incrementally and use what has been learned in the next puzzle. For example, students' identification of informed consent in 2016 and confidentiality in 2018 represented their ability to draw on their own tacit knowledge and identify ethical concepts. The cumulative learning from the students in these initial classes in 2016 and 2018 was how pivotal the concepts of confidentiality and informed consent were for qualitative research ethics. However, these definitions were only at their most basic form. Confidentiality and consent transform themselves differently in various qualitative research techniques. Thus, confidentiality and consent are robust concepts, but they need to be identified as fragile. There are limits to confidentiality, and consent is malleable.

Chapter 3 begins with a singular provocation that pervades the entire book. It focuses attention on a fictitious 200-word scenario, Eve's story that the reader absorbs in less than five minutes. Like the audio-recording device that was plopped in front of the students on day one, Eve's story is also sprung on students. Invariably, this provocation engages, if not enrages, students to draw on their basic knowledge of ethics.

Eve's story is fictitious, documenting her years collecting personal information in a domestic violence women's refuge. In this short scenario,

Eve collects a treasure trove of data about people's lives that few people would have access to. As with other scenarios in this book, the reader is asked if they would be happy to be part of this research. Would they have conducted the research in a similar or different manner? Novice researchers who have read Eve's story have easily deciphered both the harms to others and how by using basic common sense these harms could have been avoided, even if the researcher had not sought formal ethics review.

The chapter ends contrasting Eve's story with one of the few assigned readings used in the book or class, not written by Tolich. The reading is a chapter excerpt from Venkatesh's *Gang Leader for a Day* (Venkatesh, 2008, pp. 185–218). An electronic copy of the chapter is sent to the students prior to the second class with the expectation that they come to class ready to discuss the reading immediately. They usually arrive at the class bursting with indignation, which is channelled into Eve's story. The students discuss Venkatesh only after comprehending the ethical considerations in Eve's story. Most students see Venkatesh's chapter as identical to Eve's story.

In five-hour workshops, only the Venkatesh chapter is assigned. In a 13-week semester course there is more time to have the students read other relevant texts such as the methodological statement in Alice Goffman's book *On the Run* (Goffman, 2014, pp. 213–264). Goffman's book has similarities to both Venkatesh and Eve's story. The focus of this pedagogy is that the students are using the learning they created by analysing Eve's story to review these two established chapters.

Pedagogically, what is important here is the sequencing of the task. It is worth repeating – the students come to understand ethics through Eve's story and *take that learning* to the published texts of Goffman and Venkatesh. They develop their skills in trying to take cases apart and putting them back together again ethically. In other words, they moved from the hypothetical, "this could never happen", to the real. It did happen. Both the Goffman and Venkatesh books are sociological bestsellers that begin their research without either ethics approval or any sign of ethical reflexivity. The main learning students take from these contrasts is that it is the latter, not the former, that is problematic.

The new learning found in an analysis of Eve and Venkatesh's work reinforces the importance of gaining informed consent prior to conducting the research, and/or grasping who can have access to the data. Yet this learning is soon challenged. Ethical considerations are not black-and-white, and in Chapter 4, the students take their new ethics assumptions about mandatory informed consent to a virtual reality research situation where giving informed consent is not always practical.

Chapter 4 disrupts students' recently acquired understanding of consent by presenting research sites where a researcher cannot give participants informed consent. In a virtual reality experiment, a participant may be informed that they are going to take part in a virtual reality experiment, but it's likely the participant will not be told the nature of that experiment. If they were told in advance, this could confound the experiment's data collection. Thus, consent is not always practical or informed. This conundrum is presented as a puzzle, and students are asked to come up with ways to protect research participants in lieu of a full informed consent. Students locate answers to this question in a review of the one-page Nuremberg Code before applying them to two iconic psychology studies by Zimbardo and Milgram. Neither of these studies permitted the participants to withdraw from the study at any time.

Chapter 5 provides a fork in the road. By Chapter 5, the term "research ethics" has generally unearthed core ethical principles that can be translated as respect for persons, beneficence, and non-maleficence, all outlined in the 1979 Belmont Report. These principles are fundamental ethical considerations, but they are not rote learned, instead, they emerge organically out of the students' analysis of Eve's story, the chapters by Venkatesh and Goffman, the virtual reality study, and the Zimbardo and Milgram readings.

Chapter 5 challenges the students' assumptions that all research ethics are the same. This assumption is tested in a hypothetical mixed methods research project. The focus of the puzzle asks:

1. How easily can a research participant withdraw from a survey?
2. How easily can a research participant withdraw from a transcribed unstructured interview?

This simple puzzle leads readers to an understanding that ethical principles are the same for all research, yet distinct epistemologies mean ethics manifest differently. The fork in the road exposes an epistemological wedge between qualitative and quantitative research ethics, especially in the terms "anonymity" used by quantitative researchers and "confidentiality" used by qualitative researchers. These terms are mutually exclusive. Once survey data are collected, the puzzle reveals both the respondent's identity and what they said are unknown, making this quantitative data anonymous. Can qualitative research ever be anonymous when qualitative researchers always know the identity of their participants and know what they said? What they say cannot be unknown. The only way that this identity can be altered is if the data is de-identified. But de-identified data is never anonymous.

The lessons in Chapters 6 and 7 focus solely on qualitative research techniques. Qualitative research techniques may have an identical epistemology, but how their ethical considerations manifest are technique-specific. A review of each of these six techniques demonstrates that each possesses a unique set of ethical considerations.

Chapter 6 contrasts the ethical consideration of confidentiality usually offered to participants in unstructured interviews with those found in focus groups. The strength of unstructured interviews are the robust confidentiality assurances offered between the researcher and the participant. Even after the interview has taken place and has been transcribed, a participant can withdraw a part of the interview or the whole interview. Ethical considerations offered to focus group participants are not the same. Focus group researchers cannot provide robust confidentiality assurances for focus group participants. A researcher cannot prevent a participant from telling other people outside the focus group what others have said.

Chapter 7 explores the multidimensional concept of consent as it is practised in autoethnography, narrative research, and observation research in public spaces and photovoice. There is no uniform practice in the various techniques presented.

To replicate autoethnography, students are encouraged to write a short 10-line story about a childhood celebration. Invariably these stories involve others organising or sharing the celebration. Once texts are deconstructed, students grapple with the question: Do they need to gain the consent of the people mentioned in the story, or do they own their children's story that they are telling?

Narrative research within a multistage interview with one person makes informed consent problematic, if not an oxymoron (Josselson, 1996). How is consent managed when the research question transforms iteratively within and between a series of interviews with one person? What is the strength or status of the original informed consent to take part in the narrative research? What steps should researchers do to bolster an ongoing consent process?

Observational ethics are explored in an everyday setting in Chapter 7 where students are asked to collect data during their weekly grocery shopping. No informed consent is sought from the supermarket employee, as this observation takes place in public space. Nonetheless, this task usually is conducted with some discomfort that engenders in-depth discussion about the student's moral compass.

Photovoice's ethics are presented as exemplary: the poster child of qualitative research ethics. Photovoice researchers use anticipatory ethics before taking their first photograph.

Chapter 8 provides one of the two Capstone review exercises in the book that strengthens the students' learning. In architecture, a capstone is the stone that secures all the stones beneath it. In an academic context, a capstone is the final class that completes a student's curriculum (Seybold, 2017). The first Capstone (in Chapter 8) is a continuation of a set of exercises that assume the researcher is responsible for the ethical considerations of those people who take part in research projects.

This first Capstone focuses on ethical considerations the researcher controls when exempt from formal ethics review. The task involves creating a hypothetical case study of a social agency. In many ways, this exercise is similar to Eve's story in Chapter 3, but essentially different as the researcher is engaging transparently with the social agency in good faith prior to commencing any research.

The task involves the reader choosing any social agency they have had no previous involvement with and imagining asking them if they can conduct a study with them. It is important for the exercise that the researcher have no affiliation, in fact, little knowledge of the social agency. *At no time is the reader required to approach a social agency.*

The students are told that after meeting the social agency manager for the first time, they ask a series of five questions to determine the researcher's intentions and integrity. They ask:

1. What does the statement "nothing about us, without us" mean?
2. How long will you spend with the organisation, and what is your exit strategy?
3. What skills do you have that you could leave with the social agency after you leave?
4. Are you an insider or are you an outsider to the organisation? What do you already know, or assume to know, about the organisation?
5. Are you going to research "on us or with us"?

The expectation is that the student as researcher will have sufficient tacit knowledge to answer these questions. If they do not, a simple Google search of "nothing about us, without us" produces 2,630,000 hits. The previous seven chapters outline a range of ethical considerations that prepare the reader to answer these five questions. In most cases, the answers produce a paragraph, sometimes a page of consideration at most.

Answers to these five questions generate a memorandum of understanding (MOU) between the student as researcher and the hypothetical agency. Because the memorandum is a negotiated document, it also creates an ethical statement that controls for the exercise of power, creating a level playing field. Students are encouraged to reconsider Eve's research as if she had created an MOU with Women's Refuge.

This memorandum of understanding represents a type of research commonly known as Participatory Action Research. Part of the first Capstone is evaluating the MOU in terms of the participatory action research model.

A notable omission from the list of five questions is a sixth question that sets up the second capstone in Chapter 9. The sixth question asks, does the researcher need to gain institutional ethics approval before commencing the research? Even though these interactions are hypothetical, students engage with them personally as if they were real. The third cartoon, Figure 3 (see Chapter 8), captures how this lesson was taught at Aveiro, Portugal, in

September 2019. One of the postgraduate students in the workshop, caught up with the immediacy of the exercise, expressed her disillusionment with the process, claiming that now she was forced to begin the exercise again with a bureaucratic ethics committee. For her, the magic had vanished. Thomas and Znaniecki (1918) explained this outcome. They said if something is defined as real, it is real in its consequences. This student's consequence was in response to the autonomy and responsibility generated answering the five questions. Now in reality they were answerable to a higher body.

Chapter 9 evaluates the impact of this sixth question, where a researcher submits a research protocol inclusive of the MOU negotiated with the social agency to formal ethics review. This action changes the focus of the book. Up until this point formal ethics review has not been featured, but in Chapters 9 and 10, formal ethics is dominant. The delay in raising these issue is deliberate.

Students are required to compare their Capstone One MOU with Mark Israel's (2015) prophecy. Page one, line one of Israel's book *Research Ethics and Integrity for Social Scientists* throws the reader, experienced or novice, into the deep end, not exposing them to the basics of qualitative research ethics but instead locating the Achilles heel of qualitative research ethics with formal research ethics. Israel (2015) begins his book with the following:

> Social scientists are angry and frustrated. Still. They believe their work is constrained and distorted by regulators of ethical practice who neither understand social science research nor the social, political, economic and cultural contexts within which researchers work.
>
> (p. 1)

This statement is true and important, but it is a confusing and daunting start. In *Finding Your Ethical Research Self*, these discussions about anger and frustration are given a place in Chapter 9, not in the opening chapter. By Chapter 9 the reader has grasped why qualitative researchers at Aveiro University in Portugal were disappointed that now they had to submit their five-part negotiated statement to an ethics review system. If they don't, they soon will learn their MOU negotiated in Capstone One has little standing in an ethics committee review process.

Capstone Two involves the students engaging with formal ethics review by drawing on resources in Chapter 10 to write three participant information sheets on behalf of Eve's story:

- one for the women's refuge organisation, the second for the women's refuge volunteers, and
- the third for the clients who make use of women's refuge.

A self-reflective exercise has the students evaluate these three participant information sheets, asking:

1. Are the research ethics outlined in Capstone 2 of a more comprehensible standard than found in Eve's story?
2. Is it more comprehensible than practised by Venkatesh?

Chapter 10 resources Chapter 9. There is an expectation that novice researchers will not have the skills to construct an ethics application without some resourcing. This resourcing is found on TREAD (https://tread.tghn. org/) "The Research Ethics Application Database." Chapter 10 describes the origins and utility of this database and encourages novice researchers to use it. The TREAD website reads:

> TREAD was established by a former ethics review committee chair who witnessed many novice researchers struggling with a clash of theory, methodology, and ethical principles meaning that core ethical issues became secondary to a form-filling exercise. TREAD does not promote a "filling-in-the-boxes" mentality when seeking approval from a research ethics review committee. TREAD's goal is to facilitate sound ethical practice by providing examples of how researchers have described the pathways used to protect their research participants from harm. Reviewing multiple examples of protocols can promote best practice for researchers by allowing them to compare and contrast their project with donated examples. Postgraduate supervisors and ethics committee members may find it valuable to read how researchers, using a variety of well-established and novel methods with a range of populations, have described their ethical pathways. Research methods teachers may find useful examples for their students which blend considerations of theory, ethical principles and methodology.

Novice researchers should not re-invent the wheel, but can read many examples of how qualitative researchers have engaged with ethics committees.

Chapter 11, titled "Researching in Harm's Way" provides an array of incidents, big ethical moments where colleagues, students or research participants call attention to a researcher's outstanding ethical issue. These examples can be read as a whole or interspersed within the previous chapters.

Chapter 12, the conclusion, returns to the fundamental thesis of the book established by the students. Knowledge of research ethics is important, but what is essential is that researchers have the integrity not only to recognise an ethical conundrum, but to address it.

CHAPTER 3

Is eve's story Venkatesh's story?

In 2016 and 2018 the first week of class was devoted to events that led to the creation of the cartoons in Figures 1 and 2. In the second week of the semester students read an unfamiliar text, a hypothetical scenario titled "Eve's story" (Tolich, 2016a). This activity, building on the last, was meant to further exercise the students' ability to recognise their ethical intuitions and interrogate them. After the experienced shift in their *frame of reference*, how would they now view other's practice? They were asked to jot down ideas if they experienced any unease with how the researcher interacted with the people in the study. Additionally, would they be happy for the researcher to use the data described in the scenario for a forthcoming PhD? If not, why not?

EVE'S STORY (FICTITIOUS)

For the past four years Eve has volunteered at a Women's Refuge in a provincial city. Eve's volunteering involved overnight stays and collecting administrative data on the women and the children as well as ensuring they had access to showers, clean clothes and a bed for the night. Beyond these official duties, Eve listened unofficially to each of the women's stories, writing up a case study of each person coming in. These cases also included Eve's observation of the persons delivering the victim to the center. These were usually the police, and in the 42 cases Eve collected, she found that policewomen had little emotional time for these women. Eve's cases had depth as 24 of the women reappeared and 6 were triple visitors to the center. In all, Eve has filled 11 A4 notebooks detailing what she calls the policing of domestic

> violence. At no time did Eve inform Women's Refuge, the police or the women she was recording these stories.
>
> Eve no longer volunteers for the refuge and is now enrolling in a PhD program in social science and she plans to use this data set for her dissertation. What are your thoughts on this course of action? Should she be able to use the data? If not, could you share a few sentences explaining your decision? Equally, under what circumstances could she use the data?

Feedback on Eve's story was vocal; in 2018 one student's response exclaimed, "What the hell was she doing?" These students were questioning, if not challenging, Eve's action. The consensus was that Eve was collecting the information for her own interest. However, they found insufficient information given in this story to establish if Eve volunteered for this position in order to collect this information. Nonetheless, this possible subterfuge introduced a new ethical concept into the classroom discussion. The students were asking if Eve established a benefit for her data collection prior to collecting the data. They wanted to know for whose benefit Eve collected the data. This question was the first mention of the concept of beneficence, and that was a significant development.

If the audio recorder in the first class prompted issues around consent, also known as respect for persons or autonomy, these students had discovered the second of three principles in the Belmont Report (National Commission for the Protection of Human Subjects of Biomedical and Behavioral Research, 1979): the first being respect for persons, the second beneficence, and they would eventually discover the third principle, justice, within the wider discussion of vulnerability.

The 2016 and 2018 students quickly identified the vulnerability of the women in Eve's story. This insight stemmed from their empathy for the women who came into the refuge and were documented in Eve's notebooks. They saw these women as having special needs given the obvious tensions of the situation in which Eve encountered them. The assumption was that these women and their children were more than likely to be in a state of crisis. The discussion that followed allowed the students to coin the concept of vulnerability.

What was impressive about the students' learning was how quickly the two student cohorts easily located key ethical concepts such as vulnerability and beneficence, having previously established informed consent. Together, these concepts were central ethical principles. Vulnerability was enshrined in the principle of respect for persons manifest as autonomy and diminished autonomy.[2] This identification was refined through the sharing of each other's knowledge and experience. That is, the initial intuition was further refined by the discussion within the group about the potential experiences of the hypothetical participants they discussed. This was a form of collective empathising, strengthening each other's ability to imagine and see others and their perspectives. From this, then, an intuition about an ethical issue became identification of the issue.

Identification of ethical issues was one side of the coin. The other side was resolving issues. Searching for solutions challenged the students. It wasn't sufficient to become good at finding issues; solutions were also needed, and this could be difficult. In many ways, Eve's scenario was an equivalent to a horse having bolted from the barn. The student's task, now, was to find solutions. Close the doors? Buy a new horse? Or could the horse be brought back safely?

The answers the students gave showed they grasped Eve's plight. However, any suggestion permitting the use of the data in a PhD opened a Pandora's box, as the students quickly discovered that although informed consent was an omission in Eve's research design, it was not the primary ethical concern. Vulnerability was. The 2018 workshop students[1] said:

> These women are vulnerable. There are issues around safety and trauma for these women, and these issues are more important than data collection.
>
> She has no consent from anyone to do this research. These women did not know that they were being interviewed or observed for a research purpose. What is more important, these women are vulnerable, and that evening as they transitioned the Women's Refuge, they were in an extremely vulnerable situation.
>
> There was some problems with the storage of data.
>
> Were these women given pseudonyms? It's not stated in the short story.
>
> Eve was clearly in a conflict of interest as a person tasked with recording details for refuge and for her own research purposes.
>
> Eve had no right to use that information. It was collected on behalf of the agency, and she had no right to use it or even hold it.

Tremendous learning was taking place as the students tried to draft instructions for Eve. The students took the role seriously, acting as if they were Eve's reference group (see Chapter 4 for a discussion on the utility of reference groups), torn between wanting to analyze Eve's conduct and to assist her to find a way forward for her data. A stumbling block was the word "trust". The students saw Eve had breached trust on so many levels. Perhaps this was the students' greatest learning from Eve's story: "What the hell was she up to?"

The word trust is not found in any ethics code, but it is a central tenet of qualitative research ethics enmeshed within the relationship between the researcher and those researched.

Any attempts by the students to put the genie back in the bottle were futile, as finding solutions on behalf of Eve was deemed impossible. Obtaining consent from the 42 women after the data had been collected was hugely problematic for a number of reasons. The workshop students continued:

> Even if Eve could obtain the addresses of these women, which was virtually impossible, the request for permission would come out of the blue, and it would complicate matters raising further ethical questions.

> Seeking permission would bring back painful memories for the women about their experience, re-traumatising them.

> Re-contacting these women risks disrupting these women's home life. If a woman's violent partner learns of their *participation* in the supposed research, there could be repercussions opening old wounds. These women had not volunteered to take part in this research. They did not know that a research project had taken place.

Eve was not the only actor in the story, and the ethical considerations went beyond the 42 women. For example, obtaining permission to use the data from the police or from women's refuge captured the impossible predicament Eve was in. Any request for retroactive permission to use the data exposes Eve's breach of trust with the police and the refuge. The students saw the trust issue as fundamental; they were not convinced that the police or the Women's Refuge would ever trust Eve, let alone give her permission to use this data. Nor would any ethics committee allow Eve to use the data or gain retrospective consent. Tolich's students' analysis was thorough and thoughtful.

These conclusions were prescient, creating the opportunity to extract as much learning out of this scenario as possible. Students considered the possibility, even though they knew it was reckless, that Eve be given the addresses of the women and to seek their informed consent retroactively. They knew this was not a good idea to visit the women or to send a transcript of the interview:

> There is a possibility that the spouse may open the letter and read the transcript, which could ignite the situation and re-traumatise the woman. If the partner was abusive or controlling, the situation could spiral out of control.

> The women would find that they were part of a research project that they did not know about. This could cause ongoing trust issues between the informants and women's refuge.

Eve's scenario was an excellent teaching tool. It was short, explicit and used in both 2016 and 2018, and also in the five-hour 2018 workshop. It was clear that these novice researchers were capable of recognising ethical misadventure in this hypothetical research project. They engaged their ethical imagination (Nash, 1987) and their ability to not only empathise with others but think through all the relevant moral outcomes and solutions and their effects on others. In this environment, they could crowdsource the possibilities. While this might not always be possible in their professional lives later, it shows them that collective moral imagining can provide a broader picture or set of options. This collective work will not always be available in practice, but here, it teaches students to recognise the limitations of their own ethical imagination and tailor their solutions appropriately. Researchers make different decisions when they feel confident in their evaluation of a situation versus when they are aware they may not have a good idea of the full picture. Thus, students learn a degree of humility as they also learn the power of ethical imagination.

In this case, these reflections found no way forward for Eve's data. There was, however, one possible use, realised not by the students but by more experienced colleagues.

A WORRYING TREND

To triangulate how the postgraduate students in 2016 were reading Eve's story, Tolich gained ethics approval from a university ethics committee to ask 25 colleagues, many of whom were past or current members of an ethics committee, to give feedback on their reading of the Eve story. Their responses were detailed and articulate; when thematically coded, they replicated what the students had identified as core ethical problems. In only one aspect did these colleagues go beyond the students' reading of the case. The results of this research with 25 colleagues documented below was published (Tolich, 2016b) as:

Tolich, M. (2016). A worrying trend: Ethical considerations of using data collected without informed consent. *Fronteiras: Journal of Social, Technological and Environmental Science*, 5(2), 14–28.

Without exception, as with the students, all 25 respondents were reluctant to permit use of the data set as it was; they were concerned at absence of the autonomy of the participants. They held an expectation that researchers should invite subjects/informants/participants to volunteer to participate in research. One respondent said:

> I feel informed consent is a keystone of ALL research and the argument for proceeding without voluntary informed consent has to be strong and robust.

The 25 responses went beyond a unilateral prohibition on the use of the data set. Most modified their responses with disclaimers attempting to find ways for Eve to proceed in her studies, salvaging something from the data but at the same time protecting Eve and the vulnerable women whose stories she recorded and the two institutions – women's refuge and the police. In many cases, even though the disclaimers were thoughtful, the eventual use of the data remained doubtful. One respondent, focusing on the trust issues the students had highlighted, wrote:

> My initial response to whether Eve could use this data is a resounding NO. I believe Eve has compromised the trust she has with Women's Refuge and the women that use this service. ... Women's Refuge is a place where these women can go for protection and by collecting and documenting a record without the specific women's permission, and with no way of contributing to their story, I believe, this is another form of abuse. ... The information Eve has collected is most likely useful to both Women's Refuge and the Police in regards to how domestic violence is managed. Therefore I wonder if there may be a way of including this information. ... If Eve fronts up to Women's Refuge, she hands over all the information she has collected regarding the 42 cases. She explains why she has collected this material (and being really clear about this), making them into case studies and how she has included her observations. She highlights some of the insights she believes she has gained and advises she wants Women's Refuge to have the material, for them to do what they wish with. She also advises Women's Refuge she is enrolling in her PhD and she would like her topic to focus on the policing of domestic violence, explaining why she believes this would be a useful project for Women's Refuge. When she submits her Ethics application she advises them she would like to speak with both Women's Refuge staff and women about their experience of policing domestic violence. The reality is that Women's Refuge will make the final decision on whether they can support this. *Women's Refuge may shred all the material she has passed over, therefore it will no longer be available.* She should be required to seek permission of all the 42 women to be allowed to include their case studies first. Women's Refuge may also refuse her access to their service at all due to the breach of trust that has already occurred. I believe it is probably unlikely Eve will be able to include this information into her project, I do believe she has a responsibility to stop recording case studies and advise Women's Refuge of what she has been collecting even if she doesn't plan to ask to use this information already collected.
>
> (our emphasis)

Informants identified Eve's failure to provide a justification for collecting the notebooks in the first place. Students in 2018 had previously coined a prescient phrase to capture Eve's conduct. They said, "What the hell was she doing?"

> This proposal seems self-serving. I do not see any benefit indicated for the women, for the Refuge, or for the police. Instead I believe there is a risk of harm that outweighs any benefits Eve perceives: there is the harm to the women seeking support caused by a betrayal of trust from a support volunteer who uses their experiences for her own ends; there is the potential for harm caused by inadvertent details coming to light about the women/families seeking support; there is the potential for a harmful impact upon the reputation of Refuge and the Police which may make women less likely to seek help; and use of any data may also be seen by women as a betrayal of trust and confidence on the part of the Police and Refuge.

Notwithstanding retrospective attempts to shore up the ethical issues, informants raised serious ethical issues based on Eve doing nothing about her data set. This data set was at risk; the storage of the detailed case studies in Eve's possession about spousal abuse was subject to subpoena:

> Are people identified or identifiable in the journals, and if so, are the journals securely held? (I'm guessing not, from this scenario.) So the immediate issue is the safe storage of the journals. Once they become research materials (rather than private observations), they are accessible by the police I suspect as well.

The consensus was the dataset was contaminated and retrospective consent was both insincere and likely to induce harm:

> Why did she not seek informed consent from the Refuge when taking up her volunteer role? If she felt it was not acceptable at the time, why would she feel it is now acceptable?

However, some experts offered respite seeing a way forward for Eve, allowing her to make use of her experience at the refuge rather than make use of the data itself. The experience could be a building block to establish a research proposal for future research. One of a number of respondents said:

> It may be that Eve could use these experiences to develop the sensitising concepts for her PhD where she will collect new information (possibly from the same shelter) that responds to the experiences/

> reflections/questions/concerns she had as a volunteer. But this writing and these experiences would not be data. Rather, these would be instructive to informing the study design and question of her PhD.

In sum, other than using the experience to establish a new research proposal to collect further information on this topic, the 25 respondents argued that Eve's story was ethically unsound and should not proceed.

Eve's story is central to this book. The students' response to it created a body of concepts which cumulatively influences the rest of the book. In Chapter 9, Eve's story returns in Capstone Two. A task is established, building upon the comments presented that suggests Eve's experiences could be developed as sensitising concepts for a PhD project. The review exercise in Capstone Two (Chapter 9) requires students to take over Eve's role and construct three participant information sheets for Women's Refuge, people who volunteer at Women's Refuge, and the clients of Women's Refuge. That self-evaluation exercise allows the reader to assess if their ethics are more robust than Eve's ethics or other researchers mentioned later in this chapter.

STRANGER THAN FICTION

Eve's story was fictitious and unlikely replicated in real life, but it does resonate. Students who discussed Eve's story were also sent a link to Chapter 6 of Venkatesh's (2008) *Gang Leader for a Day* to read, titled "The hustled and the hustler" (pp. 185–218). Thus, when the students arrived for their second class (or the second hour of the workshop), they were usually bursting with enthusiasm to discuss Venkatesh's chapter. However, this excitement got put on hold deliberately while the students discussed Eve's story. In other words, when they finally get to discuss Venkatesh's chapter, either they had written down the learning from Eve's story or had it fresh in their minds. This type of learning was characterised in Chapter 1 as an inoculation before reading more complex texts. It scaffolds learning at each stage providing tools before adding complexity. What follows now is an overview of *Gang Leader for a Day*, inclusive of how students respond to it and how they saw Eve's story as remarkably similar.

GANG LEADER FOR A DAY

In 1988 Sudhir Venkatesh was a postgraduate student in his first semester of graduate school at the University of Chicago when he began studying inner city poverty without ethical considerations. He turned up one night in a South Chicago high-rise and was confronted at knifepoint before being incarcerated by members of the Black Knights gang in a urine-soaked stairwell. Venkatesh (2008) was released only when the local drug lord named JT (who became Venkatesh's key informant) listened as Venkatesh misrepresented his research plans. Venkatesh was neither writing a book nor a dissertation.

At the time Venkatesh was a first-year graduate student completing course work, four years away from assembling a dissertation committee and seven years away from becoming a sociologist with a PhD. From this inauspicious start and with Venkatesh's life at risk, he begins his eight-year study placing those he met at risk. Venkatesh's safety and access to the high-rise subjects was assured by JT's patronage:

> I realized that I never formally asked JT about gaining access to his life and work.
>
> (Venkatesh, 2008, p. 35)

> JT was excited about writing his biography. He offered to assign me a personal driver.
>
> (Venkatesh, 2008, p. 39)

Venkatesh collected data, quoting all those he met verbatim with no attempt to inform them about his research question or to seek consent. Informed consent is a two-way street. It is first incumbent on the researcher knowing what to inform the subject about. For Venkatesh, this was impossible:

> He [JT] had no real sense of what I would actually be writing – because in truth, I didn't know myself.
>
> (Venkatesh, 2008, p. 67)

Venkatesh's study was inductive, beginning with a focus on poverty in general and moving toward a study of the informal economy of the high-rise – an account of how the tenants earn money – by babysitting, sex work, fixing cars, etc. Much of this paid work went on under the radar of both the Internal Revenue Service and, more importantly, the two high-rise power brokers – JT, the gang leader, and Ms Bailey, the high-rise manager. Both of these gatekeepers brokered, via coercion, Venkatesh's access to this informal economy.

Venkatesh did not believe what the tenants told him and sought to confirm the veracity of this data by triangulating it with his two gatekeepers. Venkatesh reported:

> "Hey, you know what, I could actually use the chance to tell you [JT and Ms Bailey] what I've been finding", I said, taking out my

notebooks. "I've been meeting so many people, and I can't be sure whether they're telling me the truth about how much they earn. I suppose I want to know whether I'm really understanding what it's like to hustle around here". ... For the next three hours, I went through my notebooks and told them what I'd learned about dozens of hustlers, male and female.

(Venkatesh, 2008, pp. 200–201)

Venkatesh divulged information about the tenants' employment practices that had been given freely to him only because he was a trusted person under the patronage of the two power brokers in the apartment complex, Ms Bailey and JT. Venkatesh had gained no informed consent, offered no confidentiality and showed little respect for persons. This resulted in the two gatekeepers using the information to seek retribution from the tenants Venkatesh had named.

Venkatesh's attempt to triangulate his data was methodologically correct, but he made many mistakes; failing to provide confidentiality to those he spoke to being only one. Recording subjects' opinions usually involves the subjects' consent, and this becomes exponentially problematic when the data recorded are illegal transactions – selling drugs, living off the proceeds of drugs, extortion, violence, sex work – all of which invariably lead to tax evasion. These are all indictable events, and the data were not stored securely. On one occasion, Ms Bailey told Venkatesh that his field notes were [insecurely] stored in JT's mother's apartment. This was one of many security lapses.

In 2016, in the class discussion of *Gang Leader for a Day*, students were engaged by Venkatesh's narrative, seeing its resemblance to Eve's story (Tolich et al., 2017, p. 248). Students were also engaged by what insights others had of both the two readings. As with Eve's story, they suggested a number of interventions Venkatesh could have adopted:

Venkatesh should have gained informed consent from the participants prior to interviewing them.

He should have stored his data more securely and not shared the data with other research participants, especially the two gatekeepers.

He should have avoided situations that put him and others in harm, such as adjudicating disputes that led to an assault.

Venkatesh provided little evidence that he was aware of basic ethical considerations ... because [the residents] were not given the knowledge of what his research was all about they couldn't actually weigh their consent.

What Venkatesh needed to do to avert most of his ethical problems was gain informed consent and the residents' voluntary participation and the consent of JT to collect information specifically about him. Each had the right to privacy.

Consent was reliant on JT knowing what [Venkatesh] was doing and when he began his project his research goals were not clearly formed, meaning informing others of his research was not possible.

Confidentiality and the storage of data provisions would have demonstrated Venkatesh's respect for the subjects, and their data.

Teachers of ethics should thank Venkatesh for his candour. He presents himself as an open book. Criticism of Venkatesh's research ethics focuses on how he used coercion – gaining access to interviewees – via the gang boss JT. This clearly violated the notion of voluntary participation. This widened the discussion in the class from the standalone concepts of consent and informed consent to voluntary participation. The residents of the Chicago high-rise were not volunteers; their autonomy was undermined.

The logistics of sending students a link to Venkatesh's chapter prior to the workshop meant when they arrived at the workshop they were primed with outrage channelling their responses through Eve's story first. When given the opportunity to discuss Venkatesh's chapter, the students' responses spoke volumes:

Is this chapter a true story? He's in a controlled environment and is putting himself in danger [and] also putting other people in danger to and he doesn't know that.

Venkatesh makes me bloody angry. Just like with Eve, he needed better training and better awareness of what he was getting into.

I found this chapter really pushed my buttons. I felt a general disbelief. Surely no person would be that naïve to conduct research like this.

What really irks me is the whole thing. Where do you start? In both cases, Eve and Venkatesh, the researchers began the research without knowing when or who s/he's going to interview. He says he wants to study poverty from the point of view of African-Americans in these neighbourhoods, but he held random conversations without considering the impact of those conversations.

There are unequal power dynamics here. The gang bosses were saying to Venkatesh just knock on the door and these people will talk to you. That made me very angry. They were not only vulnerable because they were poor or on welfare, they were also vulnerable because they were under threat from the bosses.

(Tolich et al., 2017)

When the 2018 workshop students were asked what the most important ethical concept was in the context of Eve's story and Venkatesh's book, they said it was autonomy. Their insight reshaped the conversation away from the raw concept of consent towards the more sophisticated term, autonomy. The introduction of autonomy heralded a depth of understanding about research ethics. Autonomy was one step beyond informed consent; it captured informed consent and voluntary participation in one concept.

Students were curious about Venkatesh. They wanted to know how his research came about, leading many students to read the entire book. Their questions often expressed disbelief that his research was done without any academic supervision. This, too, was similar to Eve's story. "Where was the supervisor?" In answer to this question, Venkatesh acknowledges some deception. It was doubtful Venkatesh's supervisor knew he was conducting research on the supervisor's behalf.

> I told [Professor] Wilson the barest details of the fieldwork.
>
> (Venkatesh, 2008, p. 38)

> There were times I wanted to tell my professors the real reason I missed class now and then, but I never did.
>
> (Venkatesh, 2008, p. 38)

The subtitle of *Gang Leader for a Day* is *A Rogue Sociologist Takes to the Streets*. In this subtitle Venkatesh self-defines himself outside normal supervision.

One student writing in response to a two-hour workshop where Tolich was a guest lecturer compared and contrasted the ethics practised by Venkatesh in "Hustler and Hustled", Chapter 6 of *Gang Leader for a Day*, with the hypothetical case, Eve's story, read in class time. The student wrote:

> The primary take-away from today's seminar for me is the essential pre-condition of trust and respect. Trust because that is the contract that the researcher enters into when researching phenomena involving human subjects and respect because this is the entry point for understanding the concept of "do no harm" and "beneficence". Thinking about how this applies to Eve's story and Venkatesh's story, I feel that both researchers fell well short of mark when comparing their intentions against what I think of as the essential pre-conditions of trust and respect. Eve because her intention was to use research material, which was covertly obtained while working in a position of trust, in a way that would almost certainly prove damaging to the individual subjects of that research, and Venkatesh because he breached the confidentiality of individual subjects from his research so

that he may obtain further research material or verify the veracity of that material (as well as publishing material that could clearly identify individual or groups of subjects). Is one of these researchers worse than the other? In terms of trust and respect, I don't think so. Both failed to anticipate the ramifications of their actions on the research subjects (or care about them) and both failed to practice the "do no harm" and "beneficence" principles. It is also true, however, that of these two examples Venkatesh actually did undertake actions that were harmful, while Eve's actions were not enacted. Thinking about actual harm caused, as Venkatesh did cause harm while Eve did not, then I think it is true that Venkatesh's story differs from Eve's on the point of action undertaken and harm caused. Venkatesh is clearly guilty of causing harm. Eve is not. On this basis I think they are both at fault by virtue of their lack of integrity and respect for their research subjects. But it is Venkatesh who actually caused harm to others through his lack of integrity and respect.

As one of many student responses, this piece is emblematic of the students' recognition of the key principles of importance in our interactions with others. These are not framed as what is needed to meet regulatory requirements, but what is owed to participants. These ideas of trust, respect, integrity, all were part of the cumulative collection of ethical considerations.

ETHICS ON THE RUN

In a semester-long course, students also read *On the Run* by Alice Goffman (2014, pp. 213–263). It provided a graphic account of her six years living in black Philadelphia neighbourhoods collecting field notes on their lives, especially the young men who lived on Sixth Street. As her research evolved from an undergraduate senior thesis to a PhD, the data collection targeted these men's lives and how the Philadelphia Police Department deal to inner-city Black youth. Goffman described the ongoing harassment with the men "dipping and dodging" the police 24/7 (Goffman, 2014, p. 38). Collectively, these field notes provided the data for her PhD awarded at Princeton University. The resulting book was published by the University of Chicago Press and was later presented to a mass market by Picador.

Ethical issues do not feature either formally or informally in Goffman's book. There is no explicit mention that an institutional review board (IRB) reviewed either her undergraduate thesis or her PhD dissertation. This omission would not have been a problem had Goffman provided evidence of ethical insurance in her research. Others also commented on an absence of ethical considerations.

Writing in *The New Inquiry* blog (http://thenewinquiry.com/essays/black-life-annotated/), Christina Sharpe records her concerns about Goffman's ethical dilemmas:

> I am concerned about the risks Goffman's presence posed to her subjects – increased attention by the police, undue stress on personal lives etc. I am concerned that there is no IRB protocol on file for her undergraduate thesis at the University of Pennsylvania. And while the Princeton IRB protocol on file may be backdated to include the research Goffman did as an undergraduate, that's an exceptional procedure. I am concerned, but not surprised, that critics have overwhelmingly embraced this book as it abets fantasies of black pathology.

A feature of Goffman's ethnography is her candid reporting of others' lives and her difficulties getting along as a middle-class white woman. She recalls how difficult she found following the African American Vernacular accent of the teenagers that she tutored (Goffman, 2014, p. 217). Moreover, Goffman's problematic grasp of the African American Vernacular continued when she hung out with the Sixth Street men:

> I was struggling to overcome a language barrier. Mike and Chuck used what linguists call an African American Vernacular English, and unlike Aisha's mother and aunt, they didn't shift their speech much for my benefit. They also employed more slang than Aisha and her girlfriends did. I had to work hard to learn the grammar and vocabulary they were using. … The confusion ran deeper that this language barrier: I didn't understand the significance of events as they occurred, misinterpreting people's gestures and actions.
>
> (Goffman, 2014, p. 217)

If African American Vernacular English was difficult to decipher, how did inner-city residents decipher Goffman's accent, especially the dialect known as academic research and the ethical nuances that underpin it? Unfortunately, Goffman shares little discussion about getting in and getting along; how she used codes of ethics underpinning her sociological tradition. How did she explain to her participants what she was doing recording copious notes? What would her participants have made of terms drawn from the academic vernacular like confidentiality and informed consent? What should novice researchers make of Goffman's ethical considerations (or lack thereof) protecting the confidentiality of her informants?

The students were as critical of Goffman as they were of both Venkatesh and Eve. The 2016 cohort wrote (Tolich et al., 2017, p. 249):

> Like Venkatesh, the intentions of Goffman's research were not clear either to her or her participants at the outset. She only made that discovery as she was collating her field notes. What Goffman could have done was to inform the parents of the young girls she was collecting field notes on and ask them if that was okay. She gave no evidence that she did that.
>
> From our discussions, we came to agree that if researchers set out with a framework that did not start with informed consent; they are all but guaranteed to generate other ethical issues in their research. This was readily apparent in the Venkatesh and Goffman cases. In Venkatesh's and Goffman's case they present no evidence they were working from any ethical framework, which in turn explains how Venkatesh ended up in situations where he harmed tenants and potentially put his life in danger. Goffman, on the other hand, employed a methodology that undermined subjects' autonomy when collecting data without consent.

Despite Goffman's efforts to use pseudonyms (and to some extent to skew the identity of her research site) in her attempt to protect the identity of her informants, she failed to consider how the "smallness" of the Sixth Street community might also undermine the concept of confidentiality in her research. Reporters, it turned out, had taken a photograph of Goffman to this area and been able to locate the Sixth Street boys by knocking on a door in the area, showing a photo of Goffman, claiming to be a friend of hers and asking where they might find her (McQuade, 2015). In being unaware of the limits of confidentiality, Goffman acted as a beacon to third parties. Not only were participants denied informed consent, they were extended few ethical protections such as confidentiality.

Although Alice Goffman provides no roadmap to follow for her ethical considerations, she does open a portal to an earlier historical period. She lists her father Erving Goffman's methodological treatise *On Fieldwork* (Goffman & Lofland, 1989) as her ethics guidebook. This was not sound practice; although fieldwork techniques have not changed in the ensuing years, ethical responsibilities have changed in the wake of the injustice shown to black men researched at Tuskegee and later codified in the 1979 Belmont Report.

Ethical issues such as informed consent and confidentiality did not feature in Erving Goffman's research. He was of an era where covert research was condoned. Alice Goffman's father Erving Goffman's advice on getting in and getting along in *On Fieldwork* does not involve informed consent but he recommends telling participants a story, what he calls *telling practices*.

> You have to anticipate being questioned by people whom you study so you engage in providing a story that will hold up should the facts be brought to their attention. So you engage in what are sometimes called "telling practices". ... So you have to get some story that will be – I like a story such that if they find out what you are doing, the story you presented could not be an absolute lie. If they don't find out what you're e doing, the story you presented doesn't get in your way.
>
> (Goffman & Lofland, 1989, pp. 126–127)

In the post-Belmont era where Alice Goffman researches, social scientists are compelled to address basic ethical considerations. The new *telling practices* begin with informed consent when recruiting those that volunteer to take part in research. Informed consent serves to inform the potential subjects about the background of the research and invite then to volunteer to take part in the research usually with the right to withdraw at any time. Alice Goffman provides no evidence she did that.

DISCUSSION

What learning do postgraduate students take from reading Alice Goffman's and Sudhir Venkatesh's best-selling ethnographies, given that basic ethical considerations appear non-essential in their stories of obtaining their PhDs? The ethical issues identified in both stories replicate the fictitious Eve's story. Venkatesh gained no informed consent, and he breached his informants' confidentiality when he triangulated his data. Goffman also provided no evidence of gaining informed consent, allowing reporters to expose the identity of those she studied.

Even in its brevity, Eve's story replicates that of Venkatesh and Goffman in terms of how she could have better protected her informants. The various cohorts of students, plus the 25 colleagues Tolich interviewed, were unequivocal in that they would not support Eve's future research plans. Moreover, they were wary about whether retrospective consent was possible, given both the breach of trust and the likelihood of creating more harm than good. These comparisons provided a fertile ground to become familiar with basic ethical concepts. Students in the 2016 class reflecting on the first part of the class wrote in their article (Tolich et al., 2017) about their incremental journey into qualitative research ethics:

The format of the first four weeks of the Qualitative Research Ethics class enabled us to think and do ethics out loud, at a distance appropriate to our stage as fledgling researchers. Our journey started with a simple enough question, "Is this [recording device] ethical?" Along the way we have dealt with feelings of, "that's not right ..." and through interpreting these gut instincts against a framework of ethical concepts we now have the confidence to say "that is *not* ethical and here's why". The autonomy of all those who take part in research should be respected by asking in advance if they volunteer to take part after learning what the aims are of the research. Researchers also need to provide assurances that they will take all steps necessary to ensure that no harm will befall those who volunteer to take part in the research and their identity and information will be protected. To that end we learned that there were limits on confidentiality and informants could read materials that allowed them to identify themselves and others, even though those external to the study may be oblivious to the study site. By drilling down to that next level of understanding, it became easier to see how the concepts could be applied in our own research. Through the readings for the class, we learned much more about the nuances of ethics.

Although our journey has been short, it has also been rich. Our experience has been engrossing, confronting, refreshing, empowering, and has piqued our interest in new areas of study and research. We have made new friends and are becoming trusted colleagues. But most importantly, through our increasingly candid exchanges in class we have been introduced to our ethical selves.

Evident in this student description of their experience are the concept of ethical intuitions (gut instincts), the scaffolding of learning, the practice of collective moral imagining, awareness of their moral reasoning, and the development of tools to help confront future problems. Here and in other descriptions, it is clear that they recognise their understanding can deepen, which says something about how they think of ethical thinking and practice. But importantly, they also gain confidence in their role as ethical actors to speak up or out about something they consider wrong: "We now have confidence to say 'that is not ethical and here's why'".

How will subsequent generations of sociology students read and use Goffman's and Venkatesh's books? How should social scientists, journal editors or degree-awarding institutions respond to ethnographic data collected without evidence of informed consent? Is the data useable? The cohorts of students did not think it was. Equally, colleagues who responded to Eve's story claim the data is useable only to provide sensitising concepts or insight for future data collection.

Is this criticism of Venkatesh and Goffman harsh? Some say it is.

Delamont and Atkinson (2018, p. 126) are critical of critiques of Venkatesh, saying the critiques of the book in *Sociological Forum* are po-faced "with no sensitivity to the genre or its distinctive rhetoric". The critiques offered here are different. The nature of others' critiques focus on the use of stereotypes by Venkatesh. None of these stereotypes featured in the classroom discussion of this book. The focus was on the interaction between the researcher and those who were researched. It was obvious to the students that at no time did Venkatesh show any inclination towards using ethical concepts to protect those people he studied. The consensus was that he should have. Qualitative researchers and the people they study need ethics.

The students in 2016 and 2018, as well as the 2018 Christchurch workshop students, would not agree that this criticism was harsh. They not only found fault with Venkatesh and Goffman, but they clearly saw these sociologists as having the ethics akin to Eve's story.

REVIEW QUESTIONS AND EXERCISES

Compare and contrast the ethical issues raised in Eve's story with those in Venkatesh's *Gang Leader for a Day*.

What ethical issues were identical?

Which ethical issues were unique to each case?

Of the two cases, which was the more serious breach of ethics?

What one ethical practice could Venkatesh or Eve make to enhance the protections of the persons they studied?

What practical issues might make collecting data difficult in these situations? How can these issues be addressed in an ethical manner?

NOTES

1 Permission was granted to audio record the workshop and to use the quotations.
2 Diminished autonomy may be called different things in different disciplines. Generally what is being referred to are those situations in which people have impaired capacity (whether permanent or transient) for decision-making and exercising their autonomy, making them vulnerable in certain contexts, such as research. Strategies to support people with diminished autonomy will vary by context.

CHAPTER 4

When consent is uninformed, empower participants and activate a reference group

The goal of this book is to demonstrate that research ethics is not esoteric or formulaic. That is, it's not something individuals are incapable of developing their own knowledge and skills in or just a matter of learning and applying a set of rules. We believe that research ethics is a mixture of knowledge, skills, and behaviours that can be developed by anyone to apply to different contexts appropriately. While there are differences between research ethics for researchers and research ethics experts, these are differences of degree and application, not kind. We believe developing your research ethics starts with recognising your own ethical compass, recognising, informing, and further developing your ethical intuitions, imagination, and reasoning, and building confidence in your moral agency, alongside knowledge acquisition. When you develop research ethics in this way, you are better equipped to design your project ethically from the beginning, engaging with the appropriate stakeholders as needed. But importantly, you are also better able to deal with issues that arise once your project is underway when you have to react within time constraints that do not necessarily allow a "check back" with the ethics committee.[1] Progressing through the book provides a focus on how you might think about a certain aspect of research and what you could or should consider, while explaining some of the background and ethical concepts that apply to that aspect. What is important to grasp is how to recognise, analyse, and develop ethically reasoned responses to research ethics issues. In the previous chapter, much of what Tolich's students found wrong with Eve's research design stemmed from a lack of informed consent. This was true, but in some research, informed consent is a grey area; the participant is not fully informed, meaning researchers should, but don't always, take steps to ensure ethical considerations remain robust.

Historically, some of this grey area is enshrined in Articles 1, 9, and 10 of the 1949 Nuremberg Code (BMJ, 1996, 313:1448). This response followed from the misuse of captives for research and experiments by doctors during the Nazi period in Germany leading to the development of ethical codes for research. (Flick, 2006, p. 45)

The Nuremberg Code (displayed in the following list, with Articles 1, 9, and 10 emphasised) consists of a single page. It is given out to students at the start of the third class. Clearly, if Article 1 is not viable, Article 9 is. The research participant has the power to end the study for whatever reason but this does not always happen. In the following exercise, Articles 9 and 10 are aspirational.

1. *The voluntary consent of the human subject is absolutely essential.*
2. The experiment should be such as to yield fruitful results for the good of society, unprocurable by other methods or means of study, and not random and unnecessary in nature.
3. The experiment should be so designed and based on the results of animal experimentation and a knowledge of the natural history of the disease or other problem under study that the anticipated results will justify the performance of the experiment.
4. The experiment should be so conducted as to avoid all unnecessary physical and mental suffering and injury.
5. No experiment should be conducted where there is an *a priori* reason to believe that death or disabling injury will occur; except, perhaps, in those experiments where the experimental physicians also serve as subjects.
6. The degree of risk to be taken should never exceed that determined by the humanitarian importance of the problem to be solved by the experiment.
7. Proper preparations should be made and adequate facilities provided to protect the experimental subject against even remote possibilities of injury, disability, or death.
8. The experiment should be conducted only by scientifically qualified persons. The highest degree of skill and care should be required through all stages of the experiment of those who conduct or engage in the experiment.
9. *During the course of the experiment the human subject should be at liberty to bring the experiment to an end if he has reached the physical or mental state where continuation of the experiment seems to him to be impossible.*
10. *During the course of the experiment the scientist in charge must be prepared to terminate the experiment at any stage, if he has probable cause to believe, in the exercise of the good faith, superior skill, and careful judgment required of him that a continuation of the experiment is likely to result in injury, disability, or death to the experimental subject.*

Beyond receiving a copy of this one-page code, prior to the class, students are also sent a copy of an assigned reading relevant to this lesson. The article explores the ethics of two famous psychological studies by Stanley Milgram and Philip Zimbardo:

Suggested Reading:

Tolich, M. (2014). What can Milgram and Zimbardo teach ethics committees and qualitative researchers about minimizing harm? *Research Ethics*, *10*(2), 86–96.

The article is summarised here.

Primer questions given at the outset of the lesson ask the following: Why was the 14-day Zimbardo study cancelled after six days? What were the circumstances of this cancellation? Questions about the Milgram study become self-evident; why didn't the subjects stop the study?

When the students arrive at class they once again assume that the discussion will focus on the assigned Milgram/Zimbardo article. It eventually does, but first they are presented with two puzzles, one further interrogating the power relationships revealed in the cartoon in Figure 1. The second puzzle is a hypothetical research study inviting readers to take part in a virtual reality experiment.

POWER RELATIONS

When asked to focus on the nature of the relationship between the lecturer and the students in Figure 1, students immediately identify an imbalance of power. Setting aside any socially constructed power relations based on the demographics of the lecturer and the students, in this particular situation, at minimum the lecturer has institutionally bestowed power in relation to the students based on their ability to provide grades or determine whether a student passes a course. There are of course other, subtler ways in which power is enacted within these relations between lecturer and student, related to professional progress, reputation, and confidence. However, for our purposes, recognising that the lecturer here has greater perceived power than the postgraduate students is sufficient.

Even if the lecturer does not explicitly link a student's participation (see Figure 1) in co-authoring a paper with their course grade, students are right to think that the lecturer has the potential to exploit the situation. The lecturer did not do that. He mediated any potential harm by leaving the room when the students deliberated on whether they would take part in writing a journal article. This allowed the students to present a position of solidarity in their decision. A group decision works to equal out the imbalance of power to a degree. The power dynamics within the group itself are, of course, another question. The lecturer could have done more; he could have asked a colleague to facilitate this discussion.

Looking deeper into the power relationship, the students reveal intwined relationships. The lecturer has a number of roles. He is both a teacher and a researcher. When the lecturer asked the students to deliberate about taking part in writing the journal article, was his question stated from a role as a teacher, or as a researcher. The students saw him in both roles. In ethics, these situations are called a conflict of roles or a conflict of interest. This concept was not novel to the students; it was mentioned previously in Chapter 3. There, a student spoke about Eve's various roles, saying:

> Eve was clearly in a conflict of interest as a person tasked with recording details for refuge and for her own research purposes.

Should the lecturer (or could the lecturer) have declared this conflict of interest at the beginning of the course, before activating the audio recorder? This action would be considered good practice, but it would have also undermined the experimental conditions being created. Thus, this power-related conundrum raises the question, is informed consent always mandatory? Asked another way, is informed consent always prudent? That is the focusing question for this lesson.

Flick (2006, p. 46, citing Ethik-Kodex, 1993, pp. 13–19) provides insight into the uncertainty:

> A general rule for participation in sociological investigations is that it is voluntary and it takes place on the basis of the fullest information about the goals and methods of the particular piece of research. *The principle of informed consent cannot always be applied in practice, for instance if comprehensive pre-information would distort the results of the research in an unjustifiable way.* In such cases an attempt must be made to use other possible modes of informed consent.
>
> (our emphasis)

A puzzle outlined in the information sheet that follows examines a situation where mandated informed consent practice is not practical. Tolich requires students to put themselves in the role of a potential hypothetical research participant. First, they solve these puzzles, identifying ethical problems and offering solutions in the hypothetical case before examining how these ethical conundrums exist in the Zimbardo and Milgram studies. Here is the hypothetical study:

PARTICIPANT INFORMATION SHEET

AN EMPATHETIC VIRTUAL REALITY

You are invited to take part in a research study which aims to evaluate how participants' empathy is expressed in a virtual environment. Empathy is defined as a person's ability to understand and share feelings of others.

Who should take part

Researchers are seeking 20 males and 20 females aged 18 to 34 to take part in the research.

What will I have to do

In the research project you will be required to wear special goggles and a lightweight tracking device. In addition to the glasses you will be fitted with physiological equipment designed to measure your heart rate respiration and skin responses whilst you are in the immersive virtual reality environment.

There are two parts to the study. The first will be a questionnaire completed both before and after the virtual reality experience. The second part requires the participant to take part in a number of tasks within the virtual reality environment. These tasks should take no more than 20 minutes.

The actual nature of the study is unlikely to harm individuals.

You should be aware that some people find virtual reality experience stressful. Some also experience a degree of nausea.

Any information that is shared during the study will be treated with strict confidence and once the study is completed, it will not be possible to identify individuals in the final report.

Thank you for your interest in this study.

In 2019, students in a two-hour workshop engaged with this exercise, finding the information sheet incomplete:

> If I was prone to nausea and I was taking part in a study, I would want to be able to stop the experiment at any time. It does not say that on the information sheet and it should.

The class discussion that followed that comment suggested a sentence needed to be added to the information sheet stating that the participant can stop the experiment at any time. This finding enacted Article 9 of the Nuremberg Code (BMJ, 1996, 313:1448).

> During the course of the experiment the human subject should be at liberty to bring the experiment to an end if he has reached the physical or mental state where continuation of the experiment seems to him to be impossible.

A second student focused on the safety of the participant, asking how many people were monitoring the participant's wellbeing. Was there a technician as well as a researcher observing the study? They thought this information should also have been included in the participant information sheet. This student wanted to know if it was it up to the participant to declare they wanted to leave the study. Equally, could the researcher and/or a technician also make that decision? This comment was in line of Article 10 of the Nuremberg Code, Article 10 (BMJ, 1996, 313:1448) makes it a responsibility of the researcher to end the research if the participant experiences an adverse reaction.

> During the course of the experiment the scientist in charge must be prepared to terminate the experiment at any stage, if he has probable cause to believe, in the exercise of the good faith, superior skill, and careful judgment required of him that a continuation of the experiment is likely to result in injury, disability, or death to the experimental subject.

The students' discussion raised role responsibilities beyond a simple informed consent statement. However, they did not go one step further, asking if the researcher or the technician had a conflict of interest. To do so would be to focus on the researcher's attention: was it towards the research goals, or to the health and safety of the research participant?

The fictitious virtual reality study plays the same role as Eve's story, allowing the students to discover their own ethical concerns and solutions in the puzzles. The rest of the chapter moves from the fictitious to the real. The reading (Tolich, 2014) sent to students about the Zimbardo and Milgram studies (and summarised in this chapter) raise a trove of ethical issues, beginning with a less-than-fulsome consent process informing the participant about the nature of the study. Both studies are well documented and can be viewed on YouTube:

The Stanford experiment

https://www.youtube.com/watch?v=KND_bBDE8RQ

The Milgram study

https://www.youtube.com/watch?v=rdrKCilEhC0

HORROR STORIES

Many qualitative researchers (Wiles, 2012, p. 69) view Milgram and Zimbardo as the great horror stories in social science ethics and emblematic of the need to evaluate behavioural research designs prospectively for all social sciences (Librett & Perrone, 2010). Their studies are described as: having iconic status (Haggerty, 2004), notorious (Homan, 2006; Israel & Hay, 2006; King, Henderson & Stein, 1999), disgrace (Lahman, Geist, Rodriguez, Graglia & DeRoche, 2011) infamous (Nicholls, Brehaut & Saginur, 2012; Williams-Jones & Holm, 2005) highly publicised (Lopus, Grimes, Becker & Pearson, 2007), well-known violations of participants' rights (Fitch, 2005), and enduring examples of abuse and deception of research participants (Librett & Perrone, 2010). Haggerty (2004) characterises Zimbardo and Milgram, together with Laud Humphrey's (1975) Tearoom trade as the inescapable referents in any discussion of research ethics in the social sciences. "Each study raises important questions about informed consent, deception, and manipulation of subjects, all of which REBs [ethics committees] continue to grapple with" (Haggerty, 2004, p. 399).

While we can accept this criticism, there is much to be learned from the mistakes of how Zimbardo and Milgram practised their research craft. That being said, both studies provide ample evidence of researching without being sensitive to either the Nuremberg Code or to the needs of those who are taking part in their research. That is, ethical research practice is not in and of itself intuitive. Rather, our discussion of ethical intuitions has been focused on the idea that with the particular kind of approach outlined in this book, students can recognise and develop skills and knowledge that help them identify their ethical intuitions and make their ethical intuitions and related reasoning better over time.

If we think about these famous cases in history of unethical research, we could categorise these in their simplest form in two ways. On the one hand are the cases, where the researcher or research team may have subscribed to an ends-justify-the-means type of philosophy. In so doing, they recognise that they may be treating participants unethically, but they believe their goal, if achieved outweighs these ethical infractions. The few can be sacrificed for the many. This is then a form of ethical calculation but specifically discredited by something like the Nuremberg Code and other frameworks created by societies to shield human rights. On the other hand are the cases where we might typify the research or research team as ethically unknowing or even ignorant (i.e., no ethical reasoning to fault). What is meant here is that they fail to see what is ethically salient in a given situation or ignore ethically important facts and conditions. They fail to consider people appropriately or their relationships, or communities. They might fail to think through potential consequences. This should not be mistaken for what we have earlier described as ethically important moments in the field that may occur, which we consider unpredictable. We mean here rather a failure to engage one's ethical imagination about the potential outcomes of one's work at all.

In many cases a mixture of these two may be at play, and the consequentialist approach of the first categorisation may be influenced by many different priorities. That is, conflicts in one's roles or a variety of external pressures may create a multitude of ends, to which then unethical means are justified (DuBois et al., 2016). Similarly, unknowing or ignorance can be common within a given setting, making it harder to recognise as an individual researcher or research team. Ethics committees can suffer from ethical unknowing or ignorance as much as researchers, thus complicating the picture and the evaluation of responsibility.

Ethical intuition, imagination, reasoning, and agency are key concepts and activities that are returned to often in this book as a solution to these failures.

ZIMBARDO'S PRISON STUDY

Zimbardo's (2007) prison study wanted to know how participants put into a particular role, for example, the prison guard or a prisoner, would act. Would they assume the role and be engaged with it? Or would they see the whole experience as a joke? Zimbardo's study is important for research ethics because it asks the question of why this 14-day study ended after six days. What is the learning taken from that premature closure?

Zimbardo recruited 24 students from Stanford University and paid them $15 per day. They were given psychological evaluations to test their suitability for a psychological study before being randomly assigned to two groups. Twelve were prisoners and 12 were guards. To create the research environment, the basement of the psychology department at Stanford University was redesigned as a temporary prison. To establish authenticity, Zimbardo had the local campus police arrest those assigned to the prisoner category. On entry to the prison, they were stripped naked, deloused, and required to wear a prison smock. The prison guards were given matching guard uniforms.

Zimbardo's research question asked, "Could some of the world's evil result from ordinary people, randomly assigned to one of two groups, operating in circumstances that selectively elicit bad behavior from their natures?" (Zimbardo, 2007, p. 230). Zimbardo was surprised at how rapidly both the prisoners and the prison guards assumed their aggressor and passive roles:

> At first the prisoners reacted with disbelief at their total loss of privacy, constant surveillance by the guards, and the oppression under which they were living. They tried to rebel, but their rebellion was put down by the guards. The prisoners then tried to set up an elected grievance committee, which failed to produce meaningful changes. Next, the prisoners began to turn against one another; this breakdown of group cohesion gave rise to feelings of isolation. Some of the prisoners coped by becoming extremely disturbed emotionally, as a way of demanding attention and help. Others became excessively obedient and sided with the guards against a fellow prisoner who had gone on a hunger strike. Instead of supporting the hunger strike, the prisoners treated him as a troublemaker who deserved to be punished.
> Zimbardo and others who were observing the simulation were so drawn into the situation that they did not think to end the study.
> (Sieber & Tolich, 2013, p. 60)

Was this study ethical? Apparently, it was. The Stanford University ethics committee deemed it was ethical, seeing the study as innocuous role-playing, a bit like cops and robbers:

> Neither the members of the human subjects research committee nor I imagined in advance that any such external authority was necessary in an experiment where college students had the freedom to stay or go anytime the going became rougher than they could handle. Before the experiment, it was just "kids going to play cops and robbers" and it was hard to imagine what could happen within a few days. It would have been good to have had advance hindsight operating.
> (Zimbardo, 2007, p. 235)

The learning Tolich's students take from an ethics approval is that ethics committees are not infallible, and in this case they overlooked the conflict of interest that Zimbardo had as researcher and prison warden.

A second learning is the aborted length of the study. The fact that the 14-day study ended abruptly after 6 days exposes an important ethical consideration. Why did it end, and what is the principle underlying that action? Zimbardo describes the ending:

It is likely, however that I would have terminated the study on Sunday, at the end of a full week, as a "natural ending" had not Christina Maslach's intervention forced premature closure ...

In retrospect, I believe that the main reason I did not end the study sooner, when it began to get out of hand, resulted from the conflict created in me by *my dual roles as principal investigator and thus guardian of the research ethics of the experiment,* and as prison superintendent, eager to maintain the integrity and stability of my prison at all costs. I would like to believe that had someone else been playing the superintendent's role I would have seen the light and blown the whistle sooner. I now realise that there should have been someone with authority above mine, someone in charge of oversight of the experiment.

(Zimbardo, 2007, pp. 234–235, our emphasis)

Christina Maslach was a singular *reference group* even though Zimbardo's study had a quasi-reference group in place in the psychology department at Stanford University. This quasi-reference group consisted of colleagues and graduate students who took a great interest in the escalation of the suffering but little interest in the effects of the suffering experienced by the prison inmates. Maslach explains what made Maslach so different:

The answer, I think, lies in two facts: I was a late entrant into the situation, and I was an "outsider". Unlike everyone else, I had not been a consenting participant in the study. Unlike everyone else, I had no socially defined role within that prison context, unlike everyone else, I was not there every day being carried along as the situation changed and escalated bit by bit. Thus the situation I entered at the end of the week was not truly the "same" as it was for everyone else. I lacked the prior consensual history, place and perspective. For them, the situation was constructed as being still within the range of normalcy; for me it was not – it was a madhouse.

As an outsider, I did not have the option of specific social rules that I could disobey, so my dissent took a different form – of challenging the situation itself. This challenge has been seen by some as a heroic action, but at the time it did not feel especially heroic. To the contrary, it was [a] very scary and lonely experience being the deviant, doubting my judgement of both situations and people, and maybe even my worth as a research social psychologist.

(in Zimbardo, 2007, p. 458)

Who was at fault here for the escalation of violence? Maybe it was the Stanford University ethics review committee who failed to acknowledge a basic feature of Zimbardo's research design: the conflict of interest producing a domino effect on the entire study. The lessons here for Tolich's students and the reader is that ethics committees can be useful but they are not foolproof, and similarly, researchers can be blind to ethical issues in their own studies without external input, a critical associate or in this case a graduate student, and that speaking up is challenging, but necessary. At the end of the day the researcher was ultimately responsible. Yet clearly Zimbardo's conflict of interest as the principal investigator and the warden resulted in his failure to perceive the possible harm to his participants (both prisoners and guards) in the rapid escalation of violence.

There are ways to avoid this situation. One of them is to enforce the Nuremberg Code that allows the participant to withdraw from the study or the researcher to withdraw the participant at any time. However, that didn't work in this situation. A backup solution is to have a reference group, in this case made up of Zimbardo's colleagues. This too did not protect the participants. It was only an outsider, Christina Maslach, who heroically curtailed the 14 day trial at day six.

The Nuremberg Code written in 1947, 20 years prior to Zimbardo's study, was undermined by Zimbardo's conflict of interest, and participants were not given a clear pathway to opt out of the trial. The researchers purposely diminished the autonomy of participants.

This problem stems from the conflict of interest, the researcher wearing two hats; first to collect data from participants; and second to protect those participants during the study. These problems are common and can develop at any time in a study. In Chapter 2 of this volume, Punch (1994) was quoted as saying:

> [Ethical issues] often have to be resolved situationally, and even spontaneously, without the luxury of being able to turn first to consult a more experienced colleague.

> (p. 89)

A precaution for this likely event is to create a standing reference group made up of intelligent people who have no stake in the research. Here is an example, "Dan's passing" that Tolich uses as a workshop exercise to engage and challenge his students to locate practical solutions.

Dan's Passing: Working with an Established Reference Group

Edwards, R., & Weller, S. (2016). Ethical dilemmas around anonymity and confidentiality in longitudinal research data sharing: the death of Dan. In Tolich, M. (Ed.), *Qualitative ethics in practice* (pp. 97–108). London: Routledge.

Dan was a young man participating in a longitudinal study looking at growing up in rural England. Dan was interviewed when he was 11 years old, again at the age of 14, and finally there was an interview planned for when he was 17. There was nothing unusual about this case until the researchers Susie Weller and Roz Edwards returned to interview Dan at age 17 and found he had passed away. This was their *big ethical moment*, a moment that could not have been predicted in advance by either researcher or by an ethics committee.

Weller and Edwards were experienced researchers, and they had previously formed a reference group made up of national and international academics as well as practitioners working in a range of youth and family organisations. They turned their problem over to them asking who should have access to Dan's data. Should the family be allowed to listen to the audio recordings or read the transcripts? Assume in the interviews Dan discussed his thoughts on his parents, siblings, teachers and his friends.

- Whose interests are paramount in this situation?
- What responsibilities does the researcher have to the living and the dead?
- What are the main issues for the family? What are the main issues for Dan?

Assume Dan would have signed an *assent form* (explained further in Chapter 7) as a young person with diminished autonomy and the parents would have signed a *consent form* allowing Dan to take part. The assumption would be that all data would be confidential to both those outside the family and those within the family.

When presented with this case, Tolich's students' responses to this query showed they grasped the conflicts. They could act as an impromptu reference group, and their consensus stated:

> We need to stick very closely to issues of confidentiality and consent as these are the principles that Dan was working with.

Tolich complicates the ethical conundrum by playing on heartstrings, focusing workshop participants on the mother's grief. This trope engages a bigger ethical moment.

> I see this as an ethical and moral dilemma. The ethical dilemma is what promises were given to Dan. Was he ever told the circumstances, which is that it, would be shared with other people?

The answer is no. But morally we feel for the mother, we feel for her grief and we want to do something for her.

A second workshop group responding to this scenario captured the complexity of the situation with a succinct reply.

> If Dan entered into the study believing that his family wouldn't have access to the data then I don't think his mother should be able to read them – what if there are things in there that are negative towards her or his siblings? Surely that would break her heart even further? And it could be things that only she will interpret as negative – things that the interviewer might think is harmless might mean something quite different to her. I think you have to honour him and what he thought would happen with the data.

> If you were going to give the data to the mother, then presumably someone is going through it and thinking "Yeah, this is harmless, she can read this, there's nothing in here that is going to re-traumatise her", but who gives that person the right to make that call? Surely the only person who gets to make that call is Dan, and he can't, so that call can't be made?

Tolich's students expressed concern for the grieving mother herself.

> You might be approaching the mother a couple of years down the track and here you are re-traumatising her again, yeah, how do you approach it.

But in general the students' impromptu reference group discussion focused on the rights of Dan, not the mother.

> When he first gave consent was there the understanding that it wouldn't be shared with his parents and if so, does that not need to be upheld?

> When he signed [the assent] there was an understanding that it wouldn't be shared with his parents, then I think you uphold that.

> As a researcher I agree, but as a human, you know, it's a little bit more like ahhh, yeah, it's tricky.

> I don't think it's so much "do no harm", I think you've gotta stick with the principle regardless of what's in the data. If you agreed to confidentiality from the parents then you need to stick to that, if it wasn't agreed then there's flexibility there. And while they might still

have a veto over whether the data can be included or not, they don't necessarily have the right for it to be given back to them. Stick to the protocol, yeah

And this is what the researchers did.

In what follows, we track a delicate pathway Weller followed guided by her reference group. Weller (Edwards & Weller, 2016) takes up the story:

> [V]isiting the family felt very different; the boundaries and purpose of our discussion was less clear. I was concerned about long silences, upsetting Dan's mother further and about explaining that his interviews were confidential for fear that she might wish me to divulge all that he had said … Despite my anxieties the visit went as well as could be expected given the circumstances … At no point did she enquire what Dan had discussed and completely respected the confidentiality of his interviews. Occasionally she broke the conversation to show me photographs, sharing all they had done to keep his memory alive. She also took me to the area in the house dedicated to his memory, where his ashes stood on a small table surrounded by photographs and candles … After almost an hour we moved on to talk about ways in which she could record memories of Dan for the Timescapes Archive. She was unsure how best to do this and did not feel confident in talking in an unstructured way or in writing her thoughts. Instead she suggested I ask her questions … on leaving [I] agreed to send her a copy of the transcript of her memories before depositing them in the Archive. She also gave me a photograph, which she felt best represented her son … I wholeheartedly believe that it was the right thing to do and that Dan's mother appreciated the opportunity to share her memories. It appeared to be part of a series of activities she and her family had done to pay tribute to her son and ensure his memory lived on.

Reading Weller's activity here, we might see that it tracks with what would have been regulations or ethical principles (i.e., consent to confidentiality of data, etc.), but the activity she engaged in was much more ethically rich than just following rules. Her responsiveness to the mother, ethical agency in the moment providing clear boundaries around the tapes, and her flexibility and support, show a sophisticated ethical practice. In many ways, her work with the reference group had prepared her for this interaction with Dan's mother, being mindful that it could have gone any number of ways. Despite preparation, Weller needed to be able to exercise her own agency in the situation alone. That is, had the mother reacted differently, Weller would have had to adapt in the moment, while sticking to the decisions made in a way that was sensitive to the mother's grief.

THE MILGRAM STUDY

In 1961, psychologist Stanley Milgram set out to learn what people would do when ordered by an authority figure to possibly harm others. Milgram ran newspaper ads inviting the general public to participate in a learning experiment. Volunteers were paid four dollars, and they would be divided randomly into learners and teachers. These were deceptive instructions; the real aim was to study obedience, not learning, and all of the volunteers found themselves in the role of teacher. They were instructed to teach lists of words to learners, and to give learners increasingly severe electric shocks at every mistake. The "learners" were not wired to the shock apparatus and were actually paid actors who feigned both failures to learn and pain at being "shocked". In fact, of course, the equipment was bogus.

Milgram found that 66% of his participants would deliver what they thought were lethal-level electric shocks. If the participant wanted to leave the research study, they were assertively instructed "The experiment must go on!" by an authoritative-looking scientist at prestigious Yale University. Though they were obviously very distressed about doing so, many remained.

At the end of his research, Milgram used a novel intervention he called "debriefing" of his participants to ensure that they re-entered their world in a good frame of mind. While the practice of debriefing was momentous, it was not always successful. One of his research participants in the Obedience trials, Weiner, recorded his experience with great clarity. He said:

> I stood there. I was angry at having been deceived. I resented the whole situation. I was a little embarrassed at not having stopped earlier, or seen what was going on earlier, and I was not totally unconcerned about my heart rate. What if I had a heart condition? I went home in a cold fury.

> (Blass, 2004, p. 116)

Milgram's conflict of interest was his role as the principal investigator and the person who instructed the research participant that "the experiment must continue". The participant had no obvious way of leaving the trial.

Tolich asks his students what could Milgram have done differently given that it was essential in this research design that that research participant was always the teacher? Now familiar with prior learning, students recite the basic ethics codes Milgram had available at the time. The Nuremberg ethics focused on voluntary consent (first Nuremberg principle) and the participants' right to terminate the study (ninth principle) (BMJ, 1996, 313:1448). It is the ninth principle, the participant's right to withdraw, that was not utilised in Milgram's study. Milgram's instruction to the research participant that the study must continue obscured this principle. That was a fundamental error.

The key learning in this chapter is that even when there is limited informed consent, as in the virtual reality puzzle, the research participant should be empowered to stop the project at any time for any reason. However, when a researcher like Zimbardo sees only the Bedlam in their makeshift prison rather than human suffering, his conflict of interest undermines protections. When Milgram's participants are coerced into killing the learner, these same conflicts of interest diminish the autonomy of the human participant. Agency should have been paramount; they should be able to stop the electric shock trial. Only by recognising one's conflict of interest can the researcher protect the research participant.

UNKNOWN UNKNOWNS

The potential fallibility of researchers and ethics committees' ethical decision-making are found in the discussions provided in this chapter. Apparently they also may be found on the battlefield; see Donald Rumsfeld, https://www.youtube.com/watch?v=REWeBzGuzCc.

While quoting Donald Rumsfeld in an ethics text seems counterintuitive, the idea of known-knowns, known-unknowns, and unknown-unknowns is a helpful one in research ethics. We should address our known-known risks in research always as a minimum ethical commitment. We should make every effort to address our known-unknowns, which we do by employing our ethical imagination informed by previous experience with collaboration and consultation in our planning. The only way to be prepared for unknown-unknowns is through developing our ethical practice; by feeling capable of dealing with problems in the field as they arise. Our ethical intuitions, imagination, reasoning, and agency are the ways that we can address situations to the best of our abilities as they occur.

These things come together when researchers practice research with some humility, realising the limitations of their knowledge and the influences on their ability to make ethical judgements when occupying multiple roles with external pressures, or competing priorities. These things can be ameliorated through simple activities. For example, consult and collaborate with stakeholders and peers. Have a sounding board – the reference group, a critical friend, someone unattached to the research with the requisite knowledge – to be able to provide relevant and responsive advice or input.

Additionally, the students who took part in Tolich's class and workshops saw the potential for reference groups. They also saw how to support participants' autonomy beyond the informed consent process, and especially where the consent process may include some form of deception, i.e., the use of virtual reality. They saw how to reinforce and ensure participants understand and feel able to withdraw should they wish to during a study beyond the initial discussion at consenting. Employing dynamic ongoing consent techniques provides alternatives, that is, as the study progresses seek affirmation by getting consent verbally, repeatedly. This can be done after key steps in the research or periodically throughout an activity that is continuous.

Conducting ethical research relies on a variety of actors (ethics committees, research teams, etc.) being sufficiently ethically aware of a given context to pick out the ethically salient features and ethically knowledgeable enough to address them *and* then act on them. This is in the context of dual roles, time-pressured environments, fragmented connections and communications, etc. Uncertainties are inevitable, and mistakes are always possible. Research ethics is always a movable feast.

REVIEW QUESTIONS AND EXERCISES

1. Apply articles 1, 9, and 10 of the Nuremberg Code to both the Zimbardo and Milgram studies.

    a. How would the studies have been changed had each article being enacted?
    b. How would a conflict of interest have been resolved?

2. Make the necessary corrections to the participant information sheet for the virtual reality study by incorporating Article 9 from the Nuremberg Code.
3. In the scenario of Dan's passing, which consent has more weight for the researcher, Dan's assent or the parent's consent?

4. Role-play graduate student Christine Mallach's criticism of the Zimbardo study. Contrast that with discussions of power imbalance at the top of this chapter discussing Figure 1.
5. Consider Rumsfeld's known knowns, known unknowns, and unknown unknowns in terms of how an iterative interview guide generates an emergent research question. What can a researcher and an ethics committee know in advance, and how should the researcher address the unknowns?

NOTE

1   Also known as Institutional Review Boards or Ethics Review Boards.

CHAPTER 5

Do quantitative and qualitative research have similar ethical considerations?

Chapter 4 discussed the right of the research participants to withdraw from a virtual reality study as this entitlement was enshrined in the Nuremberg Code. Although it is enshrined, withdrawing from a research study, as this chapter shows, is not always straightforward or possible.

Unlike the previous chapter's virtual reality task, this chapter's task does not involve commenting on the participant information sheets and consent forms provided. Take the documentation as given; focus on understanding them as they set up the next task, questioning the ease by which participants can withdraw from a study. For example, can a participant withdraw from a quantitative study (e.g., a survey), as easily as they can withdraw from a qualitative study (e.g., a one-on-one interview)? The answer to this question unearths a fundamental disparity between quantitative research and qualitative research.

The relationship between quantitative researchers and qualitative researchers and their participants are not equal. One relationship is embedded while the other is ephemeral. Research ethics in quantitative research and qualitative research may draw from the same ethics well, but how they manifest themselves in reality and in the rest of this book, are different. Anonymity and confidentiality are confused and frequently used interchangeably but as is explained and emphasised here, anonymity and confidentiality are mutually exclusive concepts.

The next task requires becoming familiar with the following mixed methods (survey and unstructured interviews) research project, before answering a question. The information sheet invites participants to take part in a mixed methods study of childhood attachment. Most students found the description of this task straightforward.

PARTICIPANT INFORMATION SHEET

CHILDHOOD ATTACHMENT: A MIXED METHODS STUDY

Researchers at Qualitavia University invite you to take part in a research project examining children's first day of school as an example of attachment theory. Attachment theory is a psychological model attempting to describe the dynamics of long-term and short-term interpersonal relationships between humans.

What does the study involve?

The study is a mixed methods project using both unstructured interviews and a questionnaire asking people to recall their first day of school.

Who is being asked?

The Provost of Qualitavia University has agreed to send this participant information sheet via email to students at Qualitavia University inviting all senior undergraduates to take part in this mixed research. All seniors are invited to take part in the survey. Forty of these students are invited to register their interest in taking part in a one-on-one interview.

What will I have to do?

If you would like to take part in this research, you are asked to complete a 10-question survey. Click on this hyperlink THESURVEY to take you to the survey. *Filling in this Survey implies your informed consent.*

Only 40 students are needed to take part in the one-on-one interview. If you would like to register an interest in taking part in the one-on-one interview send an email to mychildhood@qualitavia.ed. Please provide your name. The first 20 female and 20 male persons responding will be sent an information sheet and consent form and be invited to take part in the interview asking them to recall the first day of school.

The hyperlink "THESURVEY" links to the following survey:

CHILDHOOD ATTACHMENT: A MIXED METHODS STUDY
THE QUESTIONNAIRE

Thank you for agreeing to take part in the survey. Type your answers next to the questions. Please note: Filling in this Survey implies your informed consent. You may skip any questions you do not wish to answer.

a) What is your age?
b) What is your gender?
c) What was the name of your school?
d) What is your religion?
e) Was your school a co-ed school or a single sex school?
f) On my first day of school I (circle)
 • was driven to school
 • walked
 • rode a horse
 • was home-schooled
 • caught a bus
 • other (describe)
g) When you think back on your first day of school, you have happy thoughts. Do you:

strongly agree   agree   disagree   strongly disagree

SUBMIT

Your participation in the survey is now complete. By pressing the submit button the questionnaire is dispatched to the research office. Thank you.

By submitting this survey, the participant's active involvement in the project ceases. Upon receipt of the questionnaire, the researcher automatically enters the response into an electronic data file along with hundreds of other responses.

A second participant information sheet which follows invites the first 40 respondents to take part in the one-on-one interview. It is identical to the questionnaire; the main difference is explaining what the person has to do.

PARTICIPANT INFORMATION SHEET

CHILDHOOD ATTACHMENT: A MIXED METHODS STUDY

Thank you for taking an interest in this research. We invite you take part in this study examining your experience as a child on the first day of school as an example of attachment theory.

What does the study involve?

The research is a mixed methods study using both unstructured interviews and a questionnaire asking people to briefly recall their first day of school.

Who is being asked?

This participant information sheet will be sent via email to students at Qualitavia University by the Student Information Centre with the Provost's approval. The email will invite all senior undergraduates to take part. All students who complete the survey are also invited to register their interest in taking part in a one-on-one interview.

What will I have to do?

If you would like to take part in this research, you are asked to complete a 10-question survey. Click on this hyperlink THESURVEY to take you to the survey. *Filling in this Survey implies your informed consent.* The survey will take around 10-15mins to complete and asks some simple questions relating to your first day of school. Your responses will not be identifiable. Once submitted, your survey cannot be withdrawn.

Only 40 participants are needed to take part in the one-on-one interview and we will contact only those people who register. If you would like to register an interest in taking part in the one-on-one interview send an email to mychildhood@qualitavia.ed at that time you will be sent a further information sheet and consent form specific to the interview study detailing what will be involved, where they will be held and how you can manage your participation, data, and withdrawal.

Whereas the questionnaire did not require a signed consent form – the participant was told that *filling out this questionnaire implies informed consent* – any person taking part in a one-on-one interview would normally be required to sign a consent form as outlined in the following.

CONSENT FORM FOR PARTICIPANTS

CHILDHOOD ATTACHMENT: A MIXED METHODS STUDY

I have read the Information Sheet concerning this project and understand what it is about. All my questions have been answered to my satisfaction. I understand that I am free to request further information at any stage. I know that:

1. My participation in the project is entirely voluntary;
2. I am free to withdraw from the project at any time without any disadvantage;
3. Personal identifying information on audio tapes will be destroyed at the conclusion of the project but any raw data on which the results of the project depend will be retained in secure storage for at least 5 years;
4. This project involves an open-questioning technique. The general line of questioning focuses on my memories of my first day of school. The precise nature of the questions which will be asked have not been determined in advance, but will depend on the way in which the interview develops and that in the event that the line of questioning develops in such a way that I feel hesitant or uncomfortable, I may decline to answer any particular question(s) and/or may withdraw from the project without any disadvantage of any kind.

All information given to the researchers will be held in confidence.
I agree to take part in this project.

....
(Signature of participant)   (Date)

....
(Printed Name)

In 2018, the workshop students in Christchurch took part in this mixed methods exercise, for the moment, presuming they were students at Qualitavia University. They dutifully completed the questionnaire on paper before submitting their completed questionnaire into a box filled with other completed questionnaires. When all the questionnaires were in the box, the box was shuffled.

The workshop students acted out the role of signing the consent form to take part in the one-on-one interview. Rather than spending 30 minutes on each interview, for expediency purposes, each student was invited to share one thought from their first day at school on the audio recorder. They passed the audio recorder around and recorded the following:

> My father gave me a big leather bag with a long strap. I chewed the end of it. I can still taste the leather.
>
> I was very shy. My best friends looked after me.
>
> I was barefoot.
>
> I am sitting down at a big desk.
>
> I don't remember school at all, but I am sure it was fun.

With these brief verbal comments recorded on the audio recorder and their completed questionnaires scrambled in a box with other questionnaires, the puzzle began.

Could all participants withdraw from the study as outlined in Article 9 of the Nuremberg Code? Did participants who had completed the questionnaire or had spoken onto the audio-recording device have the right to withdraw from the study? To make this question real, a hypothetical situation was created. It read:

> The teacher has learned that one student has had second thoughts about taking part in the study and they would like to withdraw from both the survey and the interview. They say these memories of their first days of school have rekindled bad memories. They would like their data destroyed.

This request is plausible, insofar as it is supported by Article 9 of the Nuremberg Code. The participant can withdraw any time. However, is it plausible for both qualitative and quantitative research?

What should or could the researchers from Qualitavia University do for this person wanting to withdraw at this stage? The answer to this question is a fundamental division between practising quantitative and qualitative research ethics. Can the researcher withdraw a person from the survey and the one-on-one interview? Is it possible? The clue is epistemology. The class considered each withdrawal request separately.

The 2018 workshop students said:

> The survey data can get lost in the 2000 other surveys. It cannot be retrieved, as its individual characteristics are protected because of the volume of other questionnaires.

This answer is correct.

Note the terms "respondent" and "informant" used in this chapter distinguish between quantitative and qualitative participants respectively.

If respondents have submitted their questionnaire into the shuffled box, the questionnaire is complete. A researcher cannot now retrieve the survey, assuming that 2000 other people took part in this questionnaire process. Nothing identifies one survey from any other survey. For example, the person's name was not on the form, nor was there any other identification. Thus, once the survey was submitted, the researcher has no capacity to locate and retrieve the document.

The workshop discussion then focused on what the researcher tells the respondent about the survey. A researcher has protected themselves at this stage from claims of unethical behaviour. They would point out that although the respondent did not physically sign a consent form, they technically did. The respondent would be told that before they began the survey they would have read "filling out this survey implies informed consent". The respondent could have withdrawn from the project at that point. Now, is it too late to withdraw?

The research participant may complain to the researcher that this consent and their participation feels short-lived. The researcher would have to agree with the respondent. The ethical considerations offered for quantitative research questionnaires are ephemeral and protected by the namelessness of the data. Because neither the research participant nor the researcher can identify what the person wrote on the survey, the person is said to be anonymous.

Students consult a dictionary brought for the occasion. They find the definition of anonymity reads in the *Oxford English Dictionary* as:

> [O]f unknown name, unknown or unclear sources or authorship, without character, featureless, impersonal.

There is a tremendous ethical strength in this unknown. Any survey placed in a collection of 2000 other surveys can be treated as being unknown. Additionally, as there is no written consent form to record the respondent's identity, the data provided to the researcher comes from an unknown source, and so in this context anonymity is a watertight ethical assurance.

This assurance does have caveats; it assumes the data collection instrument acquires no unique identifiers such as the participant's name, social security number or driver's license number. As none of these were on the questionnaire, this data is anonymous. None of this was breached in this questionnaire.

What was missing in the participant information sheet from earlier was a clear statement of this fact in the consent language at the beginning of the survey. Looking back, a simple sentence could have improved the consent information (in bold in the following):

> *Thank you for agreeing to take part in the survey. Type your answers next to the questions. Please note: Filling in this Survey implies your informed consent. You may skip any questions you do not wish to answer.* ***Once you submit your responses, they will be unable to be withdrawn.***

One possible way of breaching anonymity in surveys is if insufficient consideration is given to the ways in which some demographic data when combined may identify people in different contexts. That is, while a researcher may not ask for unique identifiers such as a person's name, if the population they are surveying and the demographics they ask for are not handled with sufficient care, they may inadvertently identify people. These things must be considered carefully when reporting data from survey work.

Another possible way of breaching anonymity is when researchers offer a prize for taking part in the research. Often researchers ask respondents to provide an email address that can be used to locate the winner. The problem with this procedure if the email address is part of the survey any researcher can identify both the person and what they said. Steps can be taken to separate the person from the data (having a separate process for entering prize-draws for example), but this still means that the respondent is at least potentially identifiable as having taken part in the survey even if they cannot be connected to their responses, and so not anonymous.

While these things have to be considered carefully, it is clear that surveys offer the possibility of anonymity. Because of this, they also make withdrawal of data impossible once submitted, and this should be made clear.

FACE-TO-FACE INTERVIEWS HAVE A DIFFERENT SET OF ETHICAL CONSIDERATIONS

If a participant wanted to withdraw from a study, they could ask the researcher to delete both the audio recording and any transcript taken from it. This is quite straightforward, as the person is likely to be remembered by the researcher and they may recall what the informant said. "I was barefoot" is memorable. A researcher can't simply erase that data from their memories. It is not that simple.

There is great learning to be gained from a comparison of the students' attempts to withdraw and delete the data from the survey and the face-to-face interview. Qualitative research ethics is more complicated. Its research data can never be unknown. Anonymity is not a valid provision for qualitative research. At least one other person, the researcher, knows the identity of the person and what the person said. This knowledge can never be unknown, and offering any assurance or ethical surety is ethically flawed. To do so, you are promising an informant something that cannot be achieved.

It is worth repeating: qualitative research cannot be made anonymous. To use the genie analogy, these stories cannot be put back in the bottle once it's open. The data can be de-identified, meaning everything that identifies the person can be redacted or changed. This may include the person's occupation, the region they live in and some odd identifiable mannerisms and the way they speak (something that is not straightforward to do). Even if the data is de-identified, it is not anonymous. The researcher always knows who said the quote.

The definition of confidentiality is straightforward, but it is far from simple. Confidentiality in qualitative research is one of the most misunderstood and complicated ethical concepts to grasp. In its most simple form, it refers both to the identity of the person and the information disclosed. The researcher knows the name of the person who said the quote and promises not to tell other persons the identity of the person when reporting this information. The following is an example literally caught in Tolich's throat; he wishes it would just go away.

Thirty years ago, he interviewed a woman who worked as a supermarket clerk. It was part of a PhD studying emotional labour and the interaction clerks had with their customers. This interview (Tolich, 1993) captured the intensity of the emotional labour relationship; what it meant for "her ladies" and for her. She said:

> My job involves checking out customers. Talking with them – I know most of *my ladies*. And a few men come through. This is on the morning shift. I know most of their personal habits; I know how they like their order bagged. We have an old people's home near us. They bring a bus-load of them shopping every Monday. It's great; I love it. And they want their names on the plastic bag, and the courtesy clerk … puts their name on it. And I know most of their names. But if I'm not there, they get very irritated.

(p. 371)

Even if Tolich wanted to erase this interview from memory, he cannot. As he reads the quote, in his mind's eye he can hear the woman's voice. At times he can also feel the Marlboro cigarette smoke at the back of his throat. In the space of a one-hour interview, she lit 10 cigarettes. Thus, this woman can never be anonymous to him. Her identity and what she said Tolich has kept in confidence within their embedded relationship. The relationship is not ephemeral.

Tolich has held this woman's confidence for 30 years. However, this confidence is fickle and can be broken. There are limits placed on confidentiality, and knowing this strengthens the concept of confidentiality.

The distinction between confidentiality and anonymity is given a lot of space here, but it is necessary to demonstrate that researchers protect participants from harm in surveys and one-on-one interviews in radically different ways. Qualitative research can never be anonymous. This is impossible, as the researcher will always know what the person said and promises not to reveal the person's identity. De-identifying the data is possible by changing people's names and contexts, but the researcher always knows. The de-identified data is not anonymous data.

As strong as confidentiality assurances are, there are also limits on confidentiality. Participants, especially in qualitative research, must be told this. For example, this puzzle about participants' first day of school can be changed dramatically by asking what would happen if the police acting on a subpoena sought access to this data. Consider the same protections if law enforcement asked the researcher for data on a specific person they knew who took part in the mixed methods study. What would, or could, the researcher do if the courts subpoenaed the two data sets? How would the effects of the subpoena be different for the survey and the interview? Even if the police had access to the 2000 surveys, could they identify any one person? The answer is that the subpoena would have very little success gaining information on any one person in a survey. The police would not be able to identify any one person from the questionnaires. The researcher could not help the police. The subpoena is useless.

In Chapter 3's discussion of Eve's story, the students found that the greatest threat to the women in that case was from the police. Would the police have been able to identify the 42 women in her field notes? Yes, this is highly likely. And given the microanalysis involved in these interviews, the data is likely to document their partner's criminal behaviour that led to these woman seeking assistance from Women's Refuge. This subpoenaed information could be used in courtroom proceedings.

Ethical issues in face-to-face interviews are different from survey data. If the police had subpoenaed data from the first day of school study or from Eve's story or Venkatesh's notebooks, the police could easily identify the person's information they sought. Thus, in Eve's case, her data collection compiling the notebooks has put all of these people she interviewed at risk. This is inclusive of the victims of abuse, the police, and the organisation, Women's Refuge.

The students saw the threat posed by Eve's notebooks as the greatest treachery in Eve's data collection. Eve would have a choice of giving up the notebooks to the police's subpoena or being held in contempt of court and going to jail.

Eve's case was a hypothetical case, but law enforcement's request for research data does happen. Researchers normally don't refuse to submit to a subpoena, but Russel Ogden is an exception.

RUSSEL OGDEN'S SUBPOENA

Russel Ogden, a former graduate student in the School of Criminology, did his MA thesis on the topic of assisted suicides among persons suffering from HIV/AIDS. His proposal, which he submitted to the Simon Fraser University Ethics Committee, noted that he would offer his research participants "absolute confidentiality". Subsequent to completing his thesis, Ogden was subpoenaed to appear in Coroner's Court, and asked to share information with the court regarding a death about which it was thought he might have knowledge. He refused to testify, and was threatened with charges of contempt of court. SFU's administration and Ethics Committee quickly disappeared, leaving Ogden to face the charges on his own. Ogden invoked the *Wigmore* criteria in support of his assertion that the information he gained was subject to researcher-participant privilege, and eventually won his case, becoming the first and only researcher in Canada ever to have researcher-participant privilege recognized in common law. SFU's only response to the situation was to give Ogden $2,000 on "compassionate" grounds (against his legal expenses, which amounted to approximately $11,500), and then to change SFU's Ethics Policy in a way that precluded researchers guaranteeing confidentiality to research participants in the future.

(https://www.sfu.ca/~palys/OgdenPge.htm)

ALICE GOFFMAN: BURNED THE DATA

Alice Goffman, the author of *On the Run* discussed in Chapter 3, is another exception. She took drastic steps to protect her data:

While most ethnographic projects are completed over a year and a half, Goffman spent more than six years working in the neighborhood, which evolved from a field site into what she still basically considers her home. Her field notes, which she kept with obsessive fidelity – often transcribing hours-long conversations as they happened in real time – ran to thousands of pages. She had to spend more than a year chopping up and organizing these notes by theme for her book: the rituals of court dates and bail hearings; relationships with women and children; experiences of betrayal and abandonment. *All those records had now been burned. Even before the controversy began, Goffman felt as though their ritual incineration was the only way she could protect her friend-informers from police scrutiny after her book was published.*

(https://www.nytimes.com/2016/01/17/magazine/the-trials-of-alice-goffman.html; our emphasis)

These cases may seem dramatic, but they serve two purposes. On the one hand, they ensure researchers recognise that qualitative data is never anonymous, only ever confidential; and that such confidentiality can have limits. Noting earlier SFU's response to the situation (to change what researchers can offer participants), researchers must be aware of the context in which they operate and must think through the uses and impact of the information they are collecting, especially in settings that include marginalised or disadvantaged populations, or activities that might be illegal or socially stigmatised. Think – if the confidentiality of your data were to be breached (for any reason), what would that mean for your informants?

ANONYMITY ≠ CONFIDENTIALITY: AN EPISTEMOLOGICAL DIFFERENCE

The ethics that govern quantitative and qualitative research are sourced from the same ethical precedents but manifest themselves as separate entities. Consider the questions asked of the people invited to take part in the first day of school study. The questions are different. The survey asks a standardised set of questions:

> When you think back on your first day of school you have happy thoughts. Do you
>
> strongly agree   agree   disagree   strongly disagree

The survey asked all 2000 people exactly the same set of questions. Compare that to the one-on-one interview. The starting point gave the informant a blank slate question – *tell me about your first day of school*. Their answer could go in any direction.

Important epistemological terminology arises from these close-ended or open-ended questions. A person who answers survey questions is a respondent; they are responding to the researcher's questions. The respondent does not actively participate in the writing of these questions. They just tick the boxes with their answers. The respondent cannot offer a more elaborate answer, even if they wanted to. In a questionnaire, there is no opportunity to provide nuance in answer to the question. The respondent may want to say they had mixed feelings on their first day at school: "I was sad when I arrived at school but after I said goodbye to my parent I made four new friends and I was very happy". This is not an option open to them.

A person who answers questions in a one-on-one interview is the informant; they are literally informing the researcher's study. The informant's role is more active than the respondent's role. The researcher relies on the informant to enlighten them both about the nature of their world but also to learn from them how to ask questions to explore this world. The informant tells the researcher that they were sad to leave their parent on day one but happy to make new friends. The information is important, but so too is the nuance. Qualitative researchers learn from the informant and are likely to change the questions they ask the next informant in the next iteration of the interview guide. They might ask, "tell me about your first day of school, from the moment you arrive until the moment you left".

The role of "informant as expert" is different in quantitative and qualitative research. In a survey, the researcher is the expert; they have conducted a literature review and established hypotheses between variables. The person filling in the questionnaire has a passive role, and this has repercussions on ethical considerations.

In qualitative research, these roles are more complex. The researcher is the learner and the informant the expert. Expertise comes from the informant's lived experience. There is no necessity for a qualitative researcher to conduct a literature review (REF), though most do, to understand what has been researched and how. The strength of not undertaking a literature review allows the researcher to open the research in a truly inductive way. Asking an opening question – tell me about your first day of school – invites the informant to be an expert and to tell the learner, the researcher, what is important about the experience.

Ethical considerations used by survey researchers and those using one-on-one interviews are different. Quantitative researcher's ethics are more predictable than qualitative researchers are. The explanation for the difference is simple. Survey research uses a standardised set of questions for pragmatic reasons. It allows them to use the limited range of answers to generalise to the whole population. When they present a survey to a respondent, they are not seeking understanding of their world. The researcher's goal is to enumerate the respondent's understanding of the world.

Randomisation strengthens standardised questions. Every person in a sampling frame has an equal chance of being selected to participate in the study. Qualitative researchers, on the other hand, do not use randomisation to build their sample size. They use a non-probability sampling. Two examples of this type of sampling are snowball sampling or convenience sampling.

A feature of qualitative sampling are the low numbers of people taking part in qualitative research. The informants describe the world from their perspective, and once the researcher has a sense that they are no longer gaining new insights from interviews, they declare they have reached saturation (Glaser & Strauss, 1967). To that end, qualitative researchers might use the following phrase to tell participants how they plan to sample their population:

> I plan to interview up to 25 informants or until I reach saturation.

Standardised survey implies a deductive, linear methodology. The research design does not change. The first respondent and the last respondent receive the same set of survey questions and the same ethical assurances. The strength of quantitative research is the research instrument, the questionnaire. The relationship between the researcher and the respondent is fleeting. The respondent answers the questions in a few moments and submits their responses. Once submitted, the respondent cannot get their questions back. They are anonymous.

In qualitative research, these relationships can last forever. For example, Tolich's muscle memory can taste Marlboro cigarettes in his throat 30 years after the event.

FAKING RAPPORT

There are exceptions to an enduring relationship in qualitative research. Not all interviewees are as memorable and this can cause embarrassment, undermining sincerity. Duncombe and Jessop's (2002) recollection of their early experiences of "faking rapport" capture this instability when participants are made to feel good about themselves in the interview, by creating rapport which leads to insincerity and inauthenticity. Jessop felt troubled with this realisation that, in order to gain a "good" interview, she frequently had to "smile, nod, and appear to collude" with views that she sometimes opposed, all of these to help build a "faked rapport", and was only used to "betray" participants into revealing valuable information (Duncombe & Jessop, 2002). A failure to reflexively question the hypocrisy of "faking friendship" exposes researchers to a disturbing ethical naivety which can marginalise the relationship shared between the participant and researcher:

> Julie interviewed one woman five times over a ten-month period after her husband and friends had abandoned her, and listened empathetically to experiences they sometimes had in common. In the last interview when Julie asked her what she had gained from the research she replied, "Well, apart from anything else, I have made a friend".

However, the claim only brought home to Julie the falseness of the situation where the interviewee did not recognise how Julie's faking friendship had been part of her job. Julie's strong personal discomfort was later compounded when she could not immediately recall the interviewee's name when they met in the street.

(Duncombe & Jessop, 2002, p. 118)

Building rapport and continuing to elicit information from informants can at times feel mercenary. Tumilty recalls in one of her early interviews as novice qualitative researcher having to continue being polite and building rapport with a male informant who told her an upsetting story (unrelated to the research) in a flippant and joking way. The story which was dismissive of a woman's sexual assault, rankled her moral sensibilities. She avoided endorsing the informant's conclusion and side-stepped into further interview material, but felt complicit by failing to confront his cruelty and misogyny for the sake of getting the research data she was paid to collect. The researcher-informant relationship is complex and may be very different in different research contexts. Being clear about one's commitments and understanding the limits of one's role and responsibilities is important in understanding the differences between building rapport and faking friendship. Treating informants with respect is to be clear about one's role in the interactions one has.

Epistemologically, qualitative research is exactly the opposite of quantitative research. It uses an inductive methodology that O'Reilly (2005) imagines to be a series of spirals leading from one interview guide to the next interview guide. The interview guide is iterative; questions asked are forever evolving as the researchers collect data and analyse it simultaneously. O'Reilly (2005) claims the spiral is nuanced:

I would argue it constitutes the crucial difference between quantitative and qualitative research and is what sometimes can make it so difficult to explain qualitative research to researchers used to quantitative methods.

(p. 38)

If questions asked in quantitative research surveys do not change, this makes the survey, the research instrument, the primacy of the method. In qualitative research, the primacy of the method is the researcher themselves. This too has implications for ethical considerations.

The primacy of the method in qualitative research is not just the questions asked; it involves the questioner, the researcher. The researcher is not only asking questions based on an interview guide, but also they are as likely to divert from the script by asking follow-up questions. What gives the researcher primacy in qualitative research unique is that they are not only listening to what the interviewee says, but they are analysing these comments in real time. The researcher begins with broad introductory questions that give the informant a platform to describe their world, while simultaneously the researcher analyses what the informant says in real time. They prompt the informant seeking further clarification. There are ethics at each moment of this interaction between the informant and the research process; within each iterative spiral the research question changes, and so too does the ethics.

The changeable nature of any qualitative research interview challenges the essence of informed consent. If questions are changeable, so too are the research goals. Informants may consent to take part in a research project and be informed about the nature of that research, but the nature of that research is changeable. Thus, informed consent has limits. Researchers need to be educated about this and take responsibility for the implementation of new ethical considerations when the research changes.

The research participant must be constantly informed about the changes in the research project. The emergent or iterative nature of qualitative research makes informed consent a work in progress. These complexities further unfold in the next two chapters when examining an array of qualitative research techniques. Each of these techniques has their own set of ethical considerations and limitations.

A reader may throw their hands up in the air and ask, "Can qualitative research offer any ethical assurances?" This would be a good question. It is not that qualitative research is flaky; it is that its epistemology is fluid, making the ethics changeable. If the reader has come to this conclusion, they have bought the right book. This book addresses the uncertainty involved in qualitative research ethics. In an ideal world, the inside cover of the book would have a metallic mirror, and the reader would be invited to look into it to find who ultimately is responsible for the ethics of their research. It is the researcher.

REVIEW QUESTIONS AND EXERCISES

1. Why does a face-to-face interview have a consent form but a survey does not?
2. What are the implications of this for the relationship between the researcher and the participants?
3. In a survey, the primacy of the method is the questionnaire. It does not change from one participant to the next. In face-to-face interviews, the questions posed to an informant routinely change. What are the implications of this for informed consent?
4. What is the difference between confidentiality and anonymity? Is anonymity possible in qualitative research?
5. Is there any difference between a research subject, a participant, an informant or a respondent?

CHAPTER 6

The limits of confidentiality in unstructured interviews and focus groups

By now, readers will have understood, as the students in the classes did, that mastering an ethics concept in one chapter does not mean that the concept will have the same meaning in the next chapter. Once established, seemingly robust concepts like confidentiality can be dissected, taking on a different shape. These concepts are like a Russian doll; inside one doll is another and then yet another. For example, in Chapter 3, Eve's story and Venkatesh's research establish the importance of the concept of informed consent. Yet in Chapter 4, the focus on the virtual reality puzzle demonstrated that informed consent is not always feasible. Other ethical assurances must be put in play, such as Article 9 of the Nuremberg Code. *The participant has the right to withdraw from the study.* Yet this right cannot be guaranteed or always practised. In the Milgram study and Zimbardo's study, basic conflicts of interest prevented the researcher from operationalising Article 9 and allowing the research subject to withdraw from the study.

Chapter 6 continues this evolving ethics landscape. The chapter champions the strength of confidentiality, yet confidentiality is presented here as both being a robust and fragile concept. Ethical concepts, within concepts keep changing. Knowing a concept is never enough; being able to imagine what that concept means in the context of your work, the implications/constraints and then reasoning through what needs to be done is always needed.

Readers are invited to make themselves familiar with the participant information sheet that follows describing a qualitative study of worker satisfaction using one-on-one unstructured interviews. The information sheet should be straightforward in terms of confidentiality and consent. The puzzle to be addressed in this chapter highlights the limits of confidentiality.

PARTICIPANT INFORMATION SHEET

A STUDY OF WORKPLACE SATISFACTION IN FIVE FACTORIES

The aim of this study is to compare and contrast worker satisfaction at five manufacturing plants that employ fewer than 100 employees. The data will be compared to existing satisfaction levels for employees in larger factories.

Who should take part?

The CEO of each factory has given their consent for the researcher to interview employees and managers from all factories. All employees are invited to take part but there is no compulsion to do so.

What will you have to do?

Take part in a one-on-one interview with the researcher asking a simple question – are you happy in your work?

How will the data be used?

Each interview will be transcribed and given a codename before being analysed with a computer software package.

Ethical considerations

Confidentiality is the main ethical concept protecting your participation. Neither your name, job title nor the name of your factory will be used in the final report.

   The study is confidential.

   You may refuse to answer any question or questions.

   Each participant will be provided with an executive summary of the results.

Guillemin and Gillam (2004) predict that big ethical moments frequently happen in the world of research, and the researcher's best-laid plans can inadvertently become unglued. These moments require the researcher to modify their ethical assurances on the spot. This chapter rehearses a number of big ethical moments, knowing that if research becomes unglued, it does not necessarily have to unglue the researcher.

The participant information sheet just presented promises to treat the informants' information confidentially, meaning that no one other than the researcher will know the name of the person interviewed, what they said. Confidentiality also promises not to disclose the name of the company the person works for. On the face of it, this participant information sheet is water-tight. That is, until a big ethical moment undermines the ethics of the study.

In this next hypothetical situation, assume the researcher has made an error. They have prematurely issued a press statement about the study including some predictions about what they might hypothetically find. Four of the CEOs of these factories read this press statement and decide that their company is at risk and will not take part in the study. Stuff like this happens all the time. Expect organisations and individuals to withdraw from the study for whatever reason.

The task the students had to decipher here was to work out what would happen to the ethical considerations if these four (of the five) CEOs rescind their permission for the research to take place in their company. Consider the task in terms of the participant information sheet. What previously had been a sound research design has so easily become dysfunctional.

In this revised situation, only one of the five companies are willing to be researched. How have the ethical considerations changed? Some points to consider:

1. Previously there were five factories, now there is one.
2. Do no harm. What are the risks now with only one company that did not exist in the previous research design with five companies?
3. How have the ethical issues changed in terms of informed consent and confidentiality?

In 2018, the Christchurch workshop student answers were impressive, immediately getting to the heart of the matter:

> With only one company, people are now more identifiable. That is *an* issue. That is *the* issue.

> The employees are at risk. The CEO of this one company could read the report and identify people. If an employee is complaining about something, the CEO might see the complaint as idiosyncratic, identifying the person.

> A person's comments could identify their particular job in the company.

The workshop participants saw through the big ethical moment created by the one company research model. Their answer also caught the spirit of the suggested reading for this puzzle which highlighted the concept of internal confidentiality. The students intuitively understood some, but not all the major ethical conditions here. The reading was:

Tolich, M. (2004). Internal confidentiality: When confidentiality assurances fail relational informants. *Qualitative Sociology 27*, 101–106.

The students' comments were prescient. They had zeroed in on a core ethical issue. With only one company now in the research, there is potential for people in that company to identify each other. The students' understanding went some way in grappling with the ham-fisted concept of confidentiality.

Students were asked a seemingly ridiculous question. "Did any of them know the name of the company mentioned in the example above?" They did not. Nor would the reader. By answering no, they did not know the name of the company, they were confirming one of the two types of confidentiality outlined in the assigned reading (Tolich, 2004). Their answer led to a wider discussion about the strength and weakness of confidentiality.

External confidentiality protects the name of the one company involved in the research. But students weren't concerned about the name of the company; their main concern focused solely on the workers in the one company. They were identifying *internal confidentiality*, not external confidentiality.

External confidentiality is often the traditional focus of confidentiality: the researcher knows the name of the manufacturing plant but promises not to tell other persons the identity of the plant. The researcher also promises not to tell outsiders what any person said when reporting this information (Tolich, 2004). But this promise doesn't address the relationship between workers themselves and between the workers and the CEO. As the one student, rightly pointed out above:

> The CEO ... could look at the report and identify people. If an employee is complaining about something, the CEO might see the complaint as idiosyncratic, identifying a person.

Without being experts in research ethics, the students were identifying a limit to the concept of confidentiality. When any researcher interviews workers in only one factory, all other workers in that factory know that all persons reported in the publication are from that single company. This undermines the concept of confidentiality. For example, if the publication identifies the oldest worker or an office receptionist or a CEO or a trade union official – these people are all identifiable to people in the company. Who they are, and what they say, is discoverable.

Internal confidentiality is a serious threat to any research project involving relational participants. These relational folks include friends of the participant, family members, fellow workers or a resident of a small town.

By researching one factory, the limits of confidentiality threatened each person within the research site as information sourced is not by strangers, but by fellow residents/occupants/workers. Each of these fellow workers can identify themselves, and by default others, within the company. Researchers must be aware of these limits on confidentiality and not offer more ethical considerations than they can secure.

The hypothetical examples discussed here in class are far from fabricated. The literature on qualitative research ethics is replete with examples of breaches of internal confidentiality that these students understood intuitively. It is as if breaches of internal confidentiality were not uncommon but endemic in qualitative research.

Internal Confidentiality Disasters for Qualitative Researchers: A Brief History

Street Corner Society (1981 [1943]), William Whyte's seminal text, is a case in point. Whyte lived for three and a half years within the community he studied. In Whyte's original text, he gave pseudonyms to the community he studied (Cornerville) and to its inhabitants (e.g., "Doc"), thus protecting external confidentiality. The appendix of his 1981 edition captures the everyday world of doing ethnographic study, but it also provides an insight into the harm caused by breaches of internal confidentiality. Participants told Whyte about how insiders recognised themselves and other insiders in the text:

> Pecci (Doc) did everything he could to discourage local reading of the book for the possible embarrassment it might cause a number of individuals, including himself.
>
> (1981, p. 347)

Despite promises of external confidentiality, when his participants read the book, they saw themselves and those close to them.

A similar case of a publication depicting an anthropological study in a rural US town caused anger and dissension among those whom they have studied. Muchmore (2002) reports:

> When the [anthropology] book was published, many townspeople were highly disturbed to see some of the most intimate details of their lives recorded in print. Even though the author had attempted to protect his informants by using pseudonyms, their true identities were

easily recognizable to anyone familiar with the area. Fifteen years later, another anthropologist who visited the town was surprised to discover that the local library's copy of the book had the real names of all the individuals pencilled in next to their pseudonyms. Even after all those years, some of the community members were still visibly upset about the ways in which they had been portrayed.

A perennial solution offered by students in 2016 and 2018 and in the short courses was to create pseudonyms as a means of protecting informants exposed by internal confidentiality. Thus, in response to Eve's story (in Chapter 3), many students said that Eve's ethics could be strengthened had she disguised the names of the 42 women's stories with pseudonyms. The thinking was that if all women had fake names, they would be immune to risk. Yet pseudonyms are likely to exacerbate internal confidentiality problems.

A lesson taken from Scheper-Hughes's (1979) *Saints, Scholars and Schizophrenics: Mental Illness in Rural Ireland* provides some clarity. In her study of the mental health in an isolated Irish village, she used pseudonyms to disguise individuals, and on her return to this village some years later, the author's use of pseudonyms was not effective. Eventually the villagers "ran her out of town". Scheper-Hughes (2000) reminisces:

> I would be inclined to avoid the "cute" and "conventional" use of pseudonyms. Nor would I attempt to scramble certain identifying features of the individuals portrayed on the naive assumption that these masks and disguises could not be rather easily de-coded by villagers themselves.
>
> (p. 128)

Through these exemplars, the students learned that pseudonyms are weak ethical considerations and further weakened by the common practice of allowing informants to provide their own pseudonym, often a nickname that is identifiable to some. The problem with this is that a pseudonym can be a personal choice that others within the research site already know, allowing others to recognise what the person has said. As a rule, not using this permissive ethical consideration and being wary of internal confidentiality in relational groups is sound ethics.

Pseudonyms have some support in the literature. Wiles (2012) claims:

> The primary way that researchers seek to protect research participants from the accidental breaking of confidentiality is through the process of anonymization, which occurs through the use of pseudonyms.
>
> (p. 50)

There are two problems in Wiles's logic. First, the use of pseudonyms is a flimsy form of disguising identity, especially when the informants are relational. Second, the problem with this protection was raised previously in Chapter 5 – the use of pseudonyms fails to acknowledge that anonymity is not possible in qualitative research. Yet anonymity and confidentiality are used as a convenient shell game justifying qualitative researchers' claims that their data can be archived and that this archiving can be done anonymously. This is impossible.

Deidentifying the Data

Qualitative data can be de-identified by redacting names and context, but it cannot be anonymised. To promise anonymity in qualitative research is to act unethically. This is commonly practiced among those who seek to archive qualitative data. For example, Saunders et al. (2015) claims "anonymity" has commonly been used either interchangeably with, or conflated, with "confidentiality". This conflates the known and unknown stating "anonymity is one form of confidentiality – that of keeping participants' identities secret" (p. 617). The essence of this confusion is that it attempts to separate the identity of the person and information they shared. Once collected, qualitative data is known by virtue of that fact it cannot be unknown to the researcher.

This point deserves restating. Once confidential data is collected, it cannot be "nearly made" anonymised. At best the data can be de-identified. In fact, de-identification proves a more practical and a more ethical term for qualitative researchers, especially in the storage of data. A definition of de-identified data would be redacted data, taking off names and locations before giving it to another researcher or before it is stored in an archive. At no time should a qualitative researcher promise a participant's anonymity. As stated in Chapter 4, the term anonymity has a dictionary meaning that participants understand. Anonymity means the data are unknown.

De-identifying not only names and locations, but also being sensitive to idiosyncrasies and context when using data for public reports or journal publications, etc., is another situation in which a reference group or person may be helpful. This work involves a recognition of the connections between information rather than risk of individual elements of information in isolation. For example, a leading qualitative research journal, *Qualitative Health Research*, has said that it will not include sample descriptors/demographics to be reported in tables as has been the norm for health research in the past (Morse & Coulehan, 2015). Recognising that in the small samples used in qualitative research, baseline demographics alongside quoted material, even with pseudonyms can risk identification. As qualitative researchers, selecting between what are often rich and valuable quotes to include in writing can be very difficult.

Paying attention to what is necessary to support the work, while also being mindful of how identifiable it may make a participant (especially because of the richness of the data) can in some cases be a challenging balance. As we have discussed elsewhere, sharing the responsibilities for these burdens with participants through process consent (Chapters 4 and 7) is one way to ensure ethical practice, acknowledging the risk of a participant's full withdrawal of their data. Interviews and interview data are a complex interplay of relationships between the researcher and the informant, and the informant and their context, being aware of that context as the students demonstrated in their discussions, and how much or little you know about it (in relation to the implications of certain data elements) is the next one.

Having mastered the ethical peculiarities of one-on-one interviews, the students turned their attention to a more complex ethical conundrum contrasting the ethical considerations employed in focus group interviews with one-on-one interviews.

FOCUS GROUPS

Tolich's 25 years serving on research ethics committees has shown him that many researchers are so zealous ethically, they feel compelled to offer a dual promise of confidentiality and anonymity as if two ethical assurances are better than one. Is this promise possible? These promises are often made to those taking part in a focus group. In what follows, the task before the reader is to grasp what ethical concepts, if any, are applicable in focus group research drawing from their learnings in previous chapters. The null hypothesis suggests there are no ethical assurances other than to state categorically that there are no ethical assurances, and those participants need to take full responsibility for the behaviour of themselves and others. The assigned reading was:

Tolich, M. (2009). The principle of caveat emptor: Confidentiality and informed consent as endemic ethical dilemmas in focus group research. *Journal of Bioethical Inquiry, 6*(1), 99–108.

The following participant information sheet seeks to recruit participants to take part in focus groups. Are the ethical issues of informed consent and confidentiality different in focus groups from one-on-one interviews?

PARTICIPANT INFORMATION SHEET

A STUDY OF WORKPLACE CONTENTMENT USING FOCUS GROUPS

The aim of this study is to compare and contrast worker satisfaction at FIVE hospital emergency departments that employ fewer than 50 employees. The data will be compared to existing contentment levels for hospital staff in larger hospitals.

Who should take part?

The CEO of each hospital has given their consent for the researcher to host Focus Groups in company time with employees. All staff are invited to take part but there is no compulsion to do so

What will you have to do?

Take part in focus group lasting 60 minutes lead by the researcher asking a simple question – are you happy in your work?

How will the data be used?

Each focus group will be audio-recorded and transcribed.

Ethical considerations

Your name, job title, and the name of your hospital will not be used in the final report.
The study is confidential.
You may refuse to answer any question or questions.
Each participant will be provided with an executive summary of the results.

Workshop participants are encouraged to apply the concepts of internal/external confidentiality and informed consent to focus groups and to one-on-one interviews:

- What can the researcher control in terms of what people in the focus groups say?
- What can the researcher control in terms of what people say in one-on-one interviews?

Assume the researcher can promise external confidentiality, they do not name the hospital, but is there anything they can do to stop focus group members from telling others outside the group what others said?

The consensus among students was that it wasn't. Confidentiality was severely limited in a focus group. This was self-evident to them. Again, the assigned caveat emptor (Tolich, 2009) reading was not required.

The students felt the participants had the right to know about this limitation before participating in a focus group. They suggested researchers be upfront with participants, explaining that taking part in focus groups involves risk and the participants need to know these risks in advance. Are participants willing to absorb those risks? Being truthful with participants would go some ways towards creating a more robust confidentiality assurance than baldly offering the study is confidential, as stated in the information sheet provided earlier.

Treating a focus group discussion as a public meeting has yet to become mainstream advice or practice, but it may be good advice given these reservations. In public meetings, participants must take responsibility for their actions.

Caveat emptor (Tolich, 2009) suggests a warning could be stated before any public meeting or on a focus group participant information sheet:

> Please note there are limits on confidentiality as there are no formal sanctions on other group participants from disclosing your involvement, identity or what you say to others outside the focus group.
> There are risks in taking part in focus group research and taking part assumes that you are willing to assume those risks.
>
> (Tolich, 2009)

A second task engaged by the students in this chapter compared and contrasted the ethical assurance of informed consent given in one-on-one interviews with those given in focus groups. Were these assurances equivalent, and if not, why not?

By their nature, one-on-one interviews offer the researcher and the participant stronger ethical assurances since the interviewee has opportunities to withdraw remarks during the interview, or if the participant reads a post-interview transcript, they can ask for deletions of their remarks. As the researcher is the only person present, they can more readily promise confidentiality not to tell another person either that the participant took part in the research or what the participant said. In focus groups, verbal statements cannot be taken back since they were evoked in the presence of others – in some sense, these statements are already in a public domain. Thus, to use the word confidentiality without clarification may be taken as offering a participant layperson more than the concept can deliver.

There are other ethical complications with focus groups. The term "focus groups" can be a misnomer. Focus groups can easily become unfocused, proving problematic for the concept of informed consent. They are unwieldy by nature, as the discussion is more than the sum of separate individual interviews, with participants both querying and explaining themselves to each other. Group interaction, rather than what each person says, is the hallmark of the method. Group participants are encouraged to pursue their own interests in relation to the proposed topic. Carey and Smith (1994) labels this interaction the *group effect,* "which require(s) the researcher to cede a degree of control to group members". The outcome is that focus group subjects may discuss topics outside what was outlined in the participant information sheet. This would challenge the informed consent process.

These ethical dilemmas are not sufficiently realised in the literature or by research ethics committees (Carey & Asbury, 2012), and if researchers address them, they are assumed to be dealt with at the last moment within the focus group moderator's preamble to the group discussion. Morgan (1998) concedes that relatively little has been written about ethical issues involved in focus groups. This view reflects a consensus that focus groups are innocuous, yet Carey and Asbury (2012) suggest that research "for very sensitive topics and for some studies with people with specials needs, the focus group facilitator needs skills to monitor the level of discomfort or distress" (p. 22). However, a facilitator's skill cannot overcome a group's unwillingness to discuss something that they might consider poses too much risk to themselves in a group setting. Consideration needs to be given as to whether a focus group is the appropriate means of collecting data for the specific research question.

Tumilty's experiences in health service research settings have shown that people sometimes think of focus groups as more practical, cheaper, or easier, than conducting one-on-one interviews. But focus groups are a method that seeks to use the group dynamic specifically to elicit different information than would be gathered in a one-on-one interview (Morgan, 1998). The interaction between participants specifically is what generates unique data with this method. Where topics are particularly sensitive, risky, difficult or upsetting, then understanding the likelihood of participants accepting the risks described here, or interacting in the group sessions in the ways necessary to generate data, is important. If not considered properly at the research design stage, the disclosure of the limits of ethical assurances described here may lead once again to poor data collection.

Beyond this courtesy of disclosure, focus group researchers are limited in what ethical assurances they can offer participants. Confidentiality is outside of their control: Researchers can place few restrictions on what focus group members say outside the group. Researchers also hold no sanction over a participant should they reveal outside the focus group what was disclosed by another focus group member. Thus, promises of confidentiality must be limited to the researcher's commitment that they will not identify any participant or what a particular individual said in any publication.

While researchers may promise not to disclose what people said in the focus group to others, they have no control over what group members tell others outside the group. Tolich (2009) suggests focus group ethics are best characterised with the principle of caveat emptor (let the buyer beware). It may be a more useful tool for those involved in focus group research: that is, let the researcher, the participants and the ethics committee beware that the only ethical assurance that can be given to focus group participants is that there are few ethical assurances. Participants must be made adequately aware of these endemic ethical dilemmas *in advance*, to allow them to consent to share responsibility for any ensuing harm. The focus group moderator is not their sole protector. As before, this recognises a participant's autonomy – their right to decide what risks they find acceptable.

The students understood the term caveat emptor; how it placed responsibilities on members of the focus group to look out for themselves and others. Being mindful of oversharing, the lesson here is that few ethical considerations are available to focus group researchers or their participants.

The students in 2018 class, as shown in Figure 2, worked out these issues among themselves in the first five minutes of the course. They saw the limitations of confidentiality among the group. The solution they spontaneously came to was giving each other an assurance that no information will be taken outside the group. Their action addressed internal confidentiality. However, are such ethical assurances realistic among strangers? Would it be practical in the study of worker satisfaction covered in this chapter?

There are limits to confidentiality. There is no solution to internal confidentiality other than making participants aware of its potential. With this caveat realised, the potential fragility of internal confidentiality becomes sounder.

REVIEW QUESTIONS AND EXERCISES

1. What is the strength/weakness of confidentiality in a focus group or a one-on-one interview?
2. What is the risk to participants in a one-on-one study that is conducted within one company or one family or a small town?
3. What is the basic difference between external confidentiality and internal confidentiality?
4. What ethical assurances can be given to people that take part in a focus group?
5. Consider the methodological and ethical implications of research that interviews married couples about their spending habits. Does the researcher gain more information from each person by interviewing them separately or together? What are the internal confidentiality implications if the couple is interviewed separately?

CHAPTER 7

Irregular types of informed consent in narrative research, autoethnography, photovoice, and participant observation

Informed consent, as we have discussed, is supposedly a straightforward process by which a researcher informs participants of what a particular project is about; what they will have to do; what will happen with the data collected from this process; and what a participant's rights are within this situation. A researcher does this so that a participant can make an autonomous decision about whether they wish to take part or not. In this chapter, we describe how the nature of methodologies of narrative research, autoethnography, photovoice and participant observation can complicate informed consent, requiring us to think about it as something dynamic and continuous, rather than static and discrete (i.e., a onetime event). In the opening exercise of this chapter, students are sent on a field trip to collect data without first gaining informed consent.

PARTICIPANT OBSERVATION

Since the 2018 workshop in Christchurch, a participant observation exercise has been added to the curriculum. It began as a leap of faith but it has developed into a reflexive teaching moment that attempts to replicate an exercise that went some way to understanding how the 2016 students responded to the audio recorder. Did these responses to this exercise engage their ethical intuitions, the tacit knowledge acquired through engagement in the learning up to this point?

The 2018 Christchurch workshop students were instructed to conduct a simple observation of their weekly supermarket shopping before attending the class and bringing a written description of that social interaction to class. The learning was less focused on what the students observed about others than on how they reflexively understood the intrusive nature of what is essentially covert research. Did the exercise evoke their ethical intuitions?

Tolich did not give the students informed consent prior to taking part in this exercise. The instruction was given in a package of information; part of that package was an invitation to take part in an observational exercise.

The instructions were unequivocal:

- During your weekly supermarket shopping, make some notes in your head about the social interaction you took part in between yourself and the checkout operator checking out your groceries;
- When you arrive at your car or a park bench, jot down some preliminary notes;
- Most importantly, assemble your feelings about doing the research in front of people without their knowledge, and write down a few notes about the experience.

The brief instructions were fleshed out by distinctions between jotted notes, mental notes and expanded field notes. The expectation was that the students would use all three forms of notes (Tolich & Davidson, 1999):

> Mental notes. Writing jotted notes is not always practical. At times you may feel conspicuous or inhibited taking notes in front of people. Equally, note taking may inhibit your informants or make you conspicuous. Use your short-term memory to collect the data in short bursts of time.

> Jotted fieldnotes. These are observations recorded in a notebook. As events happen in the location, note them down. Jotted notes are never typed. In fact, they should be scribbled as quickly as possible. They are a real-time record of your stream of consciousness while in the research setting. To make this easier to do, a notebook small enough to fit into a pocket should be used.

> Expanded fieldnotes. Expanded fieldnotes are written (or typed) using full sentences and record the scribbled details in the jotted or mental notes. They attempt to bring together the scattered jottings within the jotted nvotes in some coherent order. The expanded fieldnotes could be focused on the research themes or simply a chronology of events.

Not all workshop students wrote down their experience in expanded fieldnotes; most retained their mental notes.

The task was not labelled an ethical compass exercise in advance, but this developed organically. Tolich placed the students in a situation where they acted as covert researchers, recording how they felt about collecting the data without gaining the informed consent of the supermarket cashier, either in advance or after the purchase transaction.

The exercise was a success in 2018 and in subsequent classes. In all, six workshop students shared their written or verbal concerns about taking part in the exercise and gave permission for them to be shared here. Collectively, the words they used to describe the task was weird. Jo summed it up as:

> I felt weird. The lack of transparency of what I was doing did not sit comfortably with me because it did not align with my personal or professional values, thus moral compass. Although it is normal to be aware of others around yourself, I think due to my training, I subconsciously notice/pick up emotional state people are in more so than others (common thing a lot of social workers and counsellors talk about). However, it is one thing to notice, another thing to analyse it and other thing to go and write it down. It is private to that person, they do not get opportunity to speak to the points I wrote down, and various other reasons why it felt weird, all based on; goes against my values, or as sometimes named, moral compass. In my training, we would refer to this as values more than a moral compass.

The discussion that followed around the table established the ubiquity of this task is a moral experience. There was an awareness of unease in these observations. These workshop participants saw that I was asking them to do something that made them feel creepy. They could see unethical behaviour in what they were doing, but they could see it in others also.

As in Jo's statement, there was recognition of different layers of 'creepiness', not only the unconsented observation, but the inability of the person observed to comment, correct or confirm those observations. No space was given to justify them, or to explain them. Observation, recording and analysis are points of ethical importance.

Verbal descriptions of the creepy observation were similar:

> This is a thing I do anyway. I enjoyed it. But when I came to writing it down I thought it was a little weird. I don't know why. Transferring thoughts from my head to the paper.

> I found it quite intrusive, like I was judging someone.

> I did not find it intrusive. It was quite exciting to me – I was with my young daughter and we watched the clerk who was very shy, her head was down and she didn't want to talk to us. But when my daughter asked for a lollipop, her facial expression changed. After she gave my daughter the lollipop, she said goodbye to my daughter and my daughter said goodbye to her. I think she was quite taken by my daughter. But I didn't write anything down.

> I do this kind of [observation] thing often, looking at how people interact with me and I with them. The checkout person seemed really nervous. It was funny when I went to write how I felt about the notetaking. I wasn't totally transparent. I had tremendous empathy for the person and their nervousness and then I did not write anything down.

> I was observing the customer in front of me and how the clerk interacted with them. When I got up, I made a conversation. But I didn't write it down.

These comments on the covert exercise suggests that students were aware of their ethical boundaries, and that their observations fell outside their normal expectation of informed consent. The students turned the ethical considerations for this type of research onto the teacher asking under what conditions the researcher needs to obtain consent to observe social interaction in public spaces. For example, consider an extreme example from the one-person supermarket clerk. If a researcher enters a football stadium full of thousands of fans, does the researcher need to get the consent of each person before they collect information? Logistically, this is impossible.

An excerpt from the American Sociology Association code of ethics (https://www.asanet.org/code-ethics) was shared. This code stated in situations researchers were confronting, informed consent was not required.

> **Confidentiality is not required with respect to observations in public places,** activities conducted in public, or in other settings where no rules of privacy are provided by law or custom. Similarly, assurance of confidentiality is not required in the case of information available from public records or unrestricted internet sites.

Even with this ethical assurance, the students' behaviour felt influenced by their ethical intuitions.

Tolich sought advice from a number of philosophy colleagues. They were asked to describe the moral compass that generated the weirdness the students felt conducting this covert research without first gaining informed consent. One scholar replied succinctly in Kantian terms:

> The students don't like the exercise because it seems like they are treating the check-out person as a means not an end. The check-out operative is an object to be observed rather than a person to be respectfully interacted with. So they are not being treated as a moral equal.

Kvale (1996, p. 121) confirms Kant's maxims as:

> Treat every man as an end in itself, and never as a means only AND act as if the maximum of thy act were to become by thy will a universal law of nature.

These students' responses to the exercise was sufficient to suggest that they had a tacit skill, a moral intuition that they used in everyday life and in their research.

These students' responses to this exercise support the idea that we all have ethical intuitions and that these intuitions, when identified and thought through (with imagination and reasoning), can help guide us towards ethical actions. By engaging in this ethical self-course, these students' ethical intuitions may have been more sensitive – more primed, let's say – but this is exactly the point. Ethical practice as a researcher relies on the development of a certain kind of awareness and related skills, not knowledge of regulation or the following of ethics committee-mandated processes alone. Evolution in ethical practice of research is driven by researchers, not regulators or reviewers. Researchers work on the front lines engaging meaningfully with participants in ways that aim to honour their agency, rights, future and integrity. When thinking about training researchers, teachers need to think about helping students become better at being thoughtful, empathic and creative in solving tricky problems with ethical solutions. Throughout this book, we prompt those skills: ethical intuition, ethical reasoning, ethical imagination, and ethical integrity; while providing tools such as reference groups to help the reader become aware of what is required and start working towards becoming the ethical researcher they want to be.

NARRATIVE RESEARCH AS PROCESS CONSENT

Narrative research involves multiple in-depth interviews with the same person. These interviews invariably uncover the research question during the interviews, not before the first interview begins. These recurring data collections manifest unique ethical issues, few of which can be addressed ahead of time in a fulsome participant information sheet. The researcher can only tell the informant about the general nature of the topic – for example, a person's life history – not what aspects of that life history may be explored and to what degree.

Josselson (1996, pp. xii–xiii) astutely limits the narrative researchers' informed consent process, warning that "the concept of *informed consent* is a bit oxymoronic, given that participants can, at the outset, have only the vaguest idea of what they might be consenting to". This research design is similar in some ways to the virtual reality research discussed in Chapter 4. The virtual reality participant's information sheet could not provide a fulsome informed consent. Other ethical assurances, like the right to with-draw, propped up the consent.

Researchers cannot predict with any certainty the ethical issues that will develop in narrative research. Not only does the research question and the ethical issues evolve, so too do the roles of the informant from supplier of the data to perhaps co-author. The learning objective here modifies the consent process from informed consent to process consent.

The puzzle used in this chapter returns to the childhood attachment puzzle used in Chapter 5. That puzzle asked research participants a life his-tory question discussing their first day of school. The puzzle here is a varia-tion on that. Readers are to assume, as in the hypothetical case in Chapter 5 that the researcher wanted to understand what it was to be detached from one's parent or parents on the first day of school. The researcher may have gotten more than they bargained for, which is quite often the case in quali-tative research:

- (Hypothetically) the researcher learned that the week of the first day of school, a child's parents separated. This leads the researcher to request another interview.
- At the end of the second interview, the researcher learns that in the property distribution settlement, this child began living solely with the mother and their sibling lived with their father.
- The third interview asked about this property distribution.

How has informed consent changed between the first, second and third interviews?

- What protections are available to protect the informant? Is it likely the interviews will rekindle the informant's vulnerability? How should researchers address these evolving ethical considerations?

The students in the 2018 workshop saw these questions as straightforward. Informed consent had disintegrated after the first interview. They suggested:

> At the end of the first interview, seek a form of retrospective consent reflecting that the researcher had gone on to topics not featured in the information sheet. Check to see if the person was okay to continue to be involved in the research.

> Ask the informant at the end of the first interview if they are okay. Are they happy for their data to be used? If they are okay with this process, would they be willing to take part in another interview? At the end of the second interview, this process should be respected.

> Make sure to give the participant the opportunity to walk away after each interview.

Students here are demonstrating their ethical imagination. They've identified an ethical issue and are thinking through the various ways this impacts on the participants, and the variety of solutions available to ameliorate the problem.

These suggestions were all sensible, building on what the students had previously learned in Chapter 4 such as enacting Article 9 of the Nuremberg Code. The person has the right to withdraw from the research at any time.

The workshop students' responses to this puzzle were similar to statements found in Tolich's (2017) purpose-built article on narrative research that accompanied this puzzle. Had the students read the article, they would have found that the variations in the informed consent process they were discussing had another label, namely *process consent*.

Further reading:

Tolich, M. (2017). Purpose built ethical considerations for narrative research: Broad consent or process consent but not informed consent. In I. Goodson (Ed.) *The Routledge International Handbook on Narrative and Life History*. London: Routledge, pp. 593–604.

Gaining consent at the end of the interview as the students suggested is how Ellis (2007) defines process consent. The researcher checks at each stage to make sure participants still want to be part of the project. Process consent is an active form of consent and takes the participant's right to withdraw beyond a passive construction. Rather than leaving it up to the participant to withdraw at any time, the narrative researcher can repeatedly invite the informant to volunteer to be part of the next phase of the project. At any time the person is encouraged to think about their ongoing participation. Without process consent, the right of an informant to withdraw from the research project initially written in a consent form appears to be written in disappearing ink.

Process consent is a versatile ethical consideration applicable to any research setting, not just narrative research. As (neither an ethics committee nor) a qualitative researcher can predict with any certainty the ethical issues arising in research, asking informants at the end of any interview – are they happy for their data to be used? – activates process consent. In this way, any risks associated with participation in qualitative research can be borne equally by the researcher and the participant, creating a level playing field. Accordingly, the use of process consent equalises risk between the researcher and the participant, deliberately seeking, for genuine reasons, to bolster what is normally a passive minimalist informed consent process. Yet with some candour, Josselson (2007, p. 543) says process consent "strikes terror into researchers because it means just what it says". The researcher could lose sleep offering process consent as they could potentially lose the data. The researcher must bear this risk.

VARIATIONS IN INFORMED CONSENT

Process consent is not the only variation to informed consent. Assent is another unique form of consent when informed consent is either not possible or not permissible. Examples of situations where informed consent is not possible are projects that work with children under the age of consent (this varies by legislative context) or those who may lack competence, such as a dementia patient. Competence and capacity are sometimes used interchangeably to describe a person's ability to engage in decision-making. However, competence is a legal term determined legislatively or by the courts in individual instances, whereas capacity is a concept used medically to refer to a person's ability to make a specific decision at a specific point in time (therefore more fluid and variable). Someone can be declared incompetent based on an ongoing health condition, or a child can be considered incompetent by age. Capacity is determined in conversation with someone, determining whether they are able to understand information, weigh that information against their personal preferences and values, come to a decision and express that decision consistently (Faden & Beauchamp, 1986). Both a lack of competence and a lack of capacity may lead to the use of an assent process.

The assent process typically has stages. For example, with children: first, the researcher asks a parent or guardian for permission to recruit the child. If they consent, the researcher has permission to ask the child to take part in the research. This second stage of permission is known as assent. Even though the parent has consented, the child has the right of refusal. At times, often in medical research, where medical researchers want the child to be given a special treatment, the parents may see this as their child's last hope. If a child is given the right to assent to take part in this study, this places the parent in a conflict of interest with the child. The child can say no. Assent can therefore be very difficult to manage. It should be tailored to the level of understanding of the person being assented. The purpose of assent is to show respect for the person even if they are unable to engage in the kind of decision-making that would provide full consent. It also allows them to understand what is happening to them and respects their bodily integrity.

The same assent process occurs when vulnerable persons are recruited. People who have mental health or neurological problems that impair their decision-making capacity can give assent only after another responsible person has given consent as a substitute.

In Eve's story (discussed in Chapter 3), the researcher *could have* used a double consent process after first gaining the consent of the host organisation, Women's Refuge, to conduct the research and approach their clients. This is similar to a consent-assent process, in that it first seeks permission to approach the potential subjects from an organisation entrusted with protecting them. From discussion with participants in various workshops Tolich ran, this process would have been beneficial for all parties. First, it would have alerted Women's Refuge of the threat posed to their clients from this research. Second, the researcher would have been made aware of the vulnerability of these women. Third, the researcher even could have learned how the research exposed Women's Refuge to risk by undermining this safe haven.

Broad consent is a third type of consent, where a participant agrees that a researcher may use the data collected from their participation for more than one use, even though these uses may not be able to be specified. This uncertainty of uses is what makes broad consent unusual. These uncertain uses may sometimes be limited. For example, a participant may consent that their data can be used for further research, but only if that work is not commercial. Or sometimes Broad Consent may specify that there are no limitations per se, but that all future projects using the data will be reviewed by a group or committee to ensure appropriate usage, which can provide some reassurance to participants.

Broad consent is unique in that it allows the informant to make a decision about the use of their data in ways that historically may not have been the case, thus giving them more agency. It also avoids the problem of retrospective consent. Retrospective consent would require a researcher who wanted to reuse some data for a new project to contact all the informants that had provided it to gain permission to do so. Retrospective consent can often be impractical and in some cases impossible to achieve. This consent process is very time-consuming and often incomplete. This was what Eve would have had to have done to gain consent from the 42 women (Chapter 3). Yet students were adamant that going back to get retrospective consent was not feasible, as it was likely to re-traumatise the women.

If a researcher gains broad consent at the time of data collection to share the confidential data with other people, they would not have to go back to the informant. Not only does broad consent give agency to the informant, but the informant makes a choice about what happens to their data. This choice also can minimise the process that a researcher may have to undertake with an ethics committee depending on the rules in their setting. The ethics committee would usually have to approve the reuse of data when the data was collected by informed consent only.

AUTOETHNOGRAPHY

Autoethnography is a hands-on exercise that requires no planning on the part of the student and can be completed in 15 minutes readily fitting within any classroom teaching. For many students, this style of free writing was unfamiliar to their academic studies. Moreover, some had difficulty seeing autoethnography as a credible research technique.

Students created their own autoethnography writing a story capturing some aspect of their growing up. Before beginning, they were cautioned that there would be an expectation that they would read out the story to the class if they wanted to, and from that, a discussion about autobiographical ethics would take place. This caution, essentially internal confidentiality, was similar to that established previously in discussions of focus groups (Chapter 5).

Carol's[1] story involved learning that Santa Claus was not real. She free wrote and then read out:

> I felt like I had solved a mystery, as I had come to suspect that my parents were the culprits in my deception whilst staying at my grandparents' homes over the holidays. I left my brothers in the dark, as I felt this was the kind thing to do, to continue their belief. The handwriting on the notes on Christmas morning seemed to match previous notes from the Easter Bunny and the Tooth Fairy – which all seemed highly suspicious. Upon catching my mum putting money under my pillow along with a note (as the Tooth Fairy) a few weeks later, I put 2 + 2 together resulting in a realisation that all three childhood fixtures were in fact a role-play acted out by one person.

This story had great potential to tell about moments of growing up. If Carol wished to expand on this promising beginning and write a thesis or a journal article, this would be possible. The students' next task was to answer the question, would this author need to gain the informed consent of all persons written about in this detective story?

The Santa Claus story above identifies 11 parties. These are the two parents, four grandparents, two brothers and the tooth fairy; Santa Claus and the author should not be overlooked. Gaining students' initial responses to this question helps them recognise their ethical intuitions. Adding more examples can help flesh out these intuitions and get a sense of its nature and boundaries. Another example, to illustrate.

A student in another workshop recalled a life story about her first day of school. Rey's story included four people. She free wrote:

> My First Day of School:
>
> So, when I was around 3 or 4 in preschool, I didn't play with the other kids. I don't quite remember why, but I might have been thinking they were too stupid and mean. Anyway, one day I was playing outside and saw an anthill with all the ants coming and going in nice straight lines, and thought that it was so cool that they were so organised. Some part of me connected with the little insects who had built their home on [the] far side of the backyard playground next to the fence and I promised them that I would protect them. I'm not sure how long this

lasted (could've [been] the same day, but not more than a week) that I would bring leaves over to them and talk quietly to the bugs while they came and went. Some afternoon though there were two boys, one that I had a child crush on, who came over and started making fun of me for talking to myself. I told them that I wasn't, that I was talking to the ants and they wanted to see where. After I showed them the boy that I liked started kicking apart the anthill and stomping on them all. I felt shocked and betrayed and pushed little Trevor onto the ground. He cried a little and ran inside with his friend and I tried to reshape the anthill while crying that the bugs were in such a panicked state. I'm not sure how long I was out there, but I eventually gave up and went inside where the "teacher" started to question me and why I pushed Trevor (the boy) over so I told her, but I don't remember anything after that.

Do the four people in Rey's story or the 11 in Carol's tale need to give their consent? Students did not reach a consensus. A common assumption was because it is your life story, in this case about Santa Claus, or first days of school, ethics don't apply because it's your memories, it's your story. Reasoning through why they felt it was not necessary and coming into conflict with those that felt it was helps further develop their ethical practice. It helps to realise that not every ethical intuition is universalisable and that ethical reasons can be more or less commonly held, or agreed to.

Although these two stories can be considered trivial examples, they do raise generic ethical questions of autonomy.

The recommended reading was:

Tolich, M. (2010). A critique of current practice: Ten foundational guidelines for autoethnographers. *Qualitative Health Research*, *20*(12), 1599–1610. Reprinted in Sikes, P. (Ed.). Autoethnography Sage Benchmarks in Social Science Series, Volume 1 (pp. xxi–lii). London: Sage.

Tolich's (2010) article attempts to answer this dilemma, asking if autoethnography is some form of oxymoron. The word "auto" implies the story is only about the person writing the story, and they have proprietary rights to their story.

Clandinin and Connelly (2000) also challenge this claim, asking self-narrative writers a pointed question: Do they own a story because they tell it? For example, if you write a story about your first day of school, your first experience with alcohol or getting laid off from work, do you need to get consent from others who get written into the story? Do these other people need to give their consent? Does the researcher need to get ethics approval to conduct the study?

Chang (2008, p. 69), who wrote the textbook on autoethnographic methods, states:

> As you play a multi-faceted role as researcher, informant, and author, you should be reminded that your story is never made in a vacuum and others are always visible or invisible participants in your story.

Autoethnographers are not always aware that they do not *own* their story just because they lived it or authored it. Others mentioned in the story – family, friends and coworkers – also have rights to ethical assurances, and autoethnographers must anticipate ethical questions on behalf of these others. Internal confidentiality is relevant here, but so too is a recruitment strategy when studying people known to the researcher. The literature calls these *relational persons*.

Students are asked how they should recruit a potential participant into the autoethnography when this person is in a relationship with the researcher. This could be a researcher's child, patient, employee, or a student. In this relationship, these people are seen as having a diminished autonomy. They may feel compelled to take part. Voluntariness is a key part of consent, that is, consent free from coercion. There is a conflict of interest. How should researchers manage these conflicts of interests in their research?

The autoethnographer Lee Murray (Murray et al., 2012) wanted to study her family, and the ethics committee identified this as relational research and therefore a conflict of interest. The ethics committee thought there would be a sense of obligation from her children. Murray reports:

> The representative from the ethics committee remains concerned about the structural situation of the family. It is not reasonable, from the committee's perspective, to think that my children are free to give consent or not. I try to explain that my children and I are at a place of recovery and that we, as a family, did not come to this decision lightly. It is a difficult story to tell; it is difficult to remember; it is difficult to see it in writing (print); it is difficult to know others will read it (people we know and people we don't know; people we care about and people we find difficult to care about), and it is very difficult to expose ourselves in this way. But we also feel an obligation as a family to tell the story that needs to be told.
>
> (p. 45)

The university ethics committee required Murray to recruit her family via a third party. The third party would recruit Murray's children into the study on behalf of the parent. If the child did not want to take part, this third party would deem that to be not informed consent. Third-party recruitment was seen as the solution. While this use of a third party may remove some of the difficulty involved in saying no to someone with whom you have a relationship, it doesn't remove the relationship, and so saying "no" may still have consequences. Thinking through these issues and how to manage them in one's writing, but more importantly, for one's ongoing relationships, is vital.

Chang's *Autoethnography as Method* (2008) raises similar concerns to Tolich's piece about autoethnography's unique ethical position, claiming that protecting the privacy of others in autoethnographic stories is much more difficult than in other studies involving human subjects. She stated:

> Since most autoethnographers focus primarily on self, they may feel that ethical issues involving human subjects do not apply to their research design. This assumption is incorrect. Whichever format taken researchers need to keep in mind that other people are always present in self-narratives, either as active participants in the story or as associates in the background.
>
> (Chang, 2008, p. 68)

Chang promotes ethics committees as dispassionate bodies capable of protecting both research participants and the researcher themselves. That will depend, of course, on their constituencies and their standard operating practices.

Tolich's (2010) suggestion for autoethnographers is to treat all the persons mentioned in their text as vulnerable, including the researcher. Novice autoethnographers should be aware that the topics they choose might harm people, if not immediately, perhaps at some time in the future. They must engage their ethical imagination to consider all the ways in which having something of a particular nature be "out there" can have repercussions for themselves and those in their work. Like an inked tattoo, posting autoethnography to a website or making it part of curriculum vitae ensures the marking is permanent. There are no future skin grafts for autoethnographic doctors of philosophy (PhDs); anticipating these types of vulnerability to self is a foundational guideline for autoethnographers. Suggestions for how autoethnographers should address these issues include not publishing anything they would not show to the other persons mentioned in the text.

Tolich's (2010) review of autoethnography attempted to work through the ambiguity of ethical considerations in this method, finding others routinely drawn into another's autoethnography. In response,

Tolich (2010) wrote ten foundational guidelines for autoethnography as a starting point. These guidelines focus on consent, vulnerability and consultation, but the main learning was that what makes autoethnographies evocative are the others who helped forge this life's story. Those names have the right to be consulted about their participation and the right to read what the author creates. There is nothing new in these 10 foundational guidelines that follow.

CONSENT

1. Respect participants' autonomy and the voluntary nature of participation, and document the informed consent processes that are foundational to qualitative inquiry (Congress of Qualitative Inquiry, 2007).
2. Practice "process consent", checking at each stage to make sure participants still want to be part of the project (Ellis, 2007).
3. Recognise the conflict of interest or coercive influence when seeking informed consent after writing the manuscript (see Jago, 2002; Rambo, 2007).

Consultation

4. Consult with others, like an IRB (Chang, 2008; Congress of Qualitative Inquiry, 2007).
5. Autoethnographers should not publish anything they would not show the persons mentioned in the text (Medford, 2006).

Vulnerability

6. Beware of internal confidentiality: the relationship at risk is not with the researcher exposing confidences to outsiders, but confidences exposed among the participants or family members themselves (Tolich, 2004).
7. Treat any autoethnography as an inked tattoo by anticipating the author's future vulnerability.
8. Photovoice's anticipatory ethics claims that no photo is worth harming others. In a similar way, no story should harm others, and if harm is unavoidable, take steps to minimise harm.
9. Those unable to minimise risk to self or others should use a nom de plume (Morse, 2002) as the default.
10. Assume all people mentioned in the text will read it one day (see Ellis, 1995).

The 10 guidelines present an opportunity for revision. All of these guidelines have been addressed in the book's previous chapters.

PHOTO VOICE

Autoethnography's ethical considerations are quite likely to happen in the writing phase after the author has worked out which of the characters assembled are likely to be in the final text. Photovoice, on the other hand, is quite the opposite. It features an anticipatory ethics frame. It decides the ethical issues in advance.

The students' task for this research had them take a series of photographs on their cell phones. Usually the topic asks them to capture risk in their community. Students usually come to class with two or three photographs taken on their cell phones of their interpretation of risk in their community. In the class discussion, they talk about why this risk is important to them. This verbal task is the voice part of the exercise. Here is one example of a student who saw mirrors in their house as a risk:

I don't have a mirror in my room because it's a risk - will I be happy with the reflection? Or will I frown and prod at myself? A mirror is a risk because there is the potential for it to ruin my day.

Figure 3 Image of a Mirror and Quote.

To highlight the anticipatory nature of photovoice ethics, the suggestion ahead of the exercise is not to take pictures of people. Tolich added that Sieber and Tolich (2013) claim "the camera adds ten pounds of ethics"?

The recommended reading is:

Wang, C. C., & Redwood-Jones, Y. A. (2001). Photovoice ethics: Perspectives from Flint photovoice. *Health Education and Behavior, 28*(5), 560–572.

Wang and Redwood-Jones create a powerful inductive medium, generating rich data from naive participants, sometimes children, who are asked to characterise their world through photographs and later give voice or meaning to what those photographs represent to them. It is a relatively novel participatory action research method that enables researchers to assess the strengths and concerns of their community and communicate their views to policy makers.

The following excerpt is an excellent overview of anticipatory ethics:

> When conducting photovoice, facilitators should hold the safety of the participants above the spontaneity or power of the image. The camera is not a shield, and participants must be aware of their surroundings and potential dangers at all times, in addition to obtaining the participants' permission prior to taking the picture.
>
> To emphasise these points, photovoice training never begins with camera instruction but with a group discussion about the use of cameras, power, and ethics, as well as the responsibility and authority conferred on participants with cameras. ... As a first step in informing the community about Flint Photovoice, we created written brochures for participants to give to photographed subjects and interested community members. We also wrote letters addressed to participants' teachers and employers describing the project and establishing whether or how cameras would be used – that is, only with prior permission – at school or work. To help participants to build community ties, express appreciation, and facilitate reciprocity, we also tried to provide participants with photographs to give back to people they had photographed. In practice, this works most easily when participants use the type of camera – such as an instamatic or disposable – that allows low-cost double prints at the time of processing.
>
> (Wang & Redwood-Jones, 2001, p. 567)

In many ways, what Wang suggests always puts ethics before the camera. It also makes very clear the importance of thinking through the ethical implications of your work so you can address them pre-emptively, building trust and relationships with people and communities.

This trust and relationship building when possible is an effective means of ethical practice. A controversy in photovoice is the de-identification of people in photos. Such a practice, generally recommended by an ethics committee, asks for researchers to cover faces of people in photos that are used in public. Carlberg-Racich (2018) describes how de-identification of photos may disempower participants who take part in certain projects to have a voice. Similarly, Allen (2015) quite illustratively describes how ethics committee mandated processes of de-identification of photos may have caused more ethical issues in a project with teenagers, framing bodies in particularly problematic ways. Both Carlberg-Racich and Allen suggest that the process of de-identification, meant to improve participant safety, often came at the cost of participants' sense of agency or power. We can see in some cases that this trade-off between participant safety in terms of identification connected to the topic of research and participant agency may balance out differently. In some cases the overall risk of being identified as being someone doing something particular or living in a particular way may justify a restriction of participant agency within the confines of their engagement with a project. In others, the risk of identification may not be connected to potentially harmful ramifications. These decisions about trade-offs should be driven by participant input.

Carlberg-Racich also suggests that sometimes these restrictions (of excluding identifying elements) may make photo-taking less organic, but can support more creativity which has other benefits for the work (2018).

Photovoice is a dynamic methodology providing rich data in ways that have the potential to empower communities. Thinking through the ways in which to complete photovoice projects ethically requires all the skills we have discussed so far as well as strategies such as a process consent and reference groups (Chapter 4).

QUESTIONS FOR REVIEW

1 Why is informed consent an oxymoron in narrative research involving multiple interviews with the same person? How should a researcher manage this ethical dilemma?
2 What do Sieber and Tolich (2013) mean by their quip, "the camera adds ten pounds of ethics"? How does this statement impinge upon informed consent and confidentiality? How can readers resolve this dilemma?

3 Write a 10-line life history drawing on an event from your own life. Identify how many people are mentioned in the story. Do you own this story? Do you need to gain the consent of those mentioned?
4 Imagine inviting a 12-year-old child to take part in the photo voice exercise. What instructions would you give them?

NOTE

1   Permission to use these two examples has been given.

CHAPTER 8

Negotiating ethics within a memorandum of understanding (MOU)

Chapters 8 and 9 both focus on research ethics but from different starting points. In Chapter 9 the starting point for ethics begins when generating a hypothetical research proposal for a formal ethics review committee. In this chapter, there is no discussion of formal ethics review. The multistage task here has the researcher interrogate their ethical assumptions while attempting to gain access to a social agency without first going through a formal ethics review.

This chapter's brief is simple: concoct a hypothetical study based on a social agency the reader has had no previous contact with. The choices could be, but are not limited to:

• Habitat for Humanity
• Riding for the disabled
• A homeless shelter
• A food bank
• A Women's Refuge

If none of these agencies interest you, use an organisation of you own choosing.

In a graduate student workshop for physical education postgraduates that Tolich guest-lectured, he chose the organisation for the students. None of the physical education students were affiliated with the university's rowing club, yet the rowing club was the type of research setting most of these postgraduate students could later research.

For the exercises that follow, assume the social agency has its own research policies and its manager plans to ask the researcher five or six questions allowing the agency to evaluate the researcher and their project. This process differs from the access gained by Eve in Chapter 3. At no time did Eve let the Women's Refuge know that she was gathering research information about the 42 women who came through the refuge. A goal of this chapter is to understand how Eve could have negotiated access to the refuge by creating a memorandum of understanding (MOU) with the social agency. This MOU doubles as a basic set of ethics considerations in managing the relationship, the project, and the outcomes.

The only requirement for the task is that the reader has had no prior exposure with the social agency. Thus, the choice of agency the reader makes is not important. The task is hypothetical and thought-provoking. Yet in workshops with students, it has been shown that this reflective exercise allows students to unmask domain assumptions about their preconceived opinions about research relationships.

The first assumption considered in this puzzle is an important one. Presume that in the past the agency you have chosen to focus on in this exercise has had many similar requests to research them; some of these have proven to be beneficial for the agency, and others have not. Previously, other researchers may have approached the social agency taking an arrogant attitude, as if the researcher was there to save the organisation. Accept this assumption as if it was valid. Assume the hypothetical request to research this agency is met with disinterest at best and suspicion at worst. Also assume the request to study this social agency is not declined immediately, and the agency manager says they have some questions they ask potential researchers in situations like this. The number of questions asked is not stated, but assume there is more than one.

Please note again, this exercise is hypothetical and there is no reason to contact any social agency to take part in this exercise. Just imagine a dialogue with the manager of that social agency.

After the manager thanks you for coming by and showing an interest in the agency, the manager explains the research motto for the organisation. It is "nothing about us, without us". The manager responds to your quizzical expression on your face telling you to come back to talk to them again once you understand what you think that means.

It is important not to advance to the manager's second question until fully understanding what "nothing about us, without us" means. There is no requirement to read all of the 1.5 million hits on Google. A Wikipedia search reveals this statement:

> To quote James Charlton who authored a book by this same title, the term "Nothing About Us, Without Us", "expresses the conviction of people with disabilities that *they* know what is best for them". This mantra became the rallying call for the United Nations Convention on the Rights of Persons with Disabilities and continues to have relevance and significance more than ever. But why does it matter? It matters because people with disabilities must be front and center as visible leaders to share our voice and our experience. It matters because it reinforces the role of people without disabilities as allies and partners who share the

road toward inclusion and equality. It matters because it unites us with all the marginalized and invisible individuals and groups who are demanding a seat at the table. Most of all, however, it matters because we as people with disabilities need to be the ones whose voices must lead the way. "'Nothing about Us, Without Us'" emphasizes how people with disabilities must be valued as integral and essential contributors to every sector, industry and community including entertainment, fashion, education, sports, medicine, business and law. While people with disabilities need to be leaders of disability-focused organizations, that is not enough. We also need to be front and center in mainstream local, national and international organizations.

> (https://www.huffpost.com/entry/nothing-about-us-without-us-
> mantra-for-a-movement_b_59aea450e4b0c50640cd61cf)

Students in the 2018 Christchurch workshop saw the answer to this first question, "nothing about us, without us", as obvious:
It means the social agency wants to be included in the process. You're not doing the research to them, but with them.

> The important point is that you just don't turn up with a project all set, but you are willing to work with the agency.

> It is all about being inclusive from the outset. To have transparency in the process. Who owns the data is an important question.

> It bases a research project upon collaboration.

Workshop students noted the irony of the question as if the researcher in the Eve scenario (discussed in Chapter 3) answered the question. They questioned how Eve could have answered this question when she was covertly collecting information. At no time did Eve explain to the Women's Refuge that she planned to conduct interviews with the 42 women or the expectation to notify the organisation. If Eve had told Women's Refuge that she wanted to conduct research, there would have been a possibility of the research being conducted collaboratively. Women's Refuge may have had the opportunity to suggest or modify Eve's research question.

In a broad discussion, the Christchurch workshop students knew about the resource limitations of social agencies like Women's Refuge, a homeless shelter, or food banks. They knew how pragmatic agencies need research to help create an evidence base and evaluations that show they produce meaningful social change in order to justify continued funding or support. The social agencies would want, the workshop students said, to know their organisation made a difference. Research like that described in the Eve scenario may be viewed as a waste if not meaningfully connected to the lives of the women the agency serves or to the needs of the agency in sustaining its services. These things can be explored only in conversation and partnership.

The students also said the statement "nothing about us, without us" balances the research relationship between what the agency wants and what the researcher wants. Does the researcher seek to explore some social theory (i.e. masculinity or a feminist perspective), or do they seek to provide targeted change in the lives of the people the agency serves? The social agency may want to prioritise an applied aspect to this research or understand how theoretical work may help them provide or improve their service.

A supposition embedded in this statement "nothing about us, without us" is that it takes time to establish an essential relationship with a social organisation. If so, take the time and make the time. A researcher should view time as a necessary intangible resource to absorb into a research budget for any qualitative research project. These relationships are (or should be) built long before any work is funded or begins.

However, understanding time as a core factor of qualitative research for qualitative researchers is fundamentally contradictory. For example, a postgraduate student may look at their dissertation as a three-year, full-time (plus) commitment to completing a varied set of tasks for the dissertation, but a social agency may ask what the student's time commitment is *to them*. This question could be a confusing question given that the answer is obvious; a PhD has a finite tenure. However, the answer to this question is not obvious for a social agency. The organisation will have been in existence before this research began and will continue to exist after the research is completed. Any request for disclosures about time expose the researcher's ongoing commitment to the organisation.

Take a few minutes to jot down a few sentences describing how to answer this question about "nothing about us, without us" for the social agency selected.

The social agency's second question picks up on this temporal dimension asking about exit strategies. These questions focus on resourcing that do not place the PhD student at the apex of the organisation's universe. They may be asking, what commitment does the researcher have to this location or agency or people following the awarding of their degree (a PhD or MA)?

Exit strategies describe the ways in which researchers plan to ethically bring closure to their relationship with participants (individuals or organisations) at the end of their research (Morrison et al., 2012). Qualitative research in many ways depends on the ability of researchers to establish relationships and trust with their participants, whether these be individuals or organisations. In some cases, researchers may have an enduring relationship with certain organisations over the course of their careers, and so an exit strategy in the typical sense is maybe not needed (but closure of the project should occur). However, in many instances researchers will engage with many new organisations, groups and participants for different projects. Depending on the nature of the project, they may spend significant time with participants and organisations. These bonds and their eventual dissolution can have impacts on participants, organisations and the researchers themselves (Watts, 2008). Not only that, but clarity about who the work 'belongs' to and how it can be used over time will be necessary, and these discussions can be complicated. Exit strategies therefore are an explicit engagement in thinking about the ways to manage both relationships and products that are the outcome of the research.

For individual participants, exit strategies are in part about what is communicated in informed consent documents, but also about how a researcher communicates and manages expectations during the project, as well as how they wrap it up. The wrap-up should generally include some way of providing information back to participants. This means an informed consent document, explicating the purpose of a project, what will occur, the expectations on a participant, what their rights are within the project (privacy, withdrawal, etc.) and what will occur with the information provided, as well as how results of the project will be fed back to them (the opportunity for closure).

The ramifications for an exit strategy with an organisation however, go far beyond any informed consent process between the researcher and agency. Organisations are not only participants, but potentially partners, collaborators or facilitators/supporters. These kinds of roles bring with them extra ethical terrain to navigate. Who leads the project? Who owns the project? These may seem like similar questions, but the one dictates what is done, the other dictates what is done with the outcomes. For example, after the data is collected and analysed, does the agency require the researcher to return to the agency to seek consent to use the data? In other words, does the researcher's promise of informed consent extend to *process consent* (see Chapter 7)?

If the social agency requires the researcher to practice process consent, does this requirement place an uncertainty on both the researcher's data collection and analysis? Once the penultimate thesis or research is complete, does the organisation insist on reading it to assess if the document fits within their requirements – "nothing about us, without us"?

If the researcher has no plans to allow the agency to review the document prior to publication, the social agency has a right to be told this during these initial discussions, not after the data is collected, analysed and published. A social agency may balk at the idea of receiving a copy of the findings without a chance to collaborate in the dissemination phase.

Discussions of exit strategies are useful to address the inherent power inequality that exists in qualitative research. In the following, Stacey (1988) explains how a researcher can exit the situation after the research has been completed, but invariably, research participants cannot:

> For no matter how welcome, even enjoyable the fieldworker's presence may appear to "natives", fieldwork represents an intrusion and intervention into a system of relationships, a system of relationships that the researcher is far freer than the researched to leave. The inequality and potential treacherousness of this relationship seems inescapable. So too does the exploitative aspect of ethnographic process seem unavoidable. The lives, loves, and tragedies that fieldwork informants share with a researcher are ultimately data, grist for the ethnographic mill, a mill that has a truly grinding power.
>
> (p. 23)

Questions about time and exit strategies can flummox novice researchers enrolled in an academic study as if the question is sourced from an alternate reality. They may assume the answer is obvious, defined solely upon the finite nature of their academic degree. However, discussions about (the ethics of) an exit strategy establish the researcher's sensibilities about their plans as a conflict of interest. Their interest is gaining a degree. The social agency's interest may be enhancing their clients' wellbeing. These interests may not overlap.

Dialogue over these competing interests requires researchers to offer an honest assessment of their interests versus the interests of a social agency they may want to research. Is the researcher's study a means to an end (to gain a degree), or an end in itself? The agency is likely to see the research as an end in itself.

These discussions should be frank about potential issues. Thinking back to Chapter 4, an MOU should be both an agreement and a plan. On the one hand, MOUs lay out some of what we have described as necessary for an informed consent document (the what, why, when and how of a project, plus rights). MOUs will also cover how and when communication between the agency and the researcher occurs, as well as what commitment, roles and responsibilities each party holds. The exit strategy is a key part of this document – what will happen at the end of this work to the relationship and the outcomes/products of the work, who will own/control them and how will they be used. Lastly, thinking about Chapter 4, an MOU should also be based on an explicit discussion about what to do about the *known-knowns* and *known-unknowns* of collaborating on a research project. Furthermore, it is beneficial if not crucial in some cases that researchers and the agency engage in conversations about how to manage *unknown-unknowns*. That is, plan a process for dispute or problems, given that no definitive action can be agreed prior to any unpredicted issue arising. By engaging in conversations about potential unforeseen problems and the ways to manage them, research- ers and agencies can get a better sense of each other, build trust and have a sense of security in embarking on a project together.

The exit strategy as a fundamental part of this work relates to questions focused on chronological time. Does the researcher (i.e. PhD student) think of time in terms of a three-year project, or a lifetime commitment? These are thought-provoking reflective questions, and they challenge workshop par- ticipants. Essentially, they are ethical questions in terms of honesty embodied in the informed consent process. What is the agency consenting to?

Temporal questions require researchers to consider, maybe for the first occasion and in explicit terms of how the data will be used in the short and long term. The question also implies something about who owns the data collected. Is it the researcher/s, the agency or a combination? Workshop participants were vocal, engaged by the ethics of an exit strategy. They saw the researcher becoming aware of the power and responsibilities imposed by time limits.

> Be mindful that academic dates, the thesis is due in February. This might not fit the social agency's framework.

> The word closure fits better than exit and I would be having these conversations all the way through the research.

Consider Venkatesh's exit strategy (discussed in Chapter 3) from his *Gang Leader for a Day* study. His account of his exit was one-sided, focused solely on his interests and benefits. *Getting out* raised mixed feelings of success and guilt:

> I still feel guilty about all those years that I let JT think I would write his biography. I hope that he at least reads these pages someday. While a lot of it is my story, it plainly could never have happened without him. He let me into a new world with a level of trust I had no reason to expect; I can only hope that this book faithfully presents his life and his work.
>
> (Venkatesh, 2008, p. 290)

A positive outcome that eventuates from any exit strategy discussion is having the researcher realise that their project has boundaries. Time is one of those boundaries. When will the research end? A second boundary involves the researcher's responsibilities to the agency, to participants and to themselves.

There is a third boundary that surpasses any exit ritual. Even after the researcher exits the research site, they are bound to their participants by confidentiality assurances given to participants. These declarations never expire.

Jot down a few sentences describing how to provide the social agency selected with a timeline for your project.

These first two questions enable the researcher to explore their domain assumptions, allowing the social agency to witness metaphorically the researcher finding their research spot. In the next section, an interlude follows another researcher literally finding a spot.

AN INTERLUDE

The questions asked by the social agency manager might seem frustrating, but consider a similar set of tasks asked of anthropology PhD student Carlos Castaneda by his mystical mentor Don Juan. This excerpt remains one of Tolich's favourites from his undergraduate education.

Sunday, 25 June 1961

I stayed with Don Juan all afternoon on Friday. I was going to leave about 7 p.m. We were sitting on the porch in front of his house and I decided to ask him once more about the teaching. It was almost a routine question and I expected him to refuse again. I asked him if there was a way in which he could accept just my desire to learn, as if I were an Indian. He took a long time to answer. I was compelled to stay because he seemed to be trying to decide something. Finally he told me that there was a way, and proceeded to delineate a problem. He pointed out that I was very tired sitting on the floor, and that the proper thing to do was to find a "spot" on the floor where I could sit without fatigue. I had been sitting with my knees up against my chest and my arms locked around my calves. When he said I was tired, I realized that my back ached and that I was quite exhausted. I waited for him to explain what he meant by a "spot", but he made no overt attempt to elucidate the point. I thought that perhaps he meant that I should change positions, so I got up and sat closer to him. He protested at my movement and clearly emphasized that a spot meant a place where a man could feel naturally happy and strong. He patted the place where he sat and said it was his own spot, adding that he had posed a riddle I had to solve by myself without any further deliberation. What he had posed as a problem to be solved was certainly a riddle. I had no idea how to begin or even what he had in mind. Several times I asked for a clue, or at least a hint, as to how to proceed in locating a point where I felt happy and strong. I insisted and argued that I had no idea what he really meant because I couldn't conceive the problem. He suggested I walk around the porch until I found the spot. I got up and began to pace the floor. I felt silly and sat down in front of him. He became very annoyed with me and accused me of not listening, saying that perhaps I did not want to learn. After a while he calmed down and explained to me that not every place was good to sit or be on, and that within the confines of the porch there was one spot that was unique, a spot where I could be at my very best. It was my task to distinguish it from all the other places.

(read further at https://selfdefinition.org/shaman/Carlos-Castaneda-Teachings-of-Don-Juan.pdf)

The two questions posed thus far and the three that follow facilitate the finding of each person's ethical spot.

SHARING RESOURCES

If a social agency and the researcher can get beyond the first two questions, the social organisation may want to know what resources the researcher can give the organisation. Researchers may possess research techniques/skills acquired in their university education. The social agency may enquire which skills the researcher is willing to share by training members of the social agency. The social agency may have plans the researcher had not considered, if not now, maybe for future research. They may want their staff trained in these techniques.

The agency may see the researcher's skill set as a useful way of addressing an absent exit strategy problem. The social agency may suggest, as is common in these types of arrangements, that the researcher spend time training the social agency staff to use these techniques and to build their confidence and research competence. Here the social agency may be one step ahead of the researcher, seeing the research not just as an end in itself, but a means to an end, linking education and action in one (Ezzy, 2013, p. 186). In other words, even if the researcher leaves the research site after a finite period, the social agency may have built capacity, allowing them to conduct research projects generated by this collaboration in the future born out of a democratisation of research.

A third question the social agency manager could ask the researcher has them identify what skill set they can leave for the organisation after they exit. The researcher may not have many skills to conduct research, but an inventory of them should be shared. These may include how to run:

- Unstructured interviews
- Focus groups
- Narrative research
- Autoethnography
- Photovoice
- Participant observation

From this exercise the social agency manager may suggest synergies not apparent to the researcher. The social agency may possess research skills the researcher does not have. For example, in some mental health situations, the researcher may have the technical research skills, but not the tacit skills to address patients with acute illness face-to-face. In these situations, the researcher could train staff members regarding how to collect information (with some caveats). These staff conduct the interviews on behalf of the researcher and the researcher analyses the transcripts, checking the analysis with interviewers and interviewees. In those situations, both parties can mentor the other.

An unanticipated consequence of this resourcing question is that the researcher may realise the resources that they have but were not aware of. In the past, many workshop participants tended to take their access to the University library for granted. Researchers learn that social agencies don't have this access. One of the prized resources graduate students can share with the social agency is an up-to-date literature review. Many students are unaware that their access to an online database is something a social agency does not have. Integral to this resource is the time needed to conduct this literature review. How do comparable agencies in other countries address similar problems? Researchers working with standard agency data who have skills in database development or coding may be able to offer solutions to agency problems that have fallen low on the priority list regarding the management of data. There are a multitude of ways in which researchers can be of use to agencies through the indirect tasks of their research, so that the relationships created are one of reciprocity rather than extraction. In creating these relationships, researchers on one hand address ethical criticisms of exploitation or objectification of research participants and related organisations (seeing agencies and participants as "means to an end") but also complicate ethical roles and responsibilities. This blurring of boundaries is exactly why MOUs including clear exit strategies are needed. By having to engage in transparent discussions, the ethical terrain of the project is to some degree mapped out.

Jot down a few sentences describing the research techniques or skills that could be shared with the hypothetical social agency.

A *fourth question the social agency may ask* is likely to surprise the researcher, as the question is counterintuitive. The social agency manager may seek clarification on the insider and outsider role held by the researcher. On first reading, this question may seem unnecessary given that at the start of this chapter, the requirement was that the researcher have had no contact with the social agency. That is true, but the question is more complex.

If the researcher had had previous contact with the organisation, they may be an insider rather than an outsider. Insiders and outsiders bring different perspectives to the research. The insider/outsider question a social agency manager may ask highlights a different form of insider participation. The social agency manager may assume the researcher holds an outsider status, but the manager may want to know what assumptions the researcher already holds about the agency. For example, the physical education students discussed earlier were assigned the University rowing club as their hypothetical social agency. Even though they had no physical contact with the rowing club, some of them had opinions about the club.

The agency may want to know what assumptions the researcher has about the agency. For example, why does the researcher want to conduct research in the agency? What are their expectations? Even though they have not been inside the organisation, what have they read about it or been told about?

As described earlier, once you also become someone helping the agency, your insider/outsider perspective for your own work may be less clearly defined. Knowing your own views prior to engaging in a project and keeping note of how these change through a project is important for your relationship with the agency, but also for the work itself.

DIFFICULT MOU CONVERSATIONS: DISAGREEMENT, PRIOR RELATIONSHIPS, AND WORKAROUNDS

There are some important considerations around MOUs and exit strategies not yet discussed. One of these was recently raised by a student in Tolich's postgraduate classes as the book was being submitted for publication. Azlan Currie asked, what happens when what you are finding out may cast a negative light on the organisation you are completing the MOU with?

This is an excellent question, and another reason why an MOU is so important. Firstly, it's important to understand what exactly the nature is of the project a researcher plans to undertake. If a researcher's MOU with an organisation is not so much to discuss the organisation and whatever service it delivers, but to gain access through the organisation to a participant pool, who they wish to question about other aspects of the participants' lives, then this is relatively straightforward. An example of this would be if you wanted to talk to a specific professional group about work-life balance, and the researcher created an MOU with the professional association to help to help with recruitment, on the agreement that they would also provide the research results directly to the organization on the agreement that they would also be provided the research results to the organisation directly. This is relatively straightforward and largely unproblematic. The questions raised in this scenario are unlikely to bring up anything that might reflect poorly on the association (assuming of course, no unknown unknowns!).

However, another piece of research might be working with that same professional association to explore the role of the professional association in the lives of the professionals that are part of it. The MOU for this situation becomes slightly trickier. It may be the case that some responses reflect poorly on the association – i.e. is the professional association fulfilling it's responsiblities? This discussion has to be had in the creation of the MOU. One of the ways that an organisation may be more open to a researcher collecting and using all data, regardless of whether it's positive or negative, is to understand how the data will be framed and how sensitive a researcher will be to the organisation in their reporting. This means that a framing of negative data as areas of improvement with careful wording alongside positive feedback is more palatable than an emphasis on the negative. It may still not be considered acceptable. This is something one has to negotiate, and if a researcher believes that the organisation cannot come to an agreement in a way that maintains the integrity of the research, then the researcher may have to walk away.

Researchers can do projects without organisational support. This means finding alternative ways of recruiting and potentially missing out on data that would come from the organisation directly. But data cannot be omitted, ignored, or unrecognisably distorted for the sake of an agreement. In fact, if a researcher is aware from the beginning that what they are looking for is something negative, then they have to take a different approach. Say, for example, one wanted to explore a charitable service provider for its discrimination of some kinds of people seeking out its services. It's unlikely that a researcher would try to create an MOU with this service. Instead, they would have to aim to directly recruit participants independent of the service. It may be that the researcher also wants to collect data from the service itself, and that would have to be negotiated. This has to occur with full disclosure of the work planned, which will, of course, prejudice any negotiations a researcher would be having and would unlikely lead to the desired outcome. Sometimes workarounds can be found, but these are separate from the MOU process. So yes, in answer to Azi, being cognisant of what type of information you will likely get in your research will be important for the MOU process, and is something that is best discussed with your relevant reference group, who can help identify the things you might not think of. Sometimes an MOU might not be possible, and the project planned may have to change significantly.

The other important consideration around MOUs is those cases where the researcher has a long-established relationship with an organisation before the research occurs and they feel that relationship will continue long after the research finishes. We mention these kind of relationships later in the chapter. You may have been reading this work so far and think an "exit strategy" doesn't sound appropriate for what you are doing and that an MOU isn't necessary because of your good standing with the group in question already. Despite whatever relationship a researcher may already have with an organisation, an MOU, MOU like document, or MOU like conversation should be had (acknowledging that for some kinds of groups or communities, paperwork might be seen to undermine a relationship). The purpose of this MOU is to ensure that roles, responsibilities and boundaries FOR THE PURPOSE OF THE RESEARCH are well understood by all parties in advance as they are likely to differ from the relationship researchers may generally have with a group. What is really meant by the term "exit strategy" is closure. How does the researcher provide closure for the research project when it is done to indicate the transition back to a "normal" relationship rather than the arrangements that were necessary for the research? Therefore, MOUs and exit strategies (closure) are as necessary in situations where a researcher has an ongoing relationship as they are for situations where a researcher is instigating a new relationship for the purposes of a project and a defined time period.

Jot down a few sentences describing what you already know about the social agency selected. Equally, ask some questions. Using the rowing club examples is a case in point, do you expect there to be bullying in the rowing club? Do male and female rowers get access to the same resources? Historically, is the club on a decline or an assent? This task can be enhanced by taking part in a free-writing exercise.

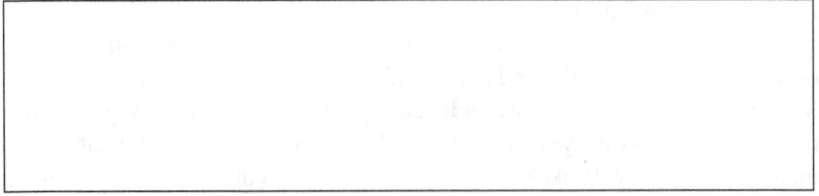

FREE-WRITING

A means to acquire answers to questions, such as whether you are an insider or an outsider, is by employing free-writing. This technique allows the researcher to describe what's inside their conscious and unconscious head about this organisation. The instruction is very clear. Simply open a blank page and write the title "The goal of this social agency is …" and start writing or typing. Write for five minutes without thinking too much – don't be surprised at what comes up. Don't be concerned at this stage with grammar or spelling. Just write and trust the process.

> In *Writing for Social Scientists: How to Start and Finish Your
> Thesis, Book, or Article*, Becker (1986) suggests free-writing before
> beginning any the research … Becker (1986: 54) usually asks his students
> to try to write whatever comes into their heads as fast as they can type,
> without reference to outline, notes, data, books or any other aids. The
> object of this exercise is to find out what the researchers wants to say
> and what all their earlier work on the topic (i.e. reading and prior classes),
> has already lead them researcher to believe. All that has to be done after
> that is find out what the respondents or the informants think!
>
> (Tolich and Davidson, 1999, p. 12)

The qualitative researcher O'Reilly (2005) suggests a more structured free-writing exercise. She suggests the following topics to start thinking and jump-start your free-writing:

> A title, or even a passage or two summarising what you are saying,
> can really help … If you can summarise what you want to say a few
> words, or sentences, it will help keep you focused as you write. As you
> go along, try to establish what it is that you are doing … [S]ometimes
> the actual act of writing can help you decide what you want to say, so
> don't keep putting it off until you are completely organised.
>
> (O'Reilly, 2005, p. 207)

Free-writing is a useful technique to use in any research project. Use it here for 5 or 10 minutes, writing answers to all the social agency questions listed here. It would be rare for anyone not to have an opinion on an agency that was of interest to you. These opinions can be shared with the agency, or they can be used by the researcher as sensitising concepts to explore the agency.

Free-writing allows the researcher to state very clearly what they think the organisation stands for. It also provides another insight for the researcher. If the writing is not shared with the agency manager, it can be put into the researcher's top drawer. Having done that, the researcher has a good idea on what they think the social agency is about. The researcher's next job is to find out what volunteers and partners of the agency think of the agency. The researcher's understanding may be quite different. This free writing could be useful in the writing stage of the research by generating what van Maanen calls a confessional starting point such as "this is what I thought when I began this research".

Van Maanen's (2011) Three Narrative Conventions provide a useful description of the different styles used in academic texts. These are realist narratives, dramatic narratives and the confessional narrative. He defines the confessional narrative as deriving from the researcher's experience:

> Confessional [narratives] relates to a style of writing dominated by an account of the author's dilemma of doing research. As the name implies, confessional tales from the field focus more explicitly on the fieldworker's experience than on the culture studied. The confessional style typically begins with an account of the assumptions that underlay your study when you first entered the field. You would then begin to confess how naive or incorrect these original assumptions were and how, via a baptism of fire, a new, better, much improved, data driven set of assumptions were being practical (Atkinson, 1990: 110). One of the strengths of such an approach is that it captures the reflexive process of doing qualitative research. The confessional narrative is persuasive because by reciting the confession the author vouches for the integrity of the new account.
>
> (Van Maanen, 2011, quote from Tolich & Davidson, 2018, p. 162)

Confessional beginnings to any writing lend legitimacy to the author's findings; sharing initial thoughts on the social agency before going on to document how informants describe their world, the author can fall on their sword and say "this is what I thought, and this is very different from what people said". The outcome generates legitimacy and authority. Engaging in this same process later in the research project or at the end will also help researchers to understand what has changed for them over time in their interactions with the agency and provides a space for them to consider, why? Not only, why, but also how does this change affect their work?

The fifth question posed here originated from two of the four reviewers who examined this book's initial proposal. They asked questions about how qualitative research changes when researching Indigenous groups. Postgraduate students in the Christchurch workshop saw this question as a straightforward restatement of nothing about us, without us:

> In Indigenous research, the expectation is that the researcher will come back to the social agency with the data found prior to dissemination and get permission to use it.

> In Indigenous research, the word exit does not translate given the research is a relationship that is ongoing; it is both meaningful and reciprocal. Any talk of exit needs to be made very clear at the start of the research relationship.

> Indigenous (first nation) research means going backwards and forwards with the organisation. They might want to ask the researcher to reword some questions or ask questions on topics you hadn't considered.

Indigenous research should begin from an Indigenous world view (Smith, 2013). These students' insights provide a starting point to consider questions from a social agency manager whose constituency had a high proportion of Indigenous clientele. The social agency may frame the question in terms of, is your research *with them, or on them*? One cannot assume that social agencies who serve Indigenous populations are Indigenous-led. Therefore social agencies may ask you, whether you are Indigenous or Non-Indigenous, how you will be responsive to these particular Indigenous people's needs and centre their voices. Where an agency fails to ask this, you should still endeavour to ask it of yourself. 'Nothing about us, without us' is here a call to ensure that not only are particular voices heard, but that an Indigenous perspective has primacy. Primacy throughout from design, to data collection, to analysis and dissemination.

For example, Indigenous. North American Indigenous groups have developed research fatigue and have begun to resist external research on them. Green and Mercer (2001) found that:

> Native American and Canadian First Nations communities, for example, after decades of serving as subjects for anthropologic and epidemiologic studies, behavioural surveys, and health education program evaluations, have put the brakes on external researchers' exploiting their circumstances while providing very little benefit to their communities. Similarly, African Americans living in inner cities have noticed that their lives have been described publicly by researchers in unflattering – if sympathetic – ways, but they have seen little come of it besides embarrassment and shame.
>
> (p. 1926)

In New Zealand, a typical critique of research involving Māori is to see research framed as research *on* Māori, not *with* Māori. This highlights a non-collaborative ethnocentric perspective held by western researchers:

> Critiques of Western approaches involved in investigating the lives of Māori people, genuinely agree that Māori are still among the most researched people in the world … As the researched, Māori people have been guinea pigs for mainly non-Māori hit-and-run researchers. While non-Māori researchers and to some extent their academic community, have accumulated career and personal benefits from the research, in too many cases the researched have seldom gained any benefits at all. Too often the outcomes of such investigations have raised the propensity for the belittlement of Māori history, knowledge and learning in the reinforcement of negative stereotypes. … As Stokes maintains, the Māori view is that doing research "… Simply for this sake of knowingness is pointless".
>
> (Holdaway, 2002, p. 47)

The authors wish to acknowledge the author of the following story that has been shared to highlight the nuance of research *on* and research *with*. It is unique.

The researcher as a non–Indigenous researcher wanted to be collaborative in his research, but when he went through a process very similar to the one outlined here, his collaboration was not seen as collaborative. Lowe's story has an epic component to it, similar to the Carlos Castaneda story earlier in this chapter. His negotiation came to an abrupt end. He recalls pitching his study to an Indigenous gatekeeper and finding himself caught red-handed in an error when saying (Lowe, George & Deger 2020, 286):

We were speaking about how I wanted to construct a practice-led, community-based project (Lowe et al., 2020).

> I recall a particular moment in a discussion I had with [a gatekeeper]) the director of a Kaupapa Māori research organisation based in rural New Zealand, my proposed primary field area. *We were speaking about how I wanted to construct a practice-led, community-based project that would create spaces for local empowerment.* "No", she remarked. "That's not right. That's the do-gooder attitude that we don't want".

What fundamental error had the researcher made?

> The gatekeeper continued by saying, "You need to come with a project and present it to the community … community involvement every step of the way [and] you'll figure out the methodology on the

ground". This encounter insistently claimed the interplay between speaking and listening (and responding) within *her* space. I could hear our words reverberate around the room as we talked, rumbling together in a two-way flow that emplaced us within our newly established set of relationships. This was more than listening *just* with ears but a listening *within* my whole body – and between our two bodies and by extension many bodies, many lives, many moments in time. The project idea that I had initially thrown out into the world was no longer *my* project. It had, over the course of the pre-ethical fieldwork, become moulded and shaped by many voices, all of which had left their mark in some form or another, accentuating the importance of building up the project *together* with others from the ground up.

Jot down the ways this one flawed nuanced negotiation with (Kaupapa Māori Research) could be seen as capturing all of the key questions asked by any social agency.

The concept of research on, not with, is not limited to Indigenous research. Venkatesh's research discussed in Chapter 3 exemplified research *on* a group. At no point was his research *with* them. Eve's story was the same.

The nuances in the Kaupapa Māori story and found in the scenarios of Venkatesh and Eve show how they failed to grasp how the creation of research can be a two-way participatory experience allowing both the researcher and the social agency (and the people they serve) an opportunity to frame the research. The exercises above, posing questions about research on, research with, "nothing about us, without us", MOUs, exit strategies, sharing resources all attempted to facilitate mental exercises that promote a two-way participation.

This kind of two-way participation is necessary in community settings for both ethical and methodological reasons. Distinctions between *research on and research with* is important for research ethics. Morse (2011) believes this leads to a cooperative inquiry, less likely to undermine the self-determination of participants. Answering these five questions promotes a cooperative inquiry because it allows any social agency or community to understand the researcher's perspective, their assumptions and whether the agency or community and the researcher would create a good fit. In essence, these five questions have conceptualised informed consent into a more meaningful dialogue. An additional outcome of the five questions could establish a template for reciprocal understanding between the researcher and the agency or community.

Taken together, a researcher's answers to these questions reveal their domain assumptions about research practice with the agency, allowing the agency greater insight into the research process than normally occurs. This allows the agency to decide which of these domain assumptions they share and which ones they do not.

PARTICIPATORY ACTION RESEARCH

Taken together, these answers serve as a succinct memorandum of understanding between the researcher and the social agency. This memorandum of understanding is an example of an informal ethics statement. The MOU also manifests itself as an example of a specific type of research known as participatory action research. The five questions represent an alternative, informal ethical review system existing outside a formal institutional ethics committee and are foundational of research conducted using a *participatory action research* model (PAR).

Participatory action research is a recognised code of practice that attempts to equalise power relationships between the researchers and the researched. Participatory action research emphasises a collaborative approach that equitably and democratically involves all partners in the research process equally at the front end of the study in the construction of the research question and at the back end, in interpreting and applying the findings.

Patton (2002, p. 185) formally describes PAR in the following seven terms. The next task asks students to compare and contrast how many of these seven points are embodied in their brief memorandum of understanding.

1. PAR recognizes the unique strengths that each partner brings. Participants in the process own the inquiry. They are involved authentically in making major focus and design decisions. They draw and apply conclusions. Participation is real, not token.
2. Participants work together as a group and the enquiry facilitator supports group cohesion and collective inquiry.
3. All aspects of the enquiry, from research focus to data analysis, are undertaken in ways that are understandable and meaningful to participants.
4. The researcher or evaluator acts as a facilitator, collaborator, and learning resource; participants are co-equal.
5. The enquiry facilitator recognises and values participants' perspectives and expertise and works to help participants recognise and value their own and each other's expertise.

6. Status and power differences between the enquiry facilitator and participants are minimised, as much as possible, practical, and authentic, without patronising or game playing.
7. The enquiry process involves participants and learning enquiry logic and skills, for example, the nature of evidence, establishing priorities, focusing questions, interpreting data, database decision-making, and connecting processes to outcomes.

(Patton, 2002, p. 185)

Typically, the PAR researcher regards the community and its leaders as equal collaborators in planning and conducting the research; the researcher is concerned with applying the findings for the good of the community. Thus, PAR is for and of the community, with the aid of an academic researcher who provides research skills and typically funding. This stance is an extreme contrast to the "Grab the data and run" or "Helicopter" approach to community research in which an academic researcher drops into the community and without giving back or acknowledging the community leadership or anything in return, or stopping to find out whether the interpretation of the findings makes sense to the community members "flies" back out.

The five questions asked in this chapter highlight a sound way to initiate research with social agencies. The researcher does not just bowl up to a social service agency and say "hey, I want to do research". They negotiate with the agency what needs to be researched. The starting point for PAR is that all people involved in the study are seen as dynamic to the study. Thus, from the outset, participants discuss and agree on what they want to research, the nature of the questions, modes of data collection and analysis, the way data are written up and how findings are distributed.

Patton (2002, p. 202) describes PAR as a philosophy that produces knowledge from the point of view of the marginalised, deprived and oppressed groups and classes. The emphasis here is on transforming social realities that the lives of such people are improved. Fals Borda (1979, p. 592) states this in stronger terms saying that the goal of PAR research is not solely to understand the world but to transform it.

PAR represents a broad, authentic attitude of mutuality and openness. It is a commitment to learning on the part of the people involved, particularly the researchers. Researchers should not assume a social agency is as keen at advancing the researcher's academic discipline. They are likely to have their own research goals.

The other side of this exercise is how it places the researcher, albeit hypothetically within an intimate relationship with a social agency. After having completed this exercise with workshop participants, Tolich has found the five questions generate accountability. And in one case, "magic".

WHERE DID THE MAGIC GO?

The five questions a prospective researcher may be asked by a social agency, especially those who are undergoing research in order to gain a degree from the university, could be incomplete. There is a sixth question not asked earlier and it can create quite a problem. It did at a qualitative ethics workshop Tolich gave at Aveiro University in Portugal in September 2019. This sixth question is revelatory about research, research ethics and the pedagogy of this book.

For researchers affiliated with a university, research ethics is not limited to how a researcher protects those that volunteer to take part in their research. Research ethics can take an institutional form, making it a three-way relationship, where a researcher from an institution i.e. a university must negotiate their ethical considerations not only with the social agency, in this case, but also with their host institution. The sixth question is relevant to this discussion. It requires the researcher to submit their research for formal ethics committee review. This sixth question is sourced from the researcher's institution and not from the social agency.

Tolich posed the sixth question late in the Aveiro workshop. It provoked a "Houston, we have a problem" moment as outlined in Figure 3. Once more in this book, workshop participants provide remarkable insight giving the instructor pause to consider how students teach ethics to the instructor.

Each of the eight workshop participants at Aveiro had worked through the proceeding five questions gaining a sense of intimacy and ownership within their hypothetical exercise to such a degree that the thought of now of starting again with their University ethics committee took the gloss off their project. The student depicted in Figure 3 who said the magic had vanished went from intimately participating in a thought experiment to being estranged from it knowing that she had to now submit these intimate negotiations (within an ethics application) to an ethics committee for formal review.

During the four-hour workshop the eight students felt listened to, they felt confident, their ethical self exposed and they were comfortable in the rich ethical perspectives they shared with their social agency. What seemed to vanish for this student was the degree of intimacy they had generated by engaging with this social agency even though the entire situation was hypothetical.

As authors of this book, we interpret this magical evaporation differently. Not a disillusionment but a singular realisation of the three goals of this book. The magic vanished confirms the three goals of this book. First, it acknowledges that students hold a great deal of knowledge about ethics within their ethical intuition, and that as teachers we can unleash this

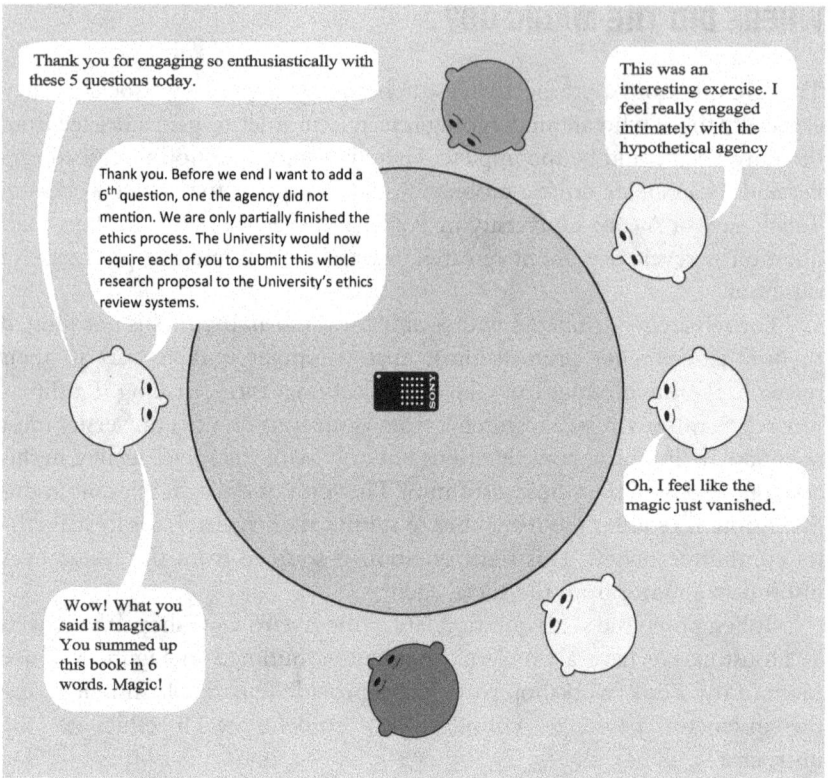

Figure 4 Did the magic vanish?

knowledge having students match their understandings with the formal concepts of research ethics. The second goal of the book was to establish situations that allowed students to voice their knowledge and further develop it in the interactions with others, hypothetical and real. At Aveiro and other places where this module has been taught, the students' answers to the five questions demonstrate that each of them could think empathetically about their research needs alongside the immediate needs of social agency. The book's third goal was aspirational, based on the hope that researchers in the field away from their supervisors and formal ethics committees would be able to practice research ethically. What the student who said "the magic just vanished" was saying was that they had the wherewithal to negotiate ethical considerations with a social agency. They felt both competent and endowed.

This sixth question and the bureaucratic evaluation it involves dominates the next two chapters.

CHAPTER 9

Formal ethics review

Research governance is not research ethics

As alluded to at the end of Chapter 8, there may have been an unintentional omission in the five questions asked by the social agency manager. They may have failed to ask a sixth question:

> Does the research need to undergo formal ethical review by an ethics committee?

If the answer is yes, and formal ethics review needs to take place prior to any negotiations, how should readers feel about all the work that went into developing a memorandum of understanding (MOU) with the social agency? It is prudent to ponder that situation when reviewing Mark Israel's (2015) claim once more:

> Social scientists are angry and frustrated. Still. They believe their work is constrained and distorted by regulators of ethical practice who neither understand social science research nor the social, political, economic and cultural contexts within which researchers work.
>
> (p. 1)

If the agency and a researcher did not know in advance that they needed to go through ethics review, this would lead to some of the frustration Israel is predicting. The students at Aveiro University mentioned at the end of Chapter 8 expressed their frustration with the process of going through formal ethics review in their statement, "the magic just vanished".

This expression of frustration is not isolated to the students from Aveiro. Van den Scott describes graduate student feelings towards research ethics review as "fear", "exasperation" and "helplessness" (2016). The authors encountered similar worries from graduate students in their work exploring a tool (see Chapter 10) to help in application writing for ethics review (Tolich & Tumilty, 2014; Tumilty et al., 2016). Supervisors and graduate students perceive the process to be costly in terms of time, costly in terms of potential changes to their work, and potentially costly in terms of their reputation and careers, if they fail to do something correctly or fail to seek approval for a significant change, where significance is poorly understood (van den Scott, 2016).

Part of the frustration stems from the researcher having to reassess one of the questions used to establish the memorandum of understanding. The question was, is the research on the organisation or with the organisation? In some ways, if research ethics review predates consultation with the agency, this is likely to create distance between parties leading the researcher to conduct research on (what they think the organisation wants), not research with the organisation. The questions, methods, analysis, and process are decided prior to collaboration so that they can be described to the ethics committee.

If they seek ethical approval after these initial conversations with organisations, the fear then becomes that ethics review may require something that contradicts what has been agreed. This, then, becomes difficult to manage – it requires either a new conversation with the organisation about the constraints of institutional ethical review (potentially undermining trust and relationships built), or advocacy and support within the ethics review process to justify and go against what might be the committee's norm. Both responses can jeopardise the project and take time – something sorely lacking in academic environments whether for graduate students or novice researchers.

The sixth question, whether formal ethics review is needed, coming after the initial consultation with the agency, explains why the magic just vanished. The intimacy of the negotiations between the agency and the researcher could now be contradicted or distorted and replaced by a bureaucratic procedure that omits the social agency.

Most countries have some form of ethical research review whether at the institutional or national level. What this review looks like, who oversees it, who conducts reviews and who is subject to review varies greatly. Australia, Brazil, Canada, the European Union, New Zealand, the United Kingdom and the United States are the countries where ethics review has the longest history of being mandatory up to a point. In these countries ethics review committees take various shapes, and not all research needs to be reviewed. As one example, in New Zealand there are two main avenues of research ethics review and they are mandatory for a large proportion of research conducted. There is review by a national Health and Disability Ethics Committee (HDEC) or by an institutional research ethics review committee. The latter are generally in tertiary education institutions. Review by a

HDEC is mandatory for any health research whether interventional or observational that includes human participants, their information or their specimens, except for where the study is considered low risk (qualitative projects are generally considered low risk within this framework). It is mandatory for researchers who are funded by government grants or who work at universities to seek research ethics review, either from the HDEC where appropriate or from their institutional committee. All other researchers not funded by a government grant, or undertaken by researchers not affiliated to or working with a university have no access to research ethics review. The rules of engagement are different in each country as are the names of the committees: Health and Disability Ethics Committee (HDEC, New Zealand), Human Research Ethics Committee (HREC, Australia), Institutional Review Boards (IRB, USA), Research Ethics Committee (REC, UK) and Ethics Committees (EU).

It is generally the case that qualitative research methodologies are considered low risk and that they have individual pathways or expedited processes (i.e., different application forms and review processes than for projects involving, say, clinical trial methodologies). The reader's country of origin and institutional affiliation gives them some clue if the research that generated the MOU in Chapter 8 needed first to go through formal ethics review. There should be no expectation that the social agency manager would have known that rule. Blame for the situation sits squarely on the researcher, not on the agency manager. If ethics review is mandatory, this situation is likely to cause a fissure in the relationship between researcher and the social agency, adding to the frustration of both parties. This problem is well documented.

A memorandum of understanding can create problems for the participatory action research model described in Chapter 8. It has nothing to do with PAR itself but everything to do with how formal research ethics colonises PAR. Some ethics committees, in the countries where there is mandatory ethics review, balk at this degree of pre-ethics consultation with a social agency. They are likely to require the researcher to gain ethics approval from them *prior to* their engaging in any dialogue with the agency. This about-face is akin to putting the horse before the cart. All the good work achieved in the negotiation of those five questions becomes redundant. Sieber and Tolich (2013) describe reasoning for this situation as:

> the regulatory structure of IRBs [ethics committee] does not give the
> community an equal say in whether a project can be undertaken. In
> many cases, the IRB does not even recognize the community as a
> partner with whom it should work, or regard risk to community (as
> opposed to risk to individual humans, or persons who are research
> subjects) as a risk that should concern them. Consequently, even if

the researcher has persuaded the community representatives that they have an equal status relationship as they design the research, the researcher must ultimately say "Now I have to go back to my university IRB to see if they will let us do this". The IRB that is unsure of how to respond to a PAR protocol may delay approval for many months, or may insist on changes that fly in the face of conditions acceptable to the community.

(pp. 86–97)

Requirements to seek ethics approval before discussing the project with a social agency disrupts the PAR framework, undermining trust created between parties. When these parties include Indigenous groups, formal ethics review can undermine sovereignty. Liebenberg et al. (2018, p. 340) provide insight into these mechanics.

Most contemporary institutional review boards are embedded in Euro-American culture, and are therefore often contradictory to Indigenous worldviews … Consequently, standardized institutional guidelines do not necessarily ensure that research is aligned with the cultural practices and belief systems of many culturally and socioeconomically disenfranchised groups … Without careful consideration of the enactment of these dominant principles, we may inadvertently engage in research that is counter to the intent of research ethics guidelines.

Liebenberg et al. (2018, p. 340) continue outlining the various factors endowing an Indigenous groups' sovereignty.

Indigenous communities (referring to First Nations, Inuit and Metis peoples in Canada) *own* their cultural knowledge, including data, collectively. Within this understanding, stewardship is awarded to an individual or institution that is responsible for the safekeeping of the knowledge, and as such is accountable to the community. Additionally, Indigenous communities have the right to *control* all components of the research, including intellectual knowledge and dissemination products, as components of their heritage. As part of ownership and control, communities should have full *access* to information about themselves and their communities, including their own data. Communities also have the right to determine who else has access to this data (for example secondary data analysis). *Possession* relates to stewardship of data and knowledge – the physical control of data and is the mechanism through which ownership is enacted and maintained.

While ethics committee review may ask you to address how your work considers relevant Indigenous issues, it is constrained and may be completed in a perfunctory manner. In some places such as a Canada or New Zealand, ethics review processes may ask you to first consult with Indigenous peoples about your work (generally through prescribed channels or processes). Where these allow meaningful consultation, they are successful. However, it is also the case that ethics review itself can present problems for working and collaborating in truly Indigenous ways. Contradictions in world views, values, and what is considered ethical can make ethical review fraught for Indigenous researchers and those partnering with Indigenous communities (Bull, 2010). Ethics committees rooted in colonialism fail to appreciate the meaning of bonds, relationships between people, roles, and responsibilities. Bull (2016) suggests that rather than completely disregarding of Indigenous values in formal ethics review, or completely rejecting traditional academic processes by Indigenous communities, working together to create shared ethical space is required. This kind of work is, however, ongoing.

Up until this point, this book has focused on research ethics highlighting the relationship between both the researcher and the person one is undertaking research with, or the social agency. As Sieber and Tolich (2013) point out, a third body, namely ethics committees, may usurp this relationship. The key concept in this relationship is *research governance*.

Research governance (rather than research ethics) provides a conceptual frame to understand the role of research ethics committees. Research governance is different from the concept of research ethics. Research ethics focuses on protecting those we undertake research with. The primary function of research governance is to protect the institution that employs the researcher from a lawsuit. This in part may also explain why many committees focus on the information sheet and consent documentation in their reviews (Stark, 2016). Not only are these easier elements for committees to review, but if research is viewed from the perspective of wanting to protect the institution from harm, then knowing participants were informed and chose freely to partake in a project becomes all the more important. Ironically, research governance performs a transformative role in research ethics, but research governance has little to do with research ethics. It is for this reason Israel is claiming social scientists are angry and frustrated with research ethics committees.

Iphofen (2011) pejoratively characterises ethics review boards as championing research governance – that is, protecting the institution from litigation rather than being primarily focused on research ethics to protect the researched. Iphofen (2011) states:

> maintaining a key distinction between research governance and the ethical review of research, the former is necessarily risk averse, while

the latter is fulfilling a key monitoring and mentoring function if it remains merely risk aware and operates in a collegial, advisory capacity. *In this way it becomes more obvious if research is being stifled or obstructed for institutional rather than ethical reason.* The main area of complaint has been in health research where the regulatory committees of the NHS have, in the past, lacked adequate knowledge of qualitative research to fairly judge design and method – once again preferring designs that come close to the experimental 'gold standard' or lend themselves to statistically quantifiable data.

(our emphasis)

Babb (2020) discusses the evolution of research ethics review from a process that early on could have been described as "collegial" but now is more appropriately described as a "compliance bureaucracy". This evolution, she suggests, is brought about by shifts in regulatory environments in general to compliance processes and increased managerialism in universities. Snook (2003), a founder of ethics review committees in New Zealand, characterises them as transformed:

far from confronting the external realities and subjecting them to critical scrutiny, ethics committees have become more inward looking and bureaucratic.

(p. 11)

Research ethics, as discussed in the first eight chapters of this book, and research governance, discussed here, do not have the same goals. Research governance ensures risk is minimised to the institution. Ethics protection of the research participant is important, but only in as much as their protection ensures less chance of reputational harm or litigation against the institution (Stark, 2012, p. 13).

While few qualitative researchers argue against the value of independent ethical review for any research project, a number of strong critiques have been voiced by qualitative researchers about how ethics committees function that warrant attention. Chief among the critiques is the misconception of the one-size-fits-all model of ethics review. This outcome leads to a hegemony of the biomedical model colonising ethics review. Haggerty (2004) claims an "ethics creep" has developed: the gradual encroachment of ethics committees into areas of research outside immediate biomedical concerns, namely qualitative research. This has raised fears among scholars that academic freedoms are being compromised. Haggerty (2004) sees this encroachment as a duality:

"Ethics creep" involves a dual process whereby the regulatory structure of the ethics bureaucracy is expanding outward, colonizing new groups, practices, and institutions, while at the same time intensifying the regulation of practices deemed to fall within its official ambit.

(p. 444)

The fear that there has been increased surveillance of qualitative research projects has resulted in serious questions about the policing of appropriate methodology and suppression of methodological innovation (Ozdemir, 2009), and it has even led to the charge that ethics committees have become grammarians (Bauer, 2001) whose primary concern is that applicants produce pristine paperwork. Staffing ethics committees with a preponderance of medical researchers as opposed to social scientists led ethics oversight to view qualitative research methods as inexact and sloppy. Case studies by Stark (2012) reported proposed studies have been declined on the basis of poor editorial work rather than a lack of rigour in considering the risks of harm to participants. Stark (2012) found that IRB reviewers believed a sloppy written application underwrote a poor research protocol. These ethics committee members said:

> If [a researcher's] attention to detail is not sufficient to know that the major heading, the words aren't spelled right. I'm worried about [other things as well as like], do I have to read this thing carefully enough to make sure that all the doses, for example, are correct, that there written the protocol correctly. I wonder what else was sloppy.

***

> if it is an excessively sloppy proposal, I'm going to be more question-ing about it ... I would be prejudiced against that it was full of typos ... I'd be questioning about the ability of the researcher.

(p. 17)

Gunsalus et al. (2006) claim when this pedantic attention to detail becomes the criteria for approval at the expense of rigorous researcher consideration of ethics, then ethics committees may come to 'undermine protection of human subjects' (p. 1441).

Van den Hoonaard's (2001) critique focuses on an incongruity between qualitative researchers using inductive methodology being reviewed by committee members whose domain assumptions are based on a hypothetico-deductive framework. Writing two decades ago, van den Hoonaard (2001) characterised this disjuncture in ethics review as a moral panic. The problem stemmed from qualitative research reviewed by ethics committees whose assumptions were sourced to a dominant deductive epistemology. He characterised the rising number of inductive researchers meeting hegemonic ethics committees as a "moral panic":

> [M]oral panic occurs throughout the research-ethics review, which so heavily relies on the deductive model of research as normative, proclaiming the rest as non-normative. Moral panics involve exaggeration of harm and risk, orchestration of the panic by elites or powerful special-interest groups, the construction of imaginary deviants, and reliance on diagnostic instruments. ... Whether as researchers or as members of research-ethics review panels, we should all become more cognizant of research ethics review as a "moral panic", to defuse the fear and anxiety that accompany the submission of research proposals for ethical review.

A decade after proclaiming a moral panic, van den Hoonaard saw little change in this hegemonic order. He corralled his anger to formal ethics review, organising the Ethics Rupture Summit in October 2012. The summit was a gathering of researchers from Australia, Brazil, Canada, Italy, New Zealand, the United Kingdom, and the United States, who are committed to enhancing ethical research practice and supporting innovative alternatives to the regulation of research ethics that might achieve this end. Item five of the eight-part New Brunswick Declaration highlighted the sense of a lack of respect for qualitative researchers: codes did not reflect practice nor "encourage regulators and administrators to nurture a regulatory culture that grants researchers the same level of respect that researchers should offer research participants" (https://the-sra.org.uk/SRA/Ethics/New-Brunswick-Declaration/SRA/Ethics/The-New-Brunswick-Declaration.aspx?hkey=2ea5b0a6-c499-45e4-9595-626bea495ff1).

The signatories of the New Brunswick declaration, including the senior author saw that ethics review committees had failed to show respect to qualitative researchers. Thus, beyond Israel's sense of frustration and anger came a sense of a lack of respect towards qualitative research. Qualitative research may fare particularly badly in the model as it exists. The problem of research governance, a philosophy that elevates the perceived potential for institutional harm above that of participant safety and public benefit, causes problems, however, for all types of research, clinical and social alike.

There have been a number of practical responses to this anger, frustration, and lack of respect. One dangerous, anarchic response to the apparent pettiness toward qualitative researchers has been for scholars to seek ways of bypassing ethics review altogether or claiming that because qualitative research is so low risk, ethics review does not apply to them (Bosk & DeVries, 2004; Dingwall, 2008; Gunsalus et al., 2006, p. 7; Hammersley &

Traianou, 2012; Schrag, 2010). In the clinical setting, this is mirrored by researchers aiming to use the grey area of quality improvement (Finkelstein et al., 2015) as a means of avoiding ethics review, given that it is not considered research proper. Qualitative researchers, like other researchers, may seek to avoid processes that they find neither helpful nor promoting of participant wellbeing. The justification for this action is understood, but it does not address the problem that qualitative researchers do have ethical issues to be reviewed prior to conducting research.

Two publications co-written by Tolich have argued for other coping strategies to address the problem with ethics review. In *Planning Ethically Responsible Research*, Sieber and Tolich (2013) acknowledged the limitations of ethics review but saw it was as unavoidable as it was partial in its ability to address qualitative research. They stated:

> As critics of the current IRB system, we are mindful of and respectful toward the overworked and under-thanked people who staff IRBs (Bosk & DeVries, 2004; Hardacre, 2012; Price, 2011); moreover, we recognize the processes of regulation as the problem, not the practice of ethics itself (Koski, 2010). Over-regulation robs researchers of a sense of autonomy in how they practice ethics, potentially resulting in alienating researchers from their planning of ethically responsible research (Gunsalus et al., 2006). We suggest essential changes of focus. Ethically responsible researchers must realize that IRBs are not the only site of ethics review. *Researchers must not only be allowed to assume more responsibility, they must take full responsibility.* Ethically responsible IRBs must realize that they are but one site of ethics review on a continuum. IRB approval of a research project does not guarantee ethical research. Consequently, researchers must be mindful of their ethical responsibilities throughout the life of the project. Planning ethically responsible research means planning far beyond the beginning of a research project i.e. the informed consent stage. Responsibility for ethics is situated throughout the research process, the analysis, publication and dissemination, including data archiving and sharing. It does not reside solely in formal ethical approval, or to use Guillemin and Gillam's (2004) term *procedural ethics.*
>
> (our emphasis)

Gunsalus had come to the same conclusion:

> all researchers must take primary responsibility for professional, ethical conduct. Our systems should reinforce that, not work against or substitute for it; the IRB should be a resource, not the source, for

> ethical wisdom. All compliance systems require the buy-in and
> collaboration of the regulated, and it will be a sad day if scholars come
> to see human protection in research as the source of frustrating delays
> and expensive paperwork.
>
> (Gunsalus et al., 2006, p. 1441)

A compromise situation is put forward here for those that agree with
Gunsalus. Researchers need to take more responsibility for their ethical
conduct, but this should not dismiss the likelihood researchers could benefit
from submitting their research for review. Three examples of research likely
to be enhanced by ethics review were discussed in Chapter 3. The research
known as Eve's story, or that conducted by Venkatesh or Alice Goffman,
would have been improved by formal ethics review. At a minimum, ethics
review would have alerted the researchers to basic ethical procedures,
informed consent would have been put in place and the researcher would
have become acquainted with basic conditions of confidentiality. Even with
this ethics review, there is no guarantee that the research would have been
conducted ethically. Eve, Venkatesh, and Goffman did not exhibit a strong
sense of ethical considerations for other people. While these three projects
could have been improved by ethics review, the impact of the review would
have been limited because formal ethics review is limited. Ethics review is
at best partial. Ethical research depends on ethical researchers.

It's All About Asking the Right Questions

Tolich and Fitzgerald (2006) pose a conundrum to expose why ethics review
is incomplete for qualitative research. Tolich and Fitzgerald suggest ethics
committees ask only three basic questions for qualitative researchers. These
incremental questions are typically asked by an ethics committee, but do
they make sense for qualitative research?

1. Tell me about the study.
2. What are the ethical issues?
3. How will you address these?

These questions are systematically unpacked in the following.

Question 1 (What is the research project about?) is what Spradley
(1979) would call a "grand tour" question, designed to elicit a verbal
description of something of significance in the informant's world, in this
case the person's research. They allow the informant, the applicant, an
opportunity to set the direction of the discussion. This question is standard.
Ethics applications usually begin by allowing the researcher to state in lay
language what the research is about. The summary states the problem and a

brief account of the methodology, along with a statement of the potential key benefits of the research and a justification of why it is necessary.

Question 2 tests the researcher's knowledge of ethics, the methodology involved and their interrelationship, gauging their ability to recognise the ethical problems likely to arise in the research project outlined in Question 1. Here the researcher will address the basic ethical principles of autonomy, beneficence, non-maleficence, and justice, as well as any issues associated with the proposed research that they wish to bring to the ethics committee's attention. In this model they are the experts, and the committee members are the learners. Thus they can use other modes of questioning, like asking explorative questions or questions of clarification (Spradley, 1979), as a means for expanding their understanding of the research and its potential ethical issues.

Question 3 requires the researcher to assume the expert role and to address their own problems using imaginative solutions that show insight into the research context, the nature of the participants and the nature of the method or methods proposed. How will the potential harm or problems identified in Question 2's response be managed or minimised? Can the researcher think critically and creatively? Do they understand the basic principles of research ethics and apply them?

After hearing answers to these three questions, the ethics committee members would then have sufficient knowledge of the research problem outlined in Question One to rate how the researcher conceived of the ethical problems likely to arise, and how they might be resolved. The committee should be able to determine if the researcher can envision ethics and ethical issues both generally and in relation to this particular kind of research.

In reality, because of the over-bureaucratisation of formal ethics review (Babb, 2020), these questions are barely recognisable in the application forms that have become longer and more formulaic, including tick-box and drop-down boxes, that facilitate ethics committee internal review and reporting. Explaining these key factors of one's work to an ethics committee, now requires the ability to translate them into "committee-speak" as constricted by the form. Tolich and Tumilty (2014) discussed this gap in communication between how researchers talk about their work (and think about it) and how ethics committees ask for and review information. It is a skill that needs to be learned. The focus is on the narrow detail around process, rather than the underlying questions, philosophies, and commitments that may have driven a researcher's work; community-centred design, addressing unequal power relations, disrupting the status quo, uncovering oppressive systems, to name but a few. These are fundamental ethical drivers of a researcher's work, yet they are rarely asked for in an ethics review form, and that's not all that's missing.

If ethics committees knew anything about qualitative research, they would know to ask a fourth question. It would be put to the applicant based on the assumption that the research problem is emergent, and many a qualitative researcher's ethical issues are unknown at the point of final ethics approval. The fourth question an ethics committee may ask might be:

> What contingencies are in place if the research project changes its focus after the research has been approved and has big ethical moments because new ethical issues arise?

This fourth question builds on the qualitative assumption that a qualitative research project is not linear but iterative and evolving. Question 4 embeds the assumption that qualitative research is highly likely to change in design as the research problem develops and asks how the researcher plans to modify or adapt the research as it unfolds. The unpredictability of qualitative research needs to be presumed and made predictable. The qualitative researcher needs to expect the unexpected.

This book is built around the fourth question. What do researchers do when the research question changes in the field, as invariably the research ethics will also change? What contingencies are in place if the research project changes its focus after the research has been approved and has begun? Whose responsibility is it to be aware of this fourth question and the ethical assurances that arise from it? This book has been written based on the assumption that this responsibility falls on the shoulders of the researcher, alone.

Taken together, Tolich and Fitzgerald's four questions transform the ethics review process, making the process more transparent and meaningful for qualitative researchers. The process also makes the researcher more accountable for his or her research's ethical considerations both in the present and the future. The four questions examine the researcher's knowledge of ethics and their ability to predict possible changes and how they may be dealt with in the field. Under this regime, respectful power relations between researcher and ethics committee are shared. Macfarlane (2010, p. 67) explains that

> Respectfulness is a virtue is closely linked with an awareness on the part of the researcher of potential and real inequalities in power relationships. The existence of unequal power relations makes the possibility of an abuse of informed consent more real.

Normally the ethics committee's approval process stops at question three, although researchers are monitored via annual reports and via their responses to any complaint or query lodged with the ethics committee. Ethics committee review is often described as a hurdle, by those who find the process unhelpful and drawn out. And in some ways it is − it serves as a minimum bar. Its role is to check that researchers don't have any glaringly obviously problems in their plans that might embarrass or harm the university by harming participants, but the real ethical work of research is done by the researcher in the development of a project, its implementation in the field, and their handling of the outcomes. This is why ethical education cannot focus on regulation (alone) but must focus on attitudes, behaviour, skills, and knowledge.

Ethics committees have not yet evolved to grasp the essential nature of qualitative research. Until that happens, qualitative researchers must be solely responsible for the ethical considerations in their research, especially when they are in the field, and they must have the courage of their convictions to enforce those unique qualitative ethics responses. As stated earlier in this chapter, this book was written to shore up the fourth question. The researcher's responsibility is to be aware of an ethics code and have the courage to practice that when the ethical moments develop in the field.

Flick (2006, p. 51) captures the root of the dilemma for researchers and ethics committees:

> [Q]ualitative research is often planned as a very open and adapted to what happens in the field. Methods here are less canonised than in quantitative research. This makes reviews by ethics committees more difficult as it is, for example, difficult to foresee what sorts of data will be collected in an ethnographic study. It also makes it sometimes difficult to ask for consent for those being researched observations are done and open spaces like marketplaces, train stations, and the like.

Moreover, given that a researcher will never know in advance when those big ethical moments will arrive, it is essential for a researcher to create a reference group that they can turn to while in the field. The greatest learning to occur in the various classes mentioned in this book did not come from the teachers, or any one student, but from the group whose brainstorming opened up doors to sound ethical practice. This collectivised engagement in ethical imagination (thinking through possible options and consequences in a way sensitive to participant realities) and ethical reasoning (working through options and understanding trade-offs between ethical values and justifications for particular choices) provides a space in which more possibilities can be envisioned and addressed, because more life experiences, knowledges, and perspectives are brought into the discussion.

A stock answer any qualitative researcher could give to answer the fourth question is to reassure the ethics committee that a reference group has been established agreeing to provide support for any big ethical moments that occur during the research. Examples of reference groups are given in Chapter 11.

The two capstones developed for the students serve different purposes. Capstone One in Chapter 8 resulted from a negotiation between the researcher and the social agency creating a level playing field by creating an ethical statement of the five questions; an elaborate informed consent process allowing both the agency and the researcher to understand the perspectives and the requirements of each party.

Capstone Two focuses on formal ethics review. Capstone Two focuses on formal ethics review; it returns to Eve's story, in Chapter 3, allowing the reader to use TREAD (The Research Ethics Application Database) introduced in Chapter 10 as a resource to create the necessary documents. Capstone Two has readers create three participant information sheets on behalf of Eve for each of the following:

- one for the Women's Refuge organisation,
- the second for the Women's Refuge volunteers,
- the third for the clients who make use of Women's Refuge.

This task is likely to be somewhat hamstrung by the requirement to write the information sheets without first negotiating with the social agency about the outcome to be produced; research on, rather than research with. This is a feature of some formal ethics review.

Readers unfamiliar with writing an ethics application or a participant information sheet should find information on how to construct those documents in Chapter 10. This includes how to access TREAD (https://tread.tghn.org).

Don't invent the (ethics) wheel

Use TREAD, The Research Ethics Application Database

Up until now the emphasis in this book has been on recognising that novice researchers and students have ethical agency in their research, that it's not just about learning rules and following them, but understanding ethical concepts in the complex settings of research in an ongoing way, from start to finish. Recognising one's own knowledge and skills and how they can be developed; one's own limits and how they can be addressed (reference groups, etc.); one's ability to adapt in the field; and the agency of participants in relation to the boundaries of one's ethical assurances and responsibilities have been the subjects of much of the discussion so far. In Chapter 9, the research ethics committee was introduced as was the discussion of people's frustration with what can sometimes feel like a pejorative processes. Throughout the book we have provided snapshots of information sheets and consents forms. At the end of the last chapter, however, readers were asked to complete their own. But where to start?

In writing about research, whether for ethics approval to do a project or in the information sheets for participants, researchers must tailor information to suit the target-reader. In an ethics application form, this is important so that the ethics review committee really understands what it is a researcher is doing, what they have considered, and how they will be managing everything. When this is done well, ethics committees feel more confident that researchers can practice ethically. Part of what is looked at very closely in ethics review is the language and content of information and consent documentation. Committees pay particular attention to the readability of language for the participants (Stark, 2016). Conveying a project in simple language is a skill – a skill not explicitly taught to research students or researchers.

The authors of this book recognised this problem, of knowing how to convey your work to ethics committees and participants throughout their time working as both committee members and researchers. Each ethics committee will have a template for their information and consent document that outlines what sections are needed, and they may have suggestions or examples of appropriate language. However, the guidelines either are too broad epistemologically in what they aim to cover, because they want to address researchers from all backgrounds and disciplines and therefore fail to convey sufficient detail to guide the novice researcher; or they are too narrowly focused on the biomedical model, and therefore sections may seem confusing or superfluous for the researcher using social science methods and especially qualitative methods (Tolich & Tumilty, 2014). What the authors knew was that most people learn how to complete ethics applications and information and consent documents, from the sharing of good exemplars between mentors/supervisors and students or between students and their peers (Tolich & Tumilty, 2014). That is, people learn by seeing the work of others and interpreting it for their work.

To that end, Tolich and Tumilty set up TREAD (formerly TEAR), The Research Ethics Application Database (2014, 2016). An open-access database of exemplary ethics application and their supporting documentation, including information and consent documentation, phone scripts, participant guides, etc. TREAD is available here: https://tread.tghn.org/about/

When logging on to TREAD's website, readers are first asked to read a Code of Conduct about the nature and philosophy of TREAD and how they should interact with documents. The exemplars are not provided as a source of material to copy, but to support thinking through how a researcher's own work might be better explained whether to a review committee or a participant. Once a TREAD visitor agrees to the Code of Conduct they can enter the database at the bottom of the page and begin to browse or search entries relevant to their work. This can be done using either category descriptors (grouping of relevant applications together) or tags (identifiers of methodology, population, topics, etc.). The applications included in TREAD are international from researchers across a range of disciplines, studying a wide variety of topics, applying to committees with very different application forms and templates.

What is common across all the applications is that they explain their work thoughtfully and thoroughly in "ethics-committee-speak" (a language ethics committees understand) and that their information sheets are appropriate for their audiences. Of note is that many of the projects deal with topics that may be considered very ethically tricky. They may include populations that have certain vulnerabilities, such as women in transitional housing,[1] or participants engaged in illegal behaviour,[2] or complex dynamics within an organisation or set of relationships.[3] For novice researchers and researchers engaging in work with new populations or in new areas, it is a rich resource evidencing the ethical reasoning of experienced researchers in many different domains. These documents can be as helpful in thinking through issues of relevance to a project one is designing as they may be in helping write an ethics application.

An example used by the authors previously (Tolich & Tumilty, 2014) is Stephanie Wahab's Photovoice Project with women in transitional housing because it provides a raft of supporting documentation that show Wahab's ethical thinking. Not only are there documents to guide participants in using cameras and taking photos in easy and accessible language, but there are also phone scripts that pay attention to checking on the participants' safety in subtle ways. Wahab's information sheet also makes explicit declarations about what things cannot be kept confidential if described in an interview, relevant to the discussions in Chapter 6:

> If you disclose actual or suspected abuse, neglect, or exploitation of a child, or disabled or elderly adult, the researcher or any member of the study staff must, and will, report this to Child Protective Services (CPS), Adult Protective Services (APS) or the nearest law enforcement agency.

Similarly, Adler's project on gambling addresses one of the issues we raise in Chapter 11. Adler's project, which is in a setting where the gambling activity being researched is illegal, includes the following text:

> **Risks:** There are some potential risks you may encounter from doing this interview. I will be asking you about a gambling activity that is technically illegal. Please be assured, however, that I will neither judge you nor identify you personally in any way. I will transcribe the interview and destroy the tape recording afterwards. If there are any subjects you would prefer not to talk about, just say so and we can go on to another subject. Everything that you say will be held in the strictest confidence. There will be no compensation, nor will you incur any expenses, for this interview.

Another exemplar, showing how a researcher has thought through some of the issue we discussed potentially arising in the field is Katie Fitzpatrick's work with high school students.[4] In one section (p. 14), where she goes through considerations for all the different elements of here work, she outlines:

Classroom Interactions:
I have focused on the following questions that may arise during time spent in classrooms:

- Should I step in if there is a problem between students in the class, such as a fight?
- Should I assist the teacher with the lesson if they are in need?

- Should I agree to supervise the class if the teacher is called away unexpectedly?
- Should I help students with their work if they are having difficulty?
- Where do I position myself in the classroom so as not to disrupt students, make them feel threatened, or cause problems for the teacher?
- Do I agree to relieve classes if the school is short of staff (as decile one schools invariably are)?
- How do my decisions affect the research and my relationships with students and staff?

All of these questions will require decisions to be made according to the environment of the classroom and the changing nature of class dynamics as well as my own ethical judgment. Because the classroom is irrevocably altered by my presence and the research is, therefore, created by the dynamic between myself and others in the school, every decision I make will affect the research. My approach will be to aim to "address processes of unfairness or injustice" (Madison, 2005) and therefore to help where I can, while remaining committed to my role in the school (that of a researcher).

Fitzgerald's application provides an excellent example of a researcher thinking through their known-knowns and known-unknowns in a thorough and ethical way.

These examples serve to show, as has been emphasised throughout this book, that these ethical situations are very real and require consideration and practical approaches that meet ethical goals and local ethics review committee requirements.

TREAD, then, as well as peers, supervisors and reference groups, are invaluable resources when sitting down to write your first application and consent documentation. But again, how to start an exercise like Capstone Two. At the end of Chapter 9, the task set was as follows:

Create three participant information sheets on behalf of Eve for each of the following:

- one for the Women's Refuge organisation,
- the second for the Women's Refuge volunteers,
- the third for the clients who make use of Women's Refuge.

WRITING YOUR OWN DOCUMENTATION

As noted in Chapter 9, there are some key things an ethics committee wants to know, and how they ask for this and what restrictions might exist in relation to how you discuss your work or what work is possible may vary greatly between different settings and jurisdictions. The key thing to remember, and the thing that people applying to ethics committees often err on, is copying and pasting work from their related grant documents or research proposals directly into applications forms.

The language and focus of research proposals and grant applications are different from those of ethics applications. While the ethics committee may want to see some rationale for your work, they do not need to see it in the same depth as a grant review committee, nor do they want to see it in the jargon that may be common in to a particular field. Remember, ethics review committees are a mixture of different experts, whether community members, clinicians, lawyers, or ethicists, and their background may not include specific knowledge of a particular research area. Therefore, clarity and explanation are crucial in adapting a previous research proposal or grant to an ethics application.

The other key difference is that for research proposals and grant applications, the format in its simplest sense is: why you want do something, what you are going to do, and how you are going to do it. Within these sections, the focus is on robustness or validity of what it is the researcher is proposing; therefore, the justifications are focused on why something makes sense theoretically or scientifically. In an ethics application the same elements are covered, but the focus is on the ethical nature of these aspects, i.e., does the rationale justify exposing participants to potential harms or wasted effort? Do the methods expose participants to unnecessary risk or harms that can be avoided? Is the way that participants are recruited, contacted, and interacted with, their data handled, etc., in some way unsafe? Therefore, the descriptions and justifications should be targeted to explaining these issues, clarifying any potential confusion and allaying any fear.

So, for example, a research proposal might say:

> We will recruit participants through purposive and snowball sampling. This sampling method will ensure that we invite an identifiable representational sample of the target population, while expanding the possibility of including those less easily identified.

An ethics committee would need to know, further, how exactly this will occur.

> We will recruit participants through purposive and snowball sampling. An invitation email, including an information sheet and contact details will be sent to public email addresses of identified individuals asking them to consider participating and sharing the invitation with anyone they think may be interested.

Figure 5 Participant relevant stages of research process

In writing an ethics application and creating an information sheet, a useful approach is to sit down with the research proposal or grant document and think through the participant journey through the project from first contact to last, where contact includes the handling of data (Figure 5).

For many qualitative researchers, they may have already thought through these aspects when writing their original grant or research proposal. However, it can be the case that researchers write grants and proposals focusing on the theoretical rather than practical and they have not yet thought through issues in any depth, if at all.

Thinking of the stages, then, in greater depth depending on previous work, a researcher can create a list of steps or a diagram (which can be helpful to provide to ethics committees) that sets out all the major points at which one should consider what is the interaction between the participant and the project and what are the ethical implications or things to pay attention to within that setting. Some suggestions on how this might be thought through are provided in what follows, noting that where a project is working with an organisation or community where initial discussions happen with that organisation or Elders in Indigenous communities, etc. that this will become a little more complex (as discussed in Chapter 8).

Recruitment – how are you contacting participants? Are you using gatekeepers? Are you using social media? How are they meant to contact you to show an interest, etc.?

Informed consent – at what stage does a potential participant receive the information sheet? How long do they have to read it and think about it? When can they ask questions? When will the consent form be signed? And so on. Will consent be an ongoing question (process consent), or one-off at the time of signing the form?

Data management – throughout the project, how will you manage contact details of participants if you have them, master lists of names and codenames, de-identification procedures, file access, long-term storage, withdrawal information and management, etc.?

Data collection arrangements – how will you be engaging with your participant – digitally, face-to-face, over the phone? How often? In what setting? In what ways do your answers require consideration in relation to privacy, safety, (yours and the participant's), location-relevant complications, etc.?

Data verification arrangements – if you are going to provide participants with the opportunity to review transcripts, how will this be managed? Or the draft analysis? If so, how will this be managed, what are the implications for your management of data and de-identification practices?

Dissemination – how will you share information at the end of the project and with whom? What kind of different ways of sharing information might be necessary? Are there any sensitives about the information that might need to be considered in advance? And so on.

These prompts are by no means exhaustive for every kind of qualitative research project but serve only as examples.

Once you have a clear idea of these factors, however, writing up an information sheet for an audience becomes easier because you know the things that you have to explain.

FURTHER CONSIDERATIONS

Another factor to consider before beginning writing is the format of an information sheet and consent form. Most ethics committees provide a template with set headings that they would like covered in informed consent documentation. We suggest that you read a number of TREAD exemplars to find the one that best fits your research purposes. It is important to note, however, that researchers can use vastly different formats as long as they cover the same material the committee is specifying.

Researchers have used colourful pamphlets with photos and diagrams. Depending on the nature of the template the ethics committee a researcher has to apply to uses, they can use a mixed approach, providing a full and complete information sheet and a pamphlet with key details and contacts. Similarly, if a researcher wanted to use a video, for example, to explain a study and what a participant will be asked to do, etc., this can be done, but would also need a written information sheet as well. In all studies participant should be able to hold on to a complete copy of the information sheet after the consent process, that they can refer back to and find contact details on for the researchers and for any complaints processes.

What is important in deciding the format of your participant information sheet and the degree to which you incorporate diagrams, images, etc., will be your knowledge and understanding of your populations' communication needs. The considerations for communicating with adolescents versus high school teachers, for example, will be very different.

It is important to be aware that information processes, whether in documents with diagrams/visual support, or videos, have been shown to be incomplete in ensuring informed consent of participants, and that a conversation with a researcher rehearsing the information before signing documentation (where that is part of the process) or the data collection process begins is the most effective (Flory & Emanuel, 2004). Therefore, whatever format or method a researcher chooses to impart information about their study to participants with, it is only one piece of the puzzle.

EDITING THE PARTICIPANT INFORMATION SHEET

Stark, in her observation of ethics review committees, noted that particular attention is paid to informed consent documentation and that committees can be rigid and formulaic in how they address language within documents (Stark, 2016). Tumilty has sat on a committee which put all informed consent documentation through a process to assess reading level. Now this too can be considered problematic, in that it treats all projects as if they have the same audience allowing for no variation in this. However, at the same time, it does ensure that lay language that is understandable by anyone is used throughout.

Considering this, a researcher may want to first write documentation in the way they find easiest, then revise language on this initial draft.

REVIEW BEFORE SUBMISSION

We suggest that for both application forms and information sheets, researchers have relevant people read through both documents and provide feedback. For an application form this might be reference group members, a peer, a mentor, or supervisor. For information sheets, this should be, where possible, a member of the target population with whom a researcher may have been partnering, a social agency, a community contact, etc. If this is not possible, then, as for the application form, a reference group member, peer, mentor, or supervisor can provide feedback. As we have discussed throughout this book, collective thinking and reasoning often helps more than isolated thinking.

We invite you to access TREAD, and on your behalf, we thank the researchers who have donated their expertise to provide a helping hand to novice researchers.

NOTES

1 Entry by Stephanie Wahab in TREAD: https://tread.tghn.org/articles/understanding-transitional-housing-programs-survivors-interpersonal-violence-qualitative-study/.
2 Entry by Patti Adler in TREAD: https://tread.tghn.org/articles/poker-house-ethnography./
3 Entry by Pat Sikes in TREAD: https://tread.tghn.org/articles/doctoral-examiners-perceptions-and-experiences-problematic-examining-situations/.
4 Entry by Katie Fitzpatrick in TREAD: https://tread.tghn.org/articles/pasifika-students-education-class-culture-and-ethnicity-new-zealand/.

CHAPTER 11

Researching in harm's way

Ethics committees cannot predict all the types of harms that occur in the field, and neither can the researcher at the time the research is designed. As was discussed in Chapter 4, there are *known-knowns* of research that are addressed in the ethical design of a project and its plan. There are *known-unknowns*, things that because of the nature of a project may occur, and while a researcher might not know exactly what they will look like, is prepared for; that is, they know what they might do if something of a particular type were to occur. In any research, there are also, however, potential *unknown-unknowns*, things that may arise out of nowhere, that researchers need to be to be able to deal with even if they cannot predict them and therefore prepare for them in a targeted way. The ability to respond to these unknown-unknowns is predicated on developing a robust ethical practice where researchers are comfortable using their ethical intuitions, ethical reasoning, ethical imagination, and ethical integrity as described throughout this book. This development of skills and awareness of one's limitations are the preparation for dealing within unknown-unknowns in the research setting.

The harms highlighted in this chapter produce an array of big ethical moments that emerge when the researcher is in the field, far from their supervisors, colleagues, and the ethics committee or even reference groups (Chapter 4) that they have brought on board for their work. Some of these harms may have been avoidable and reveal potential gaps one can have in one's knowledge; some arise in ways that cannot have been predicted. The emergent nature of qualitative research means the researcher needs to have awareness in order to identify ethical challenges as they appear and have the skills to resolve these conundrums in real time.

The book's first harm appeared at the very beginning. There the post-graduate students said "Hang on, wait a minute". This reaction happened within the first 60 seconds of Tolich's course, depicted in Figure 1. That cartoon shows the students saying to Tolich hang on, wait a minute, do you need our informed consent to turn that audio recorder on.

In Figure 2, the students did the same "Hang on a minute" thing when responding to the confidentiality assurances of the audio recordings. While these moments were artificial, created for the purpose of shaking the students' *frame of reference* in order to engage them in transformative learning, they are examples of big ethical moments the book is premised on (Mezirow, 2000). Such moments occur unpredictably and require a response – an ethical response. The assumption is that moments like these, unpredictable ethical dilemmas requiring action are common in qualitative research, and researchers need to recognise them and address them in real time in the field. This chapter provides examples that should give a researcher pause, when they or someone else says "Hang on, wait a minute". This chapter is a standalone, but teachers may find it useful to include relevant examples when reviewing previous chapters. For example, we have moved some of these "Hang on, wait a minute" moments to other chapters ourselves. Dan, the young man who died during a longitudinal study, was discussed in Chapter 4.

EXPECT THE UNEXPECTED WITH A REFERRAL SHEET

Key ideas to review in this exercise:

Do no harm.

This puzzle links to the hypothetical virtual reality study described in Chapter 4 and poses the problem of what would a researcher do if a participant had an adverse reaction. Guillemin and Gillam (2004) provide a poignant *big ethical moment* example in Sonia's story. Picture this scene and ask what would you do in this situation?

> You are a researcher working on a study examining women's experiences of heart disease. You are interviewing Sonia, a woman in her late 40s with diagnosed heart disease. Sonia lives on a remote farming property in a rural region [of Australia]. She is married and has one teenage daughter living at home. The interview is progressing well. Over a cup of tea in Sonia's kitchen, you inquire about the impact of heart disease on her life. Sonia stops and closes her eyes. After a few moments' silence, you notice tears welling up in Sonia's eyes. Sonia tells you that she is not coping – not because of her heart disease, but because she has just found out that her husband has been sexually abusing her daughter since she was a child.

What should a researcher do? Expect that the ethics committee discussed nothing like it during the formal procedural ethics evaluation. Guillemin and Gillam do not provide specific responses. Tolich's students suggest: The researcher is likely to terminate the conversation, seeing that the woman's needs are important.

> It is likely the researcher would not counsel the woman but comfort her and provide some recommendation for her to seek professional help if she wanted it.

These suggestions are correct. But researchers can do more by expecting adverse reactions. We encourage students to expect the unexpected.

A list of referrals act as a stand-in reference group. If a participant like Sonia has an adverse reaction, it is essential that the research assistant or researcher seek professional assistance. Their role is not to provide counsel. In the case of Sonia, when the researcher learns about the sexual abuse by the husband to the daughter, it is incumbent upon the researcher to cease the interview immediately and provide the participant with a list of referral agencies. These may include:

Lifeline: 0800 543 354
Suicide Crisis Helpline: 0508 828 865
Samaritans: 0800 726 666
Alcohol Drug Helpline: 0800 787 797
General mental health inquiries: 0800 443 366
The Depression Helpline: 0800 111 757

Given the uncertainty of research – expect the unexpected – researchers should customise a list like the one just presented, making it available in every research situation. Finding an informant has had an adverse reaction; they should refer the person to an agency. This cannot be predicted. In some cases, they may also need to take other actions, depending on their setting and responsibilities. Any further actions that are required should be made explicit to the participant in any situation.

DID THIS REFERENCE GROUP GIVE GOOD ADVICE?

Key ideas to review in this exercise:

Internal confidentiality, process consent, suitability of anonymity assurances in qualitative research.

Consider an invitation to join a reference group on behalf of a researcher whose big ethical moment with confidentiality is causing loss of sleep.

Drawing on advice given above in Chapter 5 about the limits of de-identification, what advice would the reader give? The researcher (cited in Macfarlane, 2010, p. 65) said:

> I'm doing multi-site case study research, in a small number of institutions in a small country where the number of such institutions is relatively small. In spite of my best efforts to anonymize my sites, projects, and respondents (using aliases, codes, and general role descriptors) any informed reader would have little difficulty identifying the sites, even the individual respondents. Deductive disclosure is a real concern. I'm assured by others that these people, given their professional roles are not naïve and have verified their transcript in full knowledge of my intention to cite or quote them. ... As a consequence I have decided that each individual respondent will verify (and amend if necessary) their own transcript. ... I'm reluctant to rock the boat by exploring into much detail, unless asked, what they actually understand by anonymity. I've spelt it out in writing, and they seem to realise what they are signing up to. Still keeps me awake at night though!

What's keeping this researcher up at night is seeking ethical solutions with the concept of confidentiality.

What advice would the reader give the researcher that would help them sleep at night?

The researcher's persistence to anonymise the data set fails to grasp how qualitative research ethics have disintegrated under the threat of internal confidentiality (Tolich, 2019). The researcher's reference group did not refocus attention away from anonymity to ongoing consent.

> I'm assured by others that these people, given their professional roles are not naïve and have verified their transcript in full knowledge of my intention to cite or quote them.

Were confidentiality and anonymity the right options? Nothing this researcher could do could make the disclosed undisclosed, so anonymity is not relevant to this case. It was too late to put the genie back in the bottle.

This researcher and their reference group needed to find alternative ethical solutions. What the researcher could have been asking informants was an ongoing form of consent, known as process consent (discussed in Chapter 7), not for additional confidentiality assurances. The assumption here is that research ethics is not static but forever a site of collaboration.

Workshop participants believed the concepts of confidentiality, anonymity, and deductive disclosure were exhausted as a line of enquiry. Instead, their focus was on consent, specifically process consent. They said:

The comment that "I'm assured by others" is also important, because the main ethical assurances should be with those who participated in this research, not with others. The researcher should gain the consent of the participants to stay in the research, even though the security of their data could be compromised. It's not that participants in the research can opt out of the research but they should be given the option to opt in.

Clandinin and Connelly's (2000) ethics guidelines, widely cited in the qualitative research literature, claim ethical considerations can and must be negotiated throughout the research process. Process consent (Ellis, 2007, p. 24) is the most common definition of this negotiation. It is an active form of consent and taking the participant's right to withdraw beyond a passive construction. Rather than leaving it up to the participant to withdraw at any time, the researcher repeatedly invites the participant to volunteer to be part of each phase of the project. Without process consent, the right of a participant to withdraw from the research project, initially written in the consent form, appears to be written in disappearing ink. Qualitative research has an interest in power relations and how they can be changed by its very nature (Cannella, 2015) Process consent addresses the internal power relations of a research project in the relationship between researcher and participant and by doing so can reinforce work in the broader setting.

As previously outlined in Chapter 7, the narrative researcher Ruth Josselson (1996, pp. xii–xiii) astutely labels the traditional informed consent process "a bit oxymoronic, given that participants can, at the outset, have only the vaguest idea of what they might be consenting to". With some candour, Josselson (2007, p. 543) says that process consent "strikes terror into researchers because it means just what it says". The researcher could have been losing sleep because offering process consent meant potentially losing the data. The researcher must bear this risk.

Explicitly offering informants' process consent in the loss of sleep scenario would have been best practice. It would have expanded participant autonomy. The participant, not the researcher, then decides whether they want to remain in the research or not. In other words, the confidentiality ethical assurances had disintegrated to such an extent that the researcher had no ethical assurances they could give the participant. This situation is not unusual in qualitative research, and it is remedial. This set of circumstances routinely happens in focus group research where research participants must take responsibility for their own safety; this may entail their withdrawing from the study, even though it strikes terror into researchers. This situation offers a researcher the opportunity to practice their ethical integrity. To acknowledge that something they had previously thought they could offer is no longer possible (confidentiality), and to address this with participants, shows a respect for the participant as a person and not just a means to your end. To treat people with respect is to practice ethically. This engagement with participants in a way that allows an ongoing negotiation and deliberation of what is ethically okay (through process consent), despite the potential risk of loss of data to a project, takes ethical courage and integrity. The current process of offering traditional informed consent is of course based in part on ethics committee review, and so ethics committees need to acknowledge that greater respect is shown to participants and their autonomy when decision-making and responsibilities are to some degree shared.

GAINING CONSENT FROM CONSENTED PARTICIPANTS

Key ideas to review in this exercise:

Informed consent, autonomous participants.

Chapter 3 records that Venkatesh, the author of *Gang Leader for a Day*, recruited his participants via coercion. When he asked a person to take part in his research, he found all of the residents had been recruited if not strong-armed by JT, the gang boss. The residents were told that they must talk to Venkatesh. If faced with a similar situation, finding all of the subjects pre-consented, what can the researcher do? It represents a hang-on-a-minute exemplar.

In the following excerpt, Tina Miller (Miller & Bell, 2002, pp. 62–63) describes the convoluted and unsatisfactory path she followed when recruiting Bangladeshi women into her study via a gatekeeper. What is wrong with this recruitment strategy, and how would you rectify it?

> The [UK-based] Bangladeshi women who came to the group where amongst other activities, English language classes were offered – were both vulnerable and largely powerless. The context in which they experienced and exercised agency was regulated by religious and cultural practices that encompassed all aspects of their lives. When, at the next meeting, Tina was introduced to the women she realized that in effect wholesale access had been provided by [J] the gate-keeper. These women would find it difficult not to agree to participate in the study as it was J who had "let her in". J was not only responsible for setting up the women's group but she also occupied a respected position in the local community: She was more powerful than the other women in terms of her perceived social class and status. However, although the women had been volunteered and access given to a hard-to-reach group, the interviews themselves provided an opportunity for the women to exercise some agency and to resist talking about certain aspects of their lives. But in situations where those in more powerful positions, for example line managers, are asked to act as

> gate-keepers to potential respondents, how feasible is it for them subsequently to resist taking part? Similarly when powerful gate-keepers are used, notions around access, coercion and, more importantly, consent can become very difficult for the researcher and participants to disentangle who is actually giving consent and to what?

What should the researcher do to manage this third-party recruitment? Third-party recruitment and/or pre-consent, by which we mean consent by a gatekeeper to approach others for potential participation, rather than consent by a gatekeeper for another to be a participant, can be extremely hard to negotiate and understand as an outsider. Examples such as those just described make a certain degree of coercion or diminishment of participants' agency quite clear. In other settings, tribal chiefs, community elders or heads of households (Holkup et al., 2004; Molyneux et al., 2005; Tindana et al., 2006) may be consulted to discuss whether research is valuable for and appropriate in their communities prior to individual participants being informed and consented for research. This consultation does not necessarily, inherently come with coercion or force; in fact, quite the opposite can be the case depending on the cultural setting, values, and norms.

The problem here is one where our ethical intuitions tells us there is something to pay attention to, but we're not quite sure what to do with it once we do. There is, or at least potentially is, an opportunity for coercion and the diminishment of autonomy of a particular party (potential participant). The ability to distinguish when third-party gatekeepers are appropriate and non-coercive is, for an outsider, very difficult if not impossible. While we can develop our ethical imagination in our ongoing interactions with others in the world and experiences conducting research, it will always be the case that different researchers may have differing gaps in their knowledge. This brings to the fore again the benefits of using a reference group. In such cases, having members of the community in question or experts with knowledge and experience of the communities is crucial in thinking through how to approach a particular population. When considering research *with* a community, considering what is meant by "with" is important.

Indigenous and Global South researchers and their communities have made it very clear that being researched "on" is no longer an option. Ethical practice in such settings calls for approaches that include consultation and partnerships, and the sharing of power if not the handing over of power entirely (Smith, 2013).[1] These kinds of principles can apply to any community, and especially those that are marginalised. Establishing relationships to truly understand the setting and what is needed is an ethical imperative.

How do you think you would approach a project working with a particular cultural or social community? What might you do first and how?

The questions raised here are similar to those raised in Chapter 8 within the negotiation of a memorandum of understanding with a social organisation. Once the organisation has agreed to allow the researcher access to the site, this doesn't mean that all members of the organisation have consented to take part. These questions are also relevant to Eve's gaining access to Women's Refuge, had she asked the organisation for permission to conduct research. The same access problems exist for Venkatesh. Although JT gave permission for the research to be conducted, each of the members of the community needed to be informed about the research and given the opportunity to consent.

At the end of Chapter 3, the following review questions were listed for consideration. Those questions are most relevant here. They asked: Compare and contrast the ethical issues raised in Eve's story with those in Venkatesh's *Gang Leader for a Day*.

> What ethical issues were identical?
>
> Which ethical issues were unique to each case?
>
> Of the two cases, which was the more serious breach of ethics.
>
> What one ethical practice could Venkatesh or Eve make to enhance the protections of the persons they studied?
>
> What practical issues might make collecting data difficult in these situations? How can these issues be addressed in an ethical manner?

As evidenced elsewhere in the book, workshop participants found all of the ethical issues raised in Eve's story and Venkatesh's book entirely predictable.

Our best protection, then, against our gaps are dialogue with others, ideally others knowledgeable of the community of interest either directly or indirectly. Talking through our work and ideas is a way of crowdsourcing ethical intuitions and imagination. We can use collective ethics praxis to figure out what it is that we need to be aware of.

DIMINISHED AUTONOMY

Key ideas to review in this exercise:

Informed consent, assent, autonomous participants.

The task here is to distinguish between autonomy and diminished autonomy in a relationship with two potential research participants:

1. A researcher asks street kids to take part in their research. They offer the street kids $10 for a 10-minute interview.

2. A researcher asks university staff to take part in a 10-minute interview, offering them $10.

What is the difference?

The workshop participants readily saw the difference. They acknowledged how the money diminished the autonomy of the street kids, but not the University staff.

> Ten dollars means more to the street kids than it does to the University staff person. Street kids are more likely to be induced to take part in the research.

This question focusing on the payment to the street kids induces them to take part in the research rather than their volunteering. This type of scenario for this problem is common, but really too simplified.

When we think about these issues, we want to consider in what ways inducements may make people consider harm and risk differently. Does the incentive change their perception of a harm or risk, which they may have previously rated differently (without the incentive). A vulnerability-responsive inducement (like food for someone who is starving) may make an incentive more motivating than an aversion to risk. At the same time, we need to consider that especially because of a person's vulnerability or lack of power, recognition of their time, effort and expertise about their setting for our research must be addressed. Feeding someone who is hungry is the ethically appropriate thing to do, but how we then consider doing research in light of this is more difficult. How do we this ethically?

Consider the cartoon, Figure 1; it reflects this question from a different angle. When the audio recorder was turned on during the first day of class, a conflict of interest between the researcher as a teacher was resolved when students were told he was only collecting information for the students, not for his own interests. The students weren't offered money, but they were offered an opportunity to co-write a journal article. Was this invitation to co-write a journal article an inducement? Did this diminish their autonomy? What is the difference between that offer of a journal article and the $10 to the street kid?

Thinking through these problems requires us to realise that vulnerability is contextual and dynamic; as Luna (2009) would say, we each have different layers of vulnerability, and as researchers we need to think through these (with the relevant communities) to come to ethical ways of addressing them.

WHEN PARTICIPANTS SELF-HARM IN A FOCUS GROUP

Key ideas to review in this exercise:
Internal confidentiality, limits on informed consent, overdisclosure.
Chapter 7 discussed how focus groups offer participants few ethical assurances. For example, focus group researchers cannot offer participants internal confidentiality because it is outside of their control: researchers can place few restrictions on focus group members. Researchers hold no ethical sanction over a participant should they reveal outside the focus group what was disclosed by another focus group member. Thus, promises of confidentiality must be limited to external confidentiality (see Chapter 5): that is, that the researcher will not identify any participant or what they said in any publication. If focus group participants are known to each other, for example if they are drawn from within the same organisation, internal confidentiality is especially problematic, setting up particular ethical issues. Expect anything said in the focus group to be gossiped about outside the focus group and be clear with participants that this is beyond the researcher's control. Such disclosure allows a participant to exercise their own agency and take responsibility for the limits of what they are comfortable saying in a group setting on the specific topic.

Group talk can disrupt the focus of the focus group as crosstalk among members raises topics not envisaged by the researcher or mentioned in the information sheet. Participants can self-disclose. Consider the following example.

> Seven men are engaged to share their opinions on a local hospital's accident and emergency service. The overall tenor of the conversation is critical of the hospital. After six participants have freely given their opinions, the facilitator asks one person who appears reluctant to share their opinion. The seventh member of the focus group explains that he has had limited experience with the hospital but he has a positive attitude. The people in the sexually transmitted disease clinic have always treated him with the utmost respect. In fact, over the years he has become well known to them.

This participant in answering a question about the hospital has disclosed information neither relevant to the question nor necessarily needed to explain his limited interaction. What it has done, however, is disclose to others some information that he may not want to be widely known. Was his perceived reluctance a weighing up of what to disclose, and his subsequent disclosure a well-thought-through response? Or was it misinterpreted? Now that he has disclosed, does he regret it? How should a researcher now handle this situation that has potential to be harmful to the participant beyond the bounds of the focus group (depending on his general level of disclosure to others outside of the group). What is the responsibility of the researcher here?

Researchers can, of course, reinforce the confidential nature of the conversation within this setting at the end of the focus group. What other approaches might they try? Recognising the limits of the researcher's responsibility and power to control a situation are also important ethical realisations.

WHEN FOCUS GROUP QUESTIONS HARM

Key ideas to review in this exercise:

Deception, leading questions, the assumption focus groups are innocuous.
"Hey, wait a minute" might occur in research when there is a feeling that there is something wrong, but it is difficult to put your finger on (an underdeveloped ethical intuition). The following puzzle has two parts, each of which raises an identical issue. The second part derives from a real situation, and the first part is contrived to match the second one. The scenarios are as follows.

> A researcher is commissioned by an unnamed far-right political party to conduct focus groups to support an extreme law-and-order reinstatement of capital punishment (that is not legal in New Zealand). The researcher provides focus group participants with a number of choices. Which execution method would be the best deterrent, and the one that the law-and-order party should campaign on?

- Stoning
- Gas chamber
- Hanging
- Firing squad
- Drowning
- Electrocution
- Lethal injection

A second example asks what is the ethical problem in the following research design? Researchers seek to run focus groups asking women in their 30s about which of the five tests used for the prescreening of the health of the foetus they prefer. Assume a brief description of each technique is given and then the focus group is asked to discuss which would be the best test that the government could offer all women who are pregnant. The participants are told that there was no right answer and the goal of the focus group was to come to some consensus on what would be the best technique to use.

Tolich was a member of an ethics committee asked to review a focus group like this. The committee was about to approve the innocuous focus group when one member of the committee said, "Hey, wait a minute", there is something wrong here. They were responding to a gut feeling (ethical intuition). The task now is to help this person out by identifying what could be the source of their intuition and finding a solution for it.

The general discussion among the workshop students who undertook this task focused on the tests and the choices before one student took a different perspective, looking at not what is written but what is not written. They asked:

> Why didn't they [the researchers] give the option of none of the above? What were they afraid of?

Solving one puzzle, means both are solved. The death penalty focus group has the same result. It offers a range of techniques to execute someone, but at no time does it offer the focus group participants the option that the death penalty is immoral.

These two examples, one hypothetical and one real, are powerful in showing us that ethics is not just about what we do in our interactions with participants, but about the very questions that we ask; either the overall research question or the individual questions we create to achieve our objectives. These issues that some may identify as ones of methodological rigour or scientific validity are also ones of ethical practice. When we distort data either in the ways we collect it, interpret/analyse it, or report it, we deceive our participants and the wider public. We also have to acknowledge that sometimes these errors occur again because of our lack of awareness or our enthusiasm for a project obscuring the ways in which it should be done.

WHEN PARTICIPANTS ARE A HARM TO OTHERS

Key ideas to review in this exercise:

Limits on informed consent.

In Bell's (Bell & Nutt, 2002) research, a big ethical moment stemmed from her dual roles as a social worker and as an academic researcher. The social worker's code of ethics requires notification to authorities when finding persons vulnerable, exposed to potential harm. The academic self does not have a similar responsibility; in fact, their responsibility is more toward protecting the research participant from harm.

> When interviewing a male foster caregiver, Bell noticed a sexually
> explicit poster in the hallway of the foster home. She had mixed
> feelings between protecting her participant's confidentiality and
> assuming her professional self's role to report the person.

What would you do?

Students reading this case study tend to side with their professional or academic selves. Trainee teachers and social workers applaud Bell's decision to report the man. Students without professional allegiances believe the reporting harmed the man as the participant information sheet was written from an academic perspective, with no warning that researcher participants could be turned in. They see the researcher as a researcher, not as a police officer or a social worker. At the same time, we might say that anyone (researcher, banker, hairdresser, neighbour) may in certain kinds of situations have an ethical obligation to seek help or report someone where there is a risk of serious harm. The question is by no means straightforward.

You do not have to answer this question. The fact is, it will have a different answer in different situations. It is a good question for the reference group of a project. But think through these different positions and their justifications.

CROSS TEACHING AND RESEARCH BOUNDARIES

Key ideas to review in this exercise:

Informed consent, verbal consent, conflicts of interest, power relations.

The mistake listed here emerged in an introduction to quantitative and qualitative research course Tolich taught in 2019 to undergraduate sociology students. The assignment set for the students examined qualitative research using unstructured interviews. The mistakes Tolich now identifies as being made were many, but there were some successes, too.

The task was team based. Three students, designated A, B, and C, would interview each other asking two questions Tolich had given them. Question 1 asked, "Why did the student choose to come to the University of Otago the previous year?" Question 2 was a hindsight question. "Was this decision to come to the University of Otago a good decision?"

After the interview, the three students were required to caucus to find a consensus for the production of a new interview guide. Were the initial questions useful? What alternative questions could be asked? What were the themes derived from the three interviews and, what, if any, consensus was gained in devising follow-up interview questions?

These groups of three students were then placed in groups of six. ABC were to interview DEF using the group's revised questions. The transcription, coding, memoing process was repeated in each group of six. At the end of the exercise, all students had access to 12 coded transcripts.

The task now was for the group of six to write one paper based on these themes, with each student taking responsibility for writing a page on a single theme. The group was also required to give the paper a title capturing the nuance of the group's findings.

As well as the general directions Tolich gave to the students in the class, he gave *verbal* instructions on ethics. He told them:

- they had the right not to answer any interview question;
- they had the right to withdraw from the study at any time.

Casualness of these (non-written) instructions reflected the innocuous research topic. The topic was asking students in their second year why they came to the University of Otago and whether that was a good decision. Two issues developed here. One was the learning about qualitative research, and the other was the ethics. The students' assignment was excellent. It was like a doctor who performs an excellent surgery only to have the patient die. What died in this assignment was ethical assurances that fit the occasion. Like most of this book's exercises, the expectation is the reader will assess the situation. Were these verbal assurances sufficient or insufficient? Should Tolich have given formal written participant information sheets to each student? Should the project have been formally reviewed by an ethics committee? If it had, it is doubtful the formal review would have predicted the problems that did emerge?

One group of six students wrote a paper based on six themes and gave the following title: "Cones, Castle Street, Couch Burning: the University of Otago Experience".

This title was somewhat expected, capturing the popular culture that pervades the University of Otago student life. Popular weekend activities by students include placing orange road cones in precarious positions, turning Castle Street in the student quarter into a single rave party, and burning couches on the street outside an apartment hosting a party. The sequel to burning couches was watching the fire brigade put it out.

Tolich describes what happened next:

> When I went to congratulate one group of six students I highlighted on their choice of title. I explained that I had read their portfolio closely as I was most familiar with how the orange cones graphically captured the Otago University experience. Having been enthusiastically positive about the output of this group, I did make one criticism noting the

students' portfolio of themes made no reference to Cones, or Castle Street or burning couches. I was very quick to point out that no points were deducted for having a misleading title. Their thematic analysis was excellent. The title bore no connection to the analysis.

Before offering my own title for the group's collective work, I took the class back over the core values of qualitative research. First, I reminded students that the goal of the project was to *understand* other students' choice of coming to this university from the other student's perspective. This type of research is inductive. I reinforced the epistemological frame, how research moves from observations to theory. They did this very well. Second, the students' project was iterative, meaning that they asked certain questions in the first interview; the transcript was coded and analysed, and then they asked different questions in the second interview. Third, qualitative research is emergent, meaning that the understanding of the world under study is not intuitive but with the right questions and the right analysis something profound will emerge. And it did. And that caused a problem.

I told the "Cones" group that their title was intuitive, not based on research evidence, but based on popular culture. I suggested an alternative title drawn from a number of the group's thematic presentations. I offered a disclaimer, that this title may shock the students. The alternative title was:

"Where Aspirations Go to Die: Otago University Resilience Stories"

The thematic analysis in the student's assignment cried out for this title.

Essentially this thematic analysis highlighted that many students in the sociology research methods in 2019 when interviewed for this project described how they had come to a different part of the University of Otago than they were currently enrolled in. Many of these students in their first year had come to Otago University to go to dental school, medical school, physiotherapy, law school, and now they were enrolled as sociology and social work majors. The quotes in the students' assignments reveal resilience. Students may have come to Otago University to do prelaw or pre-med, but that didn't work out for many students in their first year. In their second year, not having sufficient grades for these professional schools, they enrolled in social work and sociology, telling the interviewer that this new major allowed them to help many people.

This qualitative research assignment led to real learning for the students and for the teacher. Tolich had imagined the students would find innocuous topics; students talking about burning couches as part of the Otago experience. But the questions that the students asked went much deeper. As a teacher, he was delighted that this simple exercise could show the power of qualitative research. Qualitative research could be profound.

In hindsight, Tolich recognises that he made a mistake. He *should have* known that follow-up interview questions were likely to be intrusive into people's actual experience. He failed to understand how these follow-up questions would uncover students' stigma, those who did not realise their professional aspirations and found alternative pathways at the University of Otago.

When he discovered this dilemma, he sought advice from colleagues. Tolich created a reference group who validated the existence of a dilemma. They suggested that he talk to the students about this big ethical moment, which he did and apologised. He also wrote this learning into the final exam where students had a chance to review what they had learned from this assignment. While many students talked about the mistakes they made, most agreed a written form of consent would have been more appropriate.

In reviewing this together, Tolich and Tumilty recognise the assignment illustrates powerfully the magic of and the iterative nature of qualitative research. It also shows that judging what is and isn't an innocuous subject can be fraught without a clear understanding of the population under research. We want to be clear: it is also our view that even with appropriate consultation or advice, innocuous questions can lead to profound answers. This, after all, is the very thing we hope to discover with our work. Tolich acknowledges that many of the mistakes made were self-inflicted. It is this acknowledgement that Tolich and Tumilty believe is an important foundation for good ethical practice, because it requires a degree of humility, integrity, and openness to continue learning.

BEING SAFE IN UNSAFE SPACES

Key ideas to review in this exercise:

Harm to self.

Up until now, the focus of the book has been on protecting the other, the participant, but it is also ethical to protect oneself. Qualitative researchers can easily find themselves in unsafe spaces. When that happens, treat yourself as a vulnerable person.

In Chapter 3, a description of Venkatesh's first access to the high-rise apartment complex had him detained at knifepoint. He was in an unsafe space. *What steps could he have taken to protect himself?*

Imagine a similar situation. A university academic tasked with collecting data using face-to-face interviews hires a research assistant. The topic is the tenant's satisfaction with their apartment. This research takes the research assistant to the poorest parts of town. What type of strategies could the research assistant take to make this task safe? List them:

Sieber and Tolich (2013, Chapter 10) highlighted the following proactive steps any researcher could take when they found themselves in a risky situation. These steps were drawn from *A Code of Practice for the Safety of Social Researchers* (Social Research Association, n.d.), and some of these are listed here.

- *Reliability of local public transportation.* Are reputable taxis companies easy to access? Is it safe to use private cars and leave them in the area?
- *Route planning.* Plan the route in advance, and always take a map. Study a map of the area for clues as to its character. Look for schools, post offices, railway stations and other hubs of activity. Think about escape routes from dense housing areas. Avoid going by foot if feeling vulnerable.
- *Assessing safety in buildings.* In multistory buildings, think about safety when choosing elevators or staircases.
- *Using alarm devices.* Carry a screech alarm or other device to attract attention in an emergency.
- *Contact information.* Let the interviewee know that you have a schedule and that others know where you are. Stratagems include arranging for a colleague or taxi to collect you, making phone calls or arranging for calls to be made to you. Leave your mobile phone switched on.
- *Alarm system.* Carrying mobile phones or personal alarms may be helpful as long as these are considered only a part of your comprehensive safety policy. Overreliance on mobile phones and alarms must not substitute for proper training in interpersonal skills.
- *Mad money.* Researchers should always carry enough money for both expected and unexpected expenses, including the use of taxis. It is sensible to avoid the appearance of carrying a lot of money, however, and to carry a phone card in case it is necessary to use a public telephone.

A specific researcher safety strategy involves a rapid escape strategy any researcher could use when they feel sufficiently threatened in an interview with a participant in the participant's apartment. Assume that the danger is real. What could the researcher do? Consider this and practice it:

> Pull a cell phone from one's pocket as if it had vibrated, stand up answering the phone speaking with some urgency to an imaginary family member repeating the news that a relative is seriously ill and

their presence was required. The researcher need only say, "that is tragic, I will be right there", and the researcher leaves the site saying to the participant they will be in touch.

It is essential to think through these safety strategies in advance. Ethics committees do not require an applicant to provide a safety plan, but these are essential. Researchers should acknowledge the risks in their research site and plan how they will respond to these.

Sometimes these risks may be emotional (Tolich et al., 2020). Maybe an interviewee is aggressive or insulting without threatening physical violence. Maybe some content of the interview was unexpectedly emotionally distressing. Aside from the techniques used to remove oneself from the situation, organising an opportunity to debrief with a reference group member, supervisor, colleague or peer (if appropriate) after any interview that is physically or emotionally distressing is important (Pollard, 2009). Being able to continue going out on interviews can be jeopardised by feelings of unsafety or distress that are not addressed.

Caring for yourself throughout a research process is as important as caring for your participants. Your wellbeing feeds directly into the quality of the work and your ability to be responsive to others' needs.

What things work well for you in de-escalating tense situations? What verbal strategies can you practice to end conversations that you no longer wish to be part of? Who is an appropriate person in your professional sphere to establish a debrief partnership with?

Another consideration for any researcher working out in the field in contact with people is to think about completing a first aid course. While not compulsory, encountering a medical emergency with participants is one of those unknown-unknowns that are worth considering. Carrying a cell phone that is always charged can address such events to some degree also. It's worth thinking through whether the particular population you are working with has higher risks than the general population of some particular type of event. You may for instance, if working with a population of intravenous drug-users, consider carrying Naxolone if available in your local setting. You cannot imagine all unknown-unknowns (that's why they're unknown), but you can think through the things that might make you and your participants more safe given what you do know and think through what you'd want to be able to have or do if surprised.

What would you feel more comfortable knowing or having when out in the field? Think phone numbers, tools, or skills.

ONLINE RESOURCES

Here are some suggested resources, although they are a very small snapshot of what is available both online and in print and are meant to act as starting points rather than a complete set of tools.

1. Macquarie University's Online Ethics Training Module. Human Research Ethics for the Social Sciences and Humanities. https://ethics-training.mq.edu.au/
2. Research Ethics Training Curriculum (RETC), Second Edition. The HTML version of the curriculum comes with a pre-/post-test, evaluation form and certificate of completion. https://www.fhi360.org/resource/research-ethics-training-curriculum-retc-second-edition
3. The Canadian Tri-Council Policy Statement on Ethics, TCPS 2 Tutorial Course on Research Ethics (CORE). This self-paced course is a media-rich learning experience that features interactive exercises and multidisciplinary examples. CORE consists of ten modules ranging from Core Principles to REB Review. It is designed primarily for the use of researchers and REB members – though anyone may take this course and print their own certificate of http://www.pre.ethics.gc.ca/eng/education/tutorial-didacticiel/
4. Indigenous Geography Net – Research Ethics http://www.indigenousgeography.net/ethics.shtm
5. Nuffield Council of Bioethics – Research in Developing Countries https://www.nuffieldbioethics.org/publications/research-in-developing-countries
6. Working with Alcohol and Drug User Populations (Australian example)
   a. Webinar https://www.youtube.com/watch?v=ZRq64VIoVGg&feature=youtu.be
   b. Resource can be found on this page (part way down: https://community.adf.org.au/plan/key-ldat-resources/
7. Internet Research Ethics. Buchanan, Elizabeth A., and Zimmer, Michael. (2018). Internet research ethics. https://plato.stanford.edu/entries/ethics-internet-research/

In sum, these puzzles are solved by having either a reference group or a plan to exit an unsafe space or to refer someone unsafe to a safer place. Reference groups are essential, and in this book they were present on day one in Figures 1 and 2 in 2016 and 2018 when the students had no problem stepping up and telling the lecturer, "Hey, wait a minute". Where is the consent? Where are the confidentiality assurances? Reference groups do not have to be made up of experts, just intelligent people who do not have stakes in your research (Pollard, 2009).

NOTE

1   There is a wealth of work discussing indigenous methodologies, work with populations in the Global South or research with vulnerable communities. Those considering working in any of these areas are encouraged to read the literature, especially those writings by people of the community, to begin to understand how they might think about approaching their work.

CHAPTER 12

Looking back

The path was always there

Writing this qualitative research ethics book has been an inductive exercise. The focus of the book was emergent, and throughout the various chapters, the focus has refocused in an iterative process. Very little planning went into this book, but looking back at it now, there was planning – if a leap of faith, a hunch, could be called planning. The hunch was putting an audio recorder in front of graduate students on their first day as a provocation, the students' response unscripted. One student questioned the positioning of the audio recorder; yet another defined the action, critically asking where the informed consent was. The students did not need to be fully educated in the practice of informed consent; they knew this intuitively. What they needed was an incubator environment for this intuition to be realised and further developed.

The book's pedagogy was learning by doing; it was student-led with lectures following. Rather than loading up students with required reading on ethical concepts like informed consent, the students' observing the audio recorder on the table was sufficient for them to realise the concept of informed consent. This pedagogical act provided a disruption in their frame of reference to encourage transformative learning. This confirmed they had (1) the skills, (2) the confidence to identify its presence and, most importantly, (3) the willingness to use the learnings in other settings.

In hindsight, the pedagogy offered here is like walking over a frosty sports field in the early morning and looking backwards. Among the frost is a clearly delineated path; walking back to the origin, with all its twists and turns would be straightforward. When the audio recorder was placed in front of the students on that first day, there was no pathway. Yet now it seems the pathway was always there, but given the complexity of qualitative research ethics, the pathway is ephemeral. Researchers must learn what to do when the frosty pathway melts away.

The two concepts that emerged in Figures 1 and 2, informed consent and confidentiality, proved to be foundational for the book. Paradoxically, informed consent and confidentiality are strong, but they have a propensity to disintegrate, requiring qualitative researchers to take responsibility for their practice by having a thorough understanding of what qualitative research ethics are and what they are not. Qualitative researchers cannot rely on anonymity, and when they use de-identification as a proxy, (often) using pseudonyms, they put participants at risk. Nor can they rely on formal ethics committee review to bolster consent and confidentiality because formal ethics review is incomplete. Ethics review committees pose only speculative questions for qualitative researchers. They can ask researchers to (1) describe the research, (2) outline the ethical issues that will arise in this research and (3) how the researcher will address those ethical issues (Tolich & Fitzgerald, 2006). Formal ethics review cannot ask the fourth and most important question: what the researcher will do when their project's emergent research question transforms, making consent and confidentiality assurances take on an altered, less robust, character (Tolich & Fitzgerald, 2006). This book situated itself within the fourth question. Not only do formal ethics committees not ask this question, a researcher cannot predict with any certainty how their iterative research will change in the field affecting how consent and confidentiality ethical assurances are practised.

This book had students examine this uncharted territory by having them take full responsibility for ethical considerations by conceptualising deficiencies in qualitative research and when necessary using more robust forms of consent like process consent; recognising the dual faces of confidentiality, distinguishing external confidentiality from internal confidentiality (Tolich, 2004) (or deductive disclosure; Kaiser, 2009).

The book's pedagogy did not change its format after the first provocation with the audio recorder. What has changed are the form of the provocations. Whereas the first provocation was a guess – what would happen if – other chapters have been improvised and deliberately contrived to produce an outcome among the students. A continuous emphasis on the need for recognising one's ethical intuitions and building from them with others using ethical imagination and reasoning, and having the courage to act on them when necessary (ethical integrity) has been threaded throughout.

Eve's story in Chapter 3, like the placement of the audio recorder on day one, was a pivotal point in the book. Eve's story was deliberately a short description of a research project devoid of any ethical considerations. It was written in a way that locating ethical conundrums was as easy as falling off a log. Each time, in the semester-long courses or the shorter two- to five-hour workshops, students read the scenario locating the ethical problems. At the same time these cohorts had previously read Venkatesh's "Hustler and Hustled" chapter and could take their learning about ethics in Eve's story and confidently and find the same issues in Venkatesh's chapter. This scaffolding builds confidence and refines the intuitions so crucial to practising ethically throughout one's career.

A professor who invited Tolich to workshop parts of this book in his postgraduate class wrote the following about the linking of Eve's story to Venkatesh's chapter.

> Martin Tolich delivered a two-session qualitative research ethics workshop with 5 students as part of the Research Methods in Sport, Exercise and Health. This involved two interactive sessions in which Martin used a series of "real-life" scenarios to tease out key issues and considerations in conducting qualitative research projects on an ethical basis. A pre-session reading (Chapter 6) from Sudhir Venkatesh's book "Gang Leader for a Day" was assigned. The students in the workshop were engaged throughout the sessions as Martin moderated the discussion to tease out key themes and issues. Martin did this skilfully and was able to facilitate students' learning throughout drawing on two key scenarios: the case of Eve, and Sudhir Venkatesh's story. The two cases were used as working examples to reveal key considerations, and indeed, ethical pitfalls in conducting qualitative research. This was engaging and effective as it avoided a dry conceptual approach to key issues, instead, bringing the topic "alive". Furthermore, Martin was able to moderate in a way in which student contributions were the central feature of the workshop. The student feedback I solicited was very positive, suggesting they found the workshop to be both interesting and engaging. Overall, the workshop was highly effective in addressing key tenets of qualitative research ethics and in engaging and facilitating students' learning.

This staging of the various puzzles was deliberate, it was a pattern. This pattern was represented as an inoculation. After 60 seconds in this class, the students inoculated themselves against research conducted without informed consent. After five minutes reading Eve's story, they were inoculated against a range of ethical issues and able to identify them and seek to resolve their potential harm. Rather than hearing the principle of informed consent theoretically or learning about the regulatory requirements of informed consent or its process, being positioned in a way to empathise with those in these stories who were not consented ethically to take part in the projects (real or imagined), helps to instil a use of this perspective when moving forward and considering the ethics of their own work.

Each of the book's chapters uses the same pedagogy of students reading a simple exercise that exposed them to a core ethical issue which they could now use to decipher the ethics of a book chapter or a journal article. For example,

- Planning to conduct an ethnography in five companies only to find out four companies exempt themselves for the study. This provoked students to realise the limits of confidentiality as internal confidentiality.
- The virtual reality exercise in Chapter 4 confronted students' expectations that research should not be conducted outside the safety net of a robust informed consent process. In the virtual reality exercise, informed consent was not feasible.

Chapter 5 explored the epistemological basis of research ethics when a participant in a survey and an unstructured interview decided to leave the research project. The fact this was not possible in a questionnaire provided a fork in the road between qualitative and quantitative research ethics. Neither the researcher nor the respondent could identify their particular questionnaire to permit extraction. Plus, there was no signed consent form to record the respondent's participation. The relationship between the respondent filling in the questionnaire and the researcher is ephemeral. It does not matter if the researcher knows the identity of the persons who took part in the survey, as once the questionnaire is submitted, the researcher does not know how any individual person responded to the survey questions.

When students followed the qualitative research fork, they learned there was no generic qualitative research ethics. Narrative research, autoethnography, focus groups, unstructured interviews, and photovoice each had unique qualitative research ethics considerations, and the researcher was responsible for their implementation.

Chapters 8 and 9 introduced the two capstones that served to summarise the entire book. The first Capstone had the researcher negotiate with a social agency about how they could research the organisation. This exercise was essentially an elaborate consent process, with the five questions serving to inform the social agency about the researcher's domain assumptions. The exercise was revelatory for the researcher. The questions were likely to be novel, asking the researcher, for example, what exit strategy they had in mind. This is not normally a research question posed in any research proposal. Nor is the question asked by a University ethics committee. However, for the social agency, this question is essential, the assumption being that the organisation was committed to lifelong learning, not a discreet three-year research exercise.

The five questions in Capstone One linked to the second capstone. The social agency is unlikely to consider the necessity of the researcher having to gain ethics approval for the research project from the institutional research ethics committee. This sixth question creates a moment best described by Israel as evoking frustration, if not anger. What does this sixth question have to do with research relationships?

Figure 3, the cartoon generated at Aveiro, demonstrated how intimate these Capstones were for the workshop participants. Once they had generated an MOU with their social agency, the thought of starting a new ethics application was mundane.

The second Capstone task focused on writing three participant information sheets on behalf of Eve's story. These information sheets were written for (1) the organisation, (2) the volunteers, and (3) the women who found safe haven in the Women's Refuge. This task was made more difficult because it was written independently of the first Capstone. It was based on what the researcher had read or had previously known about the organisation. Invariably, the focus of the information sheets was based on the researcher's interests rather than on research developed in conjunction with the organisation, as demonstrated in the construction of the MOU in Chapter 8.

The focus of the book has been on research ethics, not on research governance or on ethics committees. Ethics committees are useful, but only as a means to an end not an end in themselves. The insights they provide are only partial and related to research at a specific time. But qualitative research does not exist at any one time; it is emergent and the research question iterative. As the research question changes, so do the research ethics.

The focus of the book has been on the person who has the responsibility for ethics, the researcher. They are responsible for understanding research ethics concepts and recognising situations where the concepts are askew. They must have the courage to speak up and say that things need to change, and the humility to recognise the limits of their knowledge and engage a reference group.

"Expect the unexpected" could have been the title of the book. It should be a basic assumption for qualitative researchers to grasp. They must know the limitations of qualitative research ethics, what to do if and when they disintegrate. Researchers need to be proactive offering participants consent at both the beginning and at the end of a project. A second proactive stance is knowing there are limits to confidentiality. Anonymity is never an option. These confidentiality limits should not come as a surprise; they are known before the research begins when researching relational persons. Relational participants need to be made aware of the threat posed by internal confidentiality. When the number of research sites diminish, so too do confidentiality assurances. Yet even when ethical assurances disintegrate totally, as happens routinely in focus group research, the researcher's responsibility is to switch ethical assurances toward a participant's autonomy, allowing them to make the decision to stay or withdraw from the research. This action creates a level playing field by subverting power relationships. This action makes the participant solely responsible for the use of their data. It also places the researcher's data at risk. The participant can withdraw at the 11th hour.

The book was framed within a second backdrop; the decade-long debate about the fraught relationship between qualitative research and research ethics (Gunsalus et al., 2006; Haggerty, 2004; Israel & Hay, 2006; van den Hoonaard, 2011). Many claim ethics review boards should be sidetracked. This is not the central thesis of this book. It argues that ethics review boards should not be deliberately sidetracked; this sidetracking occurs naturally. No ethics committee can review an ethics application and predict with any certainty what ethical issues will arise in the field. Neither can the researcher. Epistemologically, the emergent and iterative qualitative research design is sufficiently chaotic that the only person who can address the ethical issues that do arise in the field is the researcher.

To be an ethical researcher in the field is to understand that ethical practice begins from the moment a question is contemplated through to the moment a researcher spreads their work out into the world.

Everybody, whether researcher or not, has a set of values that underpin their world view, that determine what they think is right and fair, and that guide their actions. Recognising that his is necessary but insufficient to practice ethically as a researcher is a crucial first step. Research is a complex interactive engagement with a variety of parties directly and indirectly. To navigate this activity, staying true to one's values while respecting the needs and rights of others involved in the work requires a set of attitudes and behaviours as well as knowledge and skills. Ethical practice is never something that is complete, as each new situation will require new learning and development.

This book aims to help novice researchers with the knowledge and skills part of this equation – recognising intuitions, using one's ethical imagination, reasoning through the options, and acting on them. Developing ethical attitudes and behaviours is a self-practice that each individual researcher must decide on and pay attention to themselves. We encourage readers to think through their attitudes to their work and their behaviours, what are they doing, what might they like to be doing better? Openness, collaboration, humility, curiosity, courage, and integrity are just some of the values that can guide how we think about things and guide our actions.

We hope through the pedagogy provided here to support that thinking and development.

Appendix

How teachers can use the book

Teachers can use this book in a semester-long course or in a module within a research methods course.

The length of the course is not important. What is important is the establishment of an idioculture that permits students to challenge what they read or see or hear to establish a behaviour of engaging others when big ethical moments occur. Self-expression needs to be encouraged. Thus, it is not essential to cover all of the concepts or puzzles in the book. What is important in this teaching is finding the means to create a *student as researcher* idioculture where the students are encouraged to research the puzzles or scenarios and to extract their own learning and have the confidence to use that learning in the next puzzle.

Originally, the learning objectives were developed in 2016 and 2018 within a 13-week semester-long postgraduate courses. Since then it has been developed as a short course, and this book is written for a short course. The course can be taught in various formats. Two-hour slots have worked well even when acting as a guest lecturer. The two cartoons engage the students immediately. They realised the provocation and understand how the ethical concepts were generated.

ENGAGING YOUR ETHICAL RESEARCH SELF IN TWO HOURS

A minimal course outline would involve students discussing the two cartoons in Figures 1 and 2. The important finding gleaned from the students here was that the concepts of consent and confidentiality were known to them as tacit knowledge. More importantly, the cartoons demonstrate the willingness of students to speak up when they see a breach of ethical conduct.

If these two cartoons are sent to students ahead of time with the Venkatesh chapter, the second hour of the class can be devoted to Eve's story knowing that the students had previously read Venkatesh. The contrast between Eve and Venkatesh usually unveils a whole clutch of ethical concepts or principles such as respect for persons, beneficence, and nonmaleficence.

Throughout, students/readers should be encouraged to construct an ethics toolbox incrementally after each exercise. By toolbox, we mean a collection of ethical "tools" learned from the exercise that are useful for future analysis or practice.

The book's exercises can be critiqued by readers. For example, the cartoon in Figure 1 raises more ethical issues than just informed consent. The use of deception by the teacher meant the students were not informed ahead of time of what we were doing. Did the means justify the end? Astute readers could also question if the journal article promised to the students undermined or diminished their autonomy. Was promising a journal article an act of inducement? There are ethics within ethics here. Conflict of interest is the most obvious issue, as Tolich was both a researcher and teacher. All of these issues are real and are discussed.

Figure 2 introduces confidentiality. But the cartoon could also be turned in on itself to discuss the ethics of focus groups. Could the teacher in the cartoon promise confidentiality for the students? Yes, they can. But can the students assume what they say is confidential? These are standard questions in any focus group.

HOW TO ENGAGE YOUR ETHICAL SELF IN FIVE HOURS

The format that works best in a five-hour workshop is the one-page description that follows. It outlines the book's 12 chapters as seven distinct entities, each with suggested learning outcomes.

Along with this one-page description, sent to students in advance, are the two cartoons and a link to the Venkatesh chapter. Everything else in the book is developed in real time within the classroom.

QUALITATIVE RESEARCH ETHICS WORKSHOP – FIVE HOURS DURATION

1. What concept are students articulating in the first cartoon? Why did the teacher provocatively switch on the audio recorder? What concepts are the students raising for the teacher in the second cartoon? Spontaneously, these students framed the unique characteristics of qualitative research ethics. Why are consent and confidentiality robust pillars of qualitative research so fragile?

2. The workshop reads and dissects two case studies. The first is Venkatesh's "Hustler and Hustled", Chapter 6 of *Gang Leader for a Day: A Rogue Sociologist Takes to the Streets* (2008). The second is the hypothetical case, Eve's story, handed out in class and read in class time providing the focal point of the workshop's discussion.

3. Informed consent in a questionnaire and in an unstructured interview draw on the same ethical principles but manifest differently. In survey research the statement "filling out this survey implies your informed consent" is sufficient. Consent in unstructured interviews is convoluted, involving a signed consent form. Why is this, and what impact does this difference have on the concepts of confidentiality and anonymity?

4. If qualitative and quantitative ethics are different, does this mean that all qualitative research techniques have a universal set of ethical considerations? The answer is they do not. Ethical considerations in focus groups, autoethnography, narrative research, unstructured interviews, covert research and observation take different forms. There is no single qualitative research ethics. How is this difference manifest in focus groups and unstructured interviews, and why does it take these forms?

5. Two applied tasks end the workshop. Capstone One requires concocting a hypothetical study of an unfamiliar social agency. Imagine the social agency responds to the students query to research them asking a series of questions. Prepare a brief response for each of these statements:

    • Nothing about us, without us.
    • Is the research "on us or with us"?
    • What is the exit strategy?
    • What are insider and outsider research?
    • What skill set can the agency gain from the researcher?

    The sum total of these answers provides a solution and a problem. The solution takes the form of a memorandum of understanding between the researcher and the social agency. The memorandum of understanding is something akin to participatory action research. The problem is that participatory action research can represent a problem for qualitative researchers when submitting an application to an ethics committee. Many ethics committees prefer the researcher seek ethics approval before approaching an organisation.

6. Capstone Two uses Eve's hypothetical story (see point 2) as a starting point to create a formal ethics application. The application focuses on the construction of a participant information sheet and consent form

for three bodies: the social agency, volunteers in the social agency, clients of the social agency. This task is resourced by reading exemplars on TREAD (The Research Ethics Application Database; https://tread.tghn.org/), a repository of exemplary ethics applications.

7. In sum, the majority of the workshop, Tasks 1 to 5, assume the researcher is responsible for ethical considerations. In task 6, a formal ethics review process mediates the ethical considerations. This allows the class to explore, first, how this mediation changes ethics, and second, how the students' ethical considerations differ from Eve's or Venkatesh's.

References

Allen, L. (2015). Losing face? Photo-anonymisation and visual research integrity. *Visual Studies*, 30(3), 295–308. doi: 10.1080/1472586X.2015.1016741.

Asch, S. (1956). Studies of independence and conformity: A minority of one against a unanimous majority. *Psychological Monographs*, 76(9), 1–70. doi: 10.1037/h0093718.

Atkinson, P. A. (1990). *The ethnographic imagination: Textual constructions of reality*. London: Routledge.

Babb, S. L. (2020). *Regulating human research: IRBs from peer review to compliance bureaucracy*. Stanford, CA: Stanford University Press.

Bauer, P. (2001). A few simple truths about your community IRB members. *IRB: Ethics and Human Research*, 23(1), 7–8. doi: 10.2307/3563980.

Becker, H. S., & Richards, P. (1986). *Writing for social scientists: How to start and finish your thesis, book, or article*. Chicago: University of Chicago Press.

Bell, L., & Nutt, L. (2002). Divided loyalties, divided expectations: Research ethics, professional and occupational responsibilities. In M. Mauthner, M. Birch, J. Jessop, & T. Miller (Eds.), *Ethics in qualitative research* (pp. 70–90). London: Sage.

Blass, T. (2004). *The man who shocked the world: The life and legacy of Stanley Milgram*. New York: Basic Books.

BMJ. (1996). The Nuremberg Code (1947). *BMJ*, 313. doi: 10.1136/bmj.313.7070.1448.

Bosk, C., & DeVries, R. (2004). Bureaucracies of mass deception: Institutional review boards and the ethics of ethnographic research. *American Academy of Political and Social Science*, 595, 249–263. doi: 10.1177/0002716204266913.

Brinkmann, S., & Kvale, S. (2008). Ethics in qualitative psychological research. *The Sage Handbook of Qualitative Research in Psychology*, 24(2), 263–279. doi: 10.4135/9781526405555.

Buchanan, E. A., & Zimmer, M. (2018). Internet research ethics. In E. N. Zalta (Ed.), *The Stanford Encyclopedia of Philosophy* (Winter 2018 Edition). Available at \https://plato. stanford.edu/archives/win2018/entries/ethics-internet-research/.

Bull, J. (2010). Research with Aboriginal peoples: Authentic relationships as a precursor to ethical research. *Journal of Empirical Research on Human Research Ethics*, 5(4), 13–22. doi: 10.1525/jer.2010.5.4.13.

Bull, J. (2016). A two-eyed seeing approach to research ethics review: An indigenous perspective. In W. C. Van Den Hoonaard & A. Hamilton (Eds.), *The ethics rupture: Exploring alternatives to formal research ethics review* (pp. 167–186). Toronto: University of Toronto Press.

Cannella, G. S. (2015). Qualitative research as living within/transforming complex power relations. *Qualitative Inquiry*, 21(7), 594–598. doi: 10.1177/1077800414554907.

Carey, M. A., & Asbury, J. E. (2012). *Focus group research.* Walnut Creek, CA: Left Coast Press. doi: 10.4324/9781315428376.

Carey, M. A., & Smith, M. W. (1994). Capturing the group effect in focus groups: A special concern in analysis. *Qualitative Health Research*, 4(1), 123–127.

Carlberg-Racich, S. (2018). *Power and ethics in photovoice research: Exploring the implications of human subjects' protections on self-determination and the Belmont Principles.* In *Proceedings of 36th Conference Visualizing the Political Process, IVSA 2018*, Evry, France, 25–28 June. Available at: https://ivsa2018evry.sciencesconf.org/195217/document, accessed August 27, 2020.

Chang, H. (2008). *Autoethnography as method* (Vol. 1). Walnut Creek, CA: Left Coast Press.

Clandinin, D. J., & Connelly, F. M. (2000). *Narrative inquiry: Experience and story in qualitative research.* San Francisco: Jossey-Bass.

Congress of Qualitative Inquiry. (2007). *Position statement on qualitative research on IRBs* Available at: http://www.c4qi.org/PositionStatement.pdf, accessed August 27, 2020.

Delamont, S., & Atkinson, P. (2018). The ethics of ethnography. In R. Iphofen & M. Tolich (Eds.), *The SAGE handbook of qualitative research ethics* (pp. 119–132). London: Sage.

Dingwall, R. (2008). The ethical case against ethical regulation in humanities and social science research. *Twenty-First Century Society*, 3(1), 1–12. doi: 10.1080/17450140701749189.

DuBois, J. M., Chibnall, J. T., Tait, R., & Wal, J. V. (2016). Misconduct: Lessons from researcher rehab. *Nature News*, 534(7606), 173.

Ethik-Kodex der Deutschen Gesellschaft für Soziologie und des Berufsverbandes Deutscher Soziologen, *DGS-Informationen*, 1/93, 13–19.

Duncombe, J., & Jessop, J. (2002). "Doing rapport" and the ethics of "faking friendship". In M. Mauthner, M. Birch, J. Jessop, & T. Miller (Eds.), *Ethics in qualitative research* (pp. 108–123). London: Sage.

Edwards, R., & Weller, S. (2016). Ethical dilemmas around anonymity and confidentiality in longitudinal research data sharing: The death of Dan. In M. Tolich (Ed.), *Qualitative ethics in practice* (pp. 97–108). London: Routledge.

Ellis, C. (1995). Emotional and ethical quagmires in returning to the field. *Journal of Contemporary Ethnography*, 24, 711–713. doi: 10.1177/089124195024001003.

Ellis, C. (2007). Telling secrets, revealing lives: Relational ethics in research with intimate others. *Qualitative Inquiry*, 13, 3–29. doi: 10.1177/1077800406294947.

Ezzy, D. (2013). *Qualitative analysis.* London: Routledge.

Faden, R. R., & Beauchamp, T. L. (1986). *A history and theory of informed consent.* Oxford: Oxford University Press.

Fals Borda, O. (1979). Investigating reality in order to transform it: The Colombian experience. *Dialectical Anthropology*, 4(1), 33–55. doi: 10.1007/BF00417683.

Fine, G. A. (1987). *With the boys: Little league baseball and preadolescent culture.* Chicago: University of Chicago Press.

Fine, G. A. (1979). Small groups and culture creation: The idioculture of Little League baseball teams. *American Sociological Review*, 44(5), 733–745.

Finkelstein, J. A., Brickman, A. L., Capron, A., Ford, D. E., Gombosev, A., Greene, S. M., Iafrate, R. P., Kolaczkowski, L., Pallin, S. C., Pletcher, M. J., Staman, K. L., Vazquez, M. A., & Sugarman, J. (2015). Oversight on the borderline: Quality improvement and pragmatic research. *Clinical trials (London, England)*, 12(5), 457–466. doi: 10.1177/1740774515597682.

Fitch, K. (2005). Difficult interactions between IRBs and investigators: Applications and solutions. *Journal of Applied Communication Research*, 33(3), 269–276. doi: 10.1080/00909880500149486.

Flick, U. (2006). *An introduction to qualitative research*. London: Sage.

Flory, J., & Emanuel, E. (2004). Interventions to improve research participants' understanding in informed consent for research: A systematic review. *Journal of the American Medical Association*, 292(13), 1593–1601.

Gillespie, D., & Brown, K. H. (1997). "We become brave by doing brave acts": Teaching moral courage through the theater of the oppressed. *Literature and Medicine*, 16(1), 108–120. doi: 10.1353/lm.1997.0001.

Glaser, B. G., & Strauss, A. L. (1967). *The discovery of grounded theory: Strategies for qualitative research*. New York: Adline de Gruyter.

Goffman, A. (2014). *On the run: Fugitive life in an American city*. New York: Picador. doi: 10.1111/1468-2427.12245.

Goffman, E., & Lofland, L. H. (1989). On fieldwork. *Journal of Contemporary Ethnography*, 18(2), 123–132.

Green, L. W., & Mercer, S. L. (2001). Can public health researchers and agencies reconcile the push from funding bodies and the pull from communities? *American Journal of Public Health*, 91(12), 1926–1929. doi: 10.2105/ajph.91.12.1926.

Guillemin, M., & Gillam, L. (2004). Ethics, reflexivity, and "ethically important moments" in research. *Qualitative Inquiry*, 10(2), 261–280. doi: 10.1177/1077800403262360.

Gunsalus, C., Bruner, E., Burbules, N., Dash, L., Finkin, M., Goldberg, J., Greenough, W. T., Miller, G. A., & Pratt, M. G. (2006). Mission creep in the IRB world. *Science*, 312(5779), 1441. doi: 10.1126/science.1121479.

Haggerty, K. (2004). Ethics creep: Governing social science research in the name of ethics. *Qualitative Sociology*, 27(4), 391–414. doi: 10.1023/B:QUAS.0000049239.15922.a3.

Hammersley, M., & Traianou, A. (2012). *Ethics in qualitative research: Controversies and contexts*. London: Sage.

Hardacre, G. D. (2012). Navigating REBs. *Canadian Family Physician*, 58(2), 152–153.

Harland, T., & Wald, N. (2018). Curriculum, teaching and powerful knowledge. *Higher Education*, 76(4), 615–628. doi: 10.1007/s10734-017-0228-8.

Hauhart, R. C., & Grahe, J. E. (2015). *Designing and teaching undergraduate capstone courses*. Hoboken, NJ: John Wiley & Sons.

Holdaway, M. A. (2002). *A Māori model of primary health care nursing*. Doctoral thesis. Massey University, Palmerston North, New Zealand.

Holkup, P. A., Tripp-Reimer, T., Salois, E. M., & Weinert, C. (2004). Community-based participatory research: An approach to intervention research with a Native American community. *ANS: Advances in Nursing Science*, 27(3), 162. doi: 10.1097/00012272-200407000-00002.

Homan, R. (2006). Problems with codes. *Research Ethics Review*, 2(3), 98–103. doi: 10.1177/174701610600200304.

Humphreys, L. (1975). *Tearoom trade: Impersonal sex in public places*. New York: Aldine.

Iphofen, R. (2011). *Ethical decision making in social research: A practical guide*. London: Palgrave Macmillan. doi: 10.1057/9780230233768.

Israel, M. (2015). *Research ethics and integrity for social scientists: Beyond regular compliance* (2nd ed.). London: Sage. doi: 10.4135/9781473910096.

Israel, M., & Hay, I. (2006). *Research ethics for social scientists*. London: Sage. doi: 10.4135/9781849209779.

Jago, B. (2002). Chronicling an academic depression. *Journal of Contemporary Ethnography*, 31, 729–756. doi: 10.1177/089124102237823.

Josselson, R. (1996). *Ethics and process in the narrative study of lives* (Vol. 4). London: Sage.

Josselson, R. (2007). The ethical attitude in narrative research: Principles and practicalities. In J. Clandinin (Ed.), *Handbook of narrative inquiry: Mapping a methodology* (pp. 537–566). Thousand Oaks, CA: Sage. doi: 10.4135/9781452226552.n2.

Kaiser, K. (2009). Protecting respondent confidentiality in qualitative research. *Qualitative Health Research*, 19(11), 1632–1641. doi: 10.1177/1049732309350879.

Kilburn, D., Nind, M., & Wiles, R. (2014). Learning as researchers and teachers: The development of a pedagogical culture for social science research methods? *British Journal of Educational Studies*, 62(2), 191–207. doi: 10.1080/00071005.2014.918576.

King, N., Henderson, G., & Stein, J. (1999). Introduction – relationships in research: A new paradigm. In N. King, G. Henderson, & J. Stein, *Beyond regulations: Ethics in human subjects research* (pp. 1–17). Chapel Hill, NC: University of North Carolina Press.

Koski, G. (2010). "Rethinking research ethics," again: Casuistry, phronesis, and the continuing challenges of human research. *American Journal of Bioethics*, 10(10), 37–39. doi: 10.1080/15265161.2010.526444.

Kvale, S. (1996). *Inter-views: An introduction to qualitative research interviewing*. Thousand Oaks, CA: Sage.

Lahman, M., Geist, M., Rodriguez, K., Graglia, P., & DeRoche, K. (2011). Culturally responsive relational reflexive ethics in research: The three rs. *Quality and Quantity*, 45(6), 1397–1414. doi: 10.1007/s11135-010-9347-3.

Lewis, L. H., & Williams, C. J. (1994). Experiential learning: Past and present. *New Directions for Adult and Continuing Education*, 1994(62), 5–16. doi: 10.1002/ace.36719946203.

Lewthwaite, S., & Nind, M. (2016). Teaching research methods in the social sciences: Expert perspectives on pedagogy and practice. *British Journal of Educational Studies*, 64(4), 1–17. doi: 10.1080/00071005.2016.1197882.

Librett, M., & Perrone, D. (2010). Apples and oranges: Ethnography and the IRB. *Qualitative Research*, 10(6), 729–747. doi: 10.1177/1468794110380548.

Liebenberg, L., Wood, M., & Wall, D. (2018). Participatory action research with Indigenous youth and their communities. In R. Iphofen & M. Tolich (Eds.), *Handbook of qualitative research ethics* (pp. 339–353). London: Sage. doi: 10.4135/9781526435446.

Lofland, J., & Lofland, L. H. (1971). *Analyzing social settings*. Belmont, CA: Wadsworth.

Lopus, J. S., Grimes, P. W., Becker, W. E., & Pearson, R. A. (2007). Effects of human subjects requirements on classroom research: Multidisciplinary evidence. *Journal of Empirical Research on Human Research Ethics: An International Journal*, 2(3), 69–78. doi: 10.1525/jer.2007.2.3.69.

Lowe, S. J., George, L., & Deger, J. (2020). A deeper deep listening: Doing pre-ethics fieldwork in Aotearoa New Zealand. In J. Tauri, L. T. A. O. T. MacDonald, & L. George (Eds.), *Indigenous research ethics: Claiming research sovereignty beyond deficit and the colonial legacy* (pp. 275–292). Bingley, UK: Emerald Publishing Limited.

Luna, F. (2009). Elucidating the concept of vulnerability: Layers not labels. *IJFAB: International Journal of Feminist Approaches to Bioethics*, 2(1), 121–139. doi: 10.3138/ijfab.2.1.121.

Macfarlane, B. (2010). *Researching with integrity: The ethics of academic enquiry*. London: Routledge.

Madison, D. S. (2005). *Critical ethnography: Method, ethics and performance*. Thousand Oaks, CA: Sage.

McQuade, D. (2015, June 11). Alice Goffman's book on "fugitive life" in Philly under attack. *Philadelphia Magazine*.

Medford, K. (2006). Caught with a fake ID: Ethical questions about slippage in autoethnography. *Qualitative Inquiry*, 12, 853–864. doi: 10.1177/1077800406288618.

Mezirow, J. (1994). Understanding transformation theory. *Adult Education Quarterly*, 44(4), 222–232. doi: 10.1177/074171369404400403.

Mezirow, J. (2000). Learning to think like an adult: Core concepts of transformative theory. In J. Mezirow (Ed.), *Learning is transformation: Critical perspectives on the theory in progress* (pp. 3–33). San Francisco: Jossey-Bass.

Miller, T., & Bell, L. (2002). Consenting to what? Issues of access, gate-keeping and "informed" consent. In M. Mauthner, M. Birch, J. Jessop, & T. Miller (Eds.), *Ethics in qualitative research* (pp. 53–69). London: Sage.

Molyneux, C. S., Wassenaar, D. R., Peshu, N., & Marsh, K. (2005). "Even if they ask you to stand by a tree all day, you will have to do it (laughter) …!": Community voices on the notion and practice of informed consent for biomedical research in developing countries. *Social Science and Medicine*, 61(2), 443–454. doi: 10.1016/j.socscimed.2004.12.003.

Morgan, D. (1998). *The focus group guidebook.* Thousand Oaks, CA: Sage.

Morrison, Z. J., Gregory, D., & Thibodeau, S. (2012). "Thanks for using me": An exploration of exit strategy in qualitative research. *International Journal of Qualitative Methods*, 11(4), 416–427. doi: 10.1177/160940691201100408.

Morse, J. (2002). Writing my own experience. *Qualitative Health Research*, 12(9), 1159–1160. doi: 10.1177/1049732302238241.

Morse, J. M. (2011). What is qualitative health research? In N. K. Denzin & Y. S. Lincoln (Eds.), *The SAGE handbook of qualitative research* (4th ed., pp. 401–414). London: Sage.

Morse, J. M., & Coulehan, J. (2015). Maintaining confidentiality in qualitative publications. *Qualitative Health Research*, 25(2), 151–152. doi: 10.1177/1049732314563489.

Muchmore, J. A. (2002). Methods and ethics in a life history study of teacher thinking. *The Qualitative Report*, 7(4), 1–17.

Murray, L., Pushor, D., & Renihan, P. (2012). Reflections on the ethics-approval process. *Qualitative Inquiry*, 18(1), 43–54.

Narvaez, D., & Mrkva, K. (2014). The development of moral imagination. In S. Moran, D. Cropley, & J. C. Kaufman (Eds.), *The ethics of creativity* (pp. 25–45). London: Palgrave Macmillan.

Nash, R. J. (1987). Applied ethics and moral imagination: Issues for educators. *Journal of Thought*, 22(3), 68–77.

National Commission for the Protection of Human Subjects of Biomedical and Behavioral Research. (1979). *Belmont Report: Ethical principles and guidelines for the protection of human subjects of research.* Washington, DC: National Commission for the Protection of Human Subjects of Biomedical and Behavioral Research.

Nicholls, S. G., Brehaut, J., & Saginur, R. (2012). Social science and ethics review: A question of practice not principle. *Research Ethics*, 8(2), 71–78. doi: 10.1177/1747016112445435.

O'Reilly, K. (2005). *Participating and observing: Ethnographic methods.* London: Routledge.

Ozdemir, V. (2009). What to do when the risk environment is rapidly shifting and heterogeneous? Anticipatory governance and real-time assessment of social risks in multiply marginalized populations can prevent IRB mission creep, ethical inflation or underestimation of risks. *The American Journal of Bioethics*, 9(11), 65–68. doi: 10.1080/15265160903197671.

Patton, M. Q. (2002). Two decades of developments in qualitative inquiry: A personal, experiential perspective. *Qualitative Social Work*, 1(3), 261–283. doi: 10.1177/1473325002001003636.

Pollard, A. (2009). Field of screams: Difficulty and ethnographic fieldwork. *Anthropology Matters*, 11(2). doi: 10.22582/am.v11i2.10.

Price, P. L. (2011). Geography, me, and the IRB: From roadblock to resource. *The Professional Geographer*, 64(1), 34–42. doi: 10.1080/00330124.2011.596789.

Punch, M. (1994). Politics and ethics in qualitative research. In N. K. Denzin & Y. S. Lincoln (Eds.), *Handbook of qualitative research* (pp. 83–95). Thousand Oaks, CA: Sage.

Rambo, C. (2007). Handing IRB an unloaded gun. *Qualitative Inquiry*, 13(3), 353–367.

Rule, A. C. (2006). The components of authentic learning. *Journal of Authentic Learning*, 3(1), 1–10.

Saldaña, J. (2009). *The coding manual for qualitative researchers*. Thousand Oaks, CA: Sage.

Saunders, B., Kitzinger, J., & Kitzinger, C. (2015). Anonymising interview data: Challenges and compromise in practice. *Qualitative Research*, 15(5), 616–632. doi: 10.1177/1468794114550439.

Scheff, T. J. (1988). Shame and conformity: The deference-emotion system. *American Sociological Review*, 53(3), 395–406. doi: 10.2307/2095647.

Scheper-Hughes, N. (1979). *Saints, scholars, and schizophrenics: Mental illness in rural Ireland*. Berkeley, CA: University of California Press.

Scheper-Hughes, N. (2000). Ire in Ireland. *Ethnography*, 1(1), 117–140.

Schrag, Z. (2010). *Ethical imperialism*. Baltimore, MD: Johns Hopkins University Press.

Seybold, P. (2017). *The Capstone class – FAQ's*. Available at: https://liberalarts.iupui.edu/sociology/files/documents/Sociology-CapstoneFAQs.2-27-17.pdf, accessed August 27, 2020.

Sieber, J., & Tolich, M. (2013). Communicating informed consent and process consent. In J. Sieber & M. Tolich (Eds.), *Planning ethically responsible research* (pp. 115–140). Thousand Oaks, CA: Sage. doi: 10.4135/9781506335162.n7.

Silverman, D., & Marvasti, A. (2008). *Doing qualitative research: A comprehensive guide*. Thousand Oaks, CA: Sage.

Smith, L. T. (2013). *Decolonizing methodologies: Research and indigenous peoples*. London: Zed Books Ltd.

Snook, I. (2003). *Are ethics committees ethical? Paper presented to the annual conference of the New Zealand Association for Research in Education*, December, Christchurch.

Social Research Association. (n.d.). *A code of practice for the safety of social researchers*. Available at https://the-sra.org.uk/common/Uploaded%20files/SRA-safety-code-of-practice.pdf, accessed November 15, 2020.

Spradley, J. P. (1979). *The ethnographic interview*. Wadsworth, CA: Belmont.

Stacey, J. (1988, January). Can there be a feminist ethnography? *Women's Studies International Forum*, 11(1), 21–27.

Stacey, J. (1991). Can there be a feminist ethnography? In S. B. Gluck & D. Patai (Eds.), *Women's words: The feminist practice of oral history* (pp. 111–119). New York and London: Routledge.

Stark, L. (2012). *Behind closed doors: IRBs and the making of ethical research*. Chicago: University of Chicago Press.

Stark, L. (2016). The language of law: How research ethics review creates inequalities for language minorities. In W. C. van den Hoonaard & A. Hamilton (Eds.), *The ethics rupture: Exploring alternatives to formal research ethics review* (pp. 91–105). Toronto: University of Toronto Press.

Swazey, J., & Bird, S. (1997). Teaching and learning research ethics. In D. Elliott & J. E. Stern (Eds.), *Research ethics: A reader* (pp. 1–19). Lebanon, NH: University Press of New England.

Tashakkori, A., & Teddlie, C. (1998). *Mixed methodology: Combining qualitative and quantitative approaches.* Thousand Oaks, CA: Sage.

Thomas, W. I., & Znaniecki, F. (1918). *The polish peasant in Europe and America.* Boston, MA: The Gorham Press.

Tindana, P. O., Kass, N., & Akweongo, P. (2006). The informed consent process in a rural African setting: A case study of the Kassena-Nankana District of Northern Ghana. *IRB*, 28(3), 1.

Tolich, M. (2004). Internal confidentiality: When confidentiality assurances fail relational informants. *Qualitative Sociology*, 27(1), 101–106. doi: 10.1023/B:QUAS.0000015546. 20441.4a.

Tolich, M. (2009). The principle of caveat emptor: Confidentiality and informed consent as endemic ethical dilemmas in focus group research. *Journal of Bioethical Inquiry*, 6(1), 99–108.

Tolich, M. (2010). A critique of current practice: Ten foundational guidelines for autoethnographers. *Qualitative Health Research*, 20(12), 1599–1610. doi: 10.1177/1049732310376076.

Tolich, M. (2014). What can Milgram and Zimbardo teach ethics committees and qualitative researchers about minimizing harm? *Research Ethics*, 10(2), 86–96. doi: 10.1177/1747016114523771.

Tolich, M. (2016a). Fruit of the poisonous tree: Worrying trends in qualitative research. *CIAIQ 2016*, 5. Porto, Portugal.

Tolich, M. (2016b). A worrying trend: Ethical considerations of using data collected without informed consent. *Fronteiras: Journal of Social, Technological and Environmental Science*, 5(2), 14–28.

Tolich, M. (2017). Purpose built ethical considerations for narrative research: Broad consent or process consent but not informed consent. In I. Goodson, A. Antikainen, P. Sikes, & M. Andrews (Eds.), *The Routledge international handbook on narrative and life history* (pp. 605–617). London: Routledge. doi: 10.4324/9781315768199.

Tolich, M. (2019). What qualitative researchers must do when ethical assurances disintegrate? Recognise internal confidentiality, establish process consent, reference groups, referrals for participants and a safety plan. In A. Costa, L. Reis, & A. Moreira (Eds.), *WComputer Supported Qualitative Research. WCQR 2019. Advances in Intelligent Systems and ComputingWorld Conference on Qualitative Research* (pp. 22–32). Cham: Springer.

Tolich, M., Choe, L., Doesburg, A., Foster, A., Shaw, R., & Wither, D. (2017). Teaching research ethics as active learning: Reading Venkatesh and Goffman as curriculum resources. *International Journal of Social Research Methodology*, 20(3), 243–253. doi: 10.1080/13645579.2017.1287870.

Tolich, M., & Davidson, C. (1999). *Starting fieldwork: An introduction to qualitative research work in New Zealand.* Oxford: Oxford University Press.

Tolich, M., & Davidson, C. (Eds.). (2018). *Social science research in New Zealand: An introduction.* Auckland: Auckland University Press.

Tolich, M., & Fitzgerald, M. (2006). If ethics committees were designed for ethnography. *Journal of Empirical Research on Human Research Ethics*, 1(1), 71–78. doi: 10.1525/ jer.2006.1.2.71.

Tolich, M., & Tumilty, E. (2014). Making ethics review a learning institution: The Ethics Application Repository proof of concept tear.otago.ac.nz. *Qualitative Research*, 14(2), 201–212. https://doi.org/10.1177/1468794112468476.

Tolich, M., Tumilty, E., Choe, L., Hohmann-Marriott, B., & Fahey, N. (2020). Researcher emotional safety as ethics in practice: Why professional supervision should augment PhD candidates' academic supervision. In R. Iphofen (Ed.). *Handbook of research ethics and scientific integrity* (pp. 589–602). Cham: Springer. doi: 10.1007/978-3-030-16759-2_26.

Tolich, M. B. (1993). Alienating and liberating emotions at work supermarket clerks' performance of customer service. *Journal of Contemporary Ethnography*, 22(3), 361–381. doi: 10.1177/089124193022003004.

Tumilty, E., Tolich, M. B., & Dobson, S. (2016). Rupturing ethics literacy: The ethics application repository (TEAR). In W. C. van den Hoonaard & A. Hamilton (Eds.), *The ethics rupture: Exploring alternatives to formal research ethics review* (pp. 376–390). Toronto: University of Toronto Press.

Van de Pol, J., Volman, M., & Beishuizen, J. (2010). Scaffolding in teacher–student interaction: A decade of research. *Educational Psychology Review*, 22(3), 271–296. doi: 10.1007/s10648-010-9127-6.

van den Hoonaard, W. C. (2001). Is research-ethics review a moral panic? *Canadian Review of Sociology/Revue canadienne de sociologie*, 38(1), 19–36. doi: 10.1111/j.1755-618X.2001.tb00601.x.

van den Hoonaard, W. C. (Ed.). (2002). *Walking the tightrope: Ethical issues for qualitative researchers*. Toronto: University of Toronto Press.

van den Hoonaard, W. C. (2011). *The seduction of ethics: Transforming the social sciences*. Toronto: University of Toronto Press.

van den Hoonaard, W. C., & Hamilton, A. (Eds.). (2016). *The ethics rupture: Exploring alternatives to formal research-ethics review*. Toronto: University of Toronto Press.

van den Scott, L. J. K. (2016). The socialization of contemporary students by ethics boards: Malaise and ethics for graduate students. In W. C. van den Hoonaard & A. Hamilton (Eds.), *The ethics rupture: Exploring alternatives to formal research ethics review* (pp. 230–247). Toronto: University of Toronto Press.

van Maanen, J. (2011). *Tales of the field: On writing ethnography*. Chicago: University of Chicago Press.

Venkatesh, S. (2008). *Gang leader for a day: A rogue sociologist takes to the streets*. New York: Penguin.

Wang, C. C., & Redwood-Jones, Y. A. (2001). Photovoice ethics: Perspectives from Flint photovoice. *Health Education and Behavior*, 28(5), 560–572. doi: 10.1177/109019810102800504.

Watts, J. H. (2008). Emotion, empathy and exit: Reflections on doing ethnographic qualitative research on sensitive topics. *Medical Sociology Online*, 3(2), 3–14.

Wax, M. L. (1982). Research reciprocity rather than informed consent in fieldwork. In J. E. Sieber (Ed.), *The ethics of social research*, Springer Series in Social Psychology (pp. 33–48). New York: Springer. doi: 10.1007/978-1-4612-5722-6_2.

Whyte, W. F. (1981 [1943]). *Street corner society: The social structure of an Italian slum*. Chicago: University of Chicago Press.

Wiles, R. (2012). *What are qualitative research ethics?* London: Bloomsbury Academic.

Williams-Jones, B., & Holm, S. (2005). A university wide model for the ethical review of human subjects research. *Research Ethics Review*, 1(2), 39–44. doi: 10.1177/174701610500100203.

Zimbardo, P. (2007). *The Lucifer effect*. London: Random House.

Index

For Product Safety Concerns and Information please contact our EU
representative GPSR@taylorandfrancis.com
Taylor & Francis Verlag GmbH, Kaufingerstraße 24, 80331 München, Germany